W9-CCB-875

Exploring Our National Wildlife Refuges

Other books by Devereux Butcher:

EXPLORING OUR NATIONAL PARKS AND MONUMENTS
Houghton Mifflin Company, Boston 7, Mass.

EXPLORING THE NATIONAL PARKS OF CANADA
National Parks Association, Washington 6, D. C.

EXPLORING OUR NATIONAL WILDLIFE REFUGES

by

DEVEREUX BUTCHER

Second Edition Revised

The first edition was
published under the title
*Seeing America's Wildlife
In Our National Refuges*

HOUGHTON MIFFLIN COMPANY, BOSTON
1963

This book is dedicated

to everyone who enjoys wildlife

solely for the pleasure of seeing it.

Houghton Mifflin Company
2 Park Street, Boston 7

Library of Congress Catalogue Card No. 63-13319

Printed in the United States of America
Press of
JUDD AND DETWEILER, INC.

FOREWORD

Have you ever wondered how abundant our wildlife might be today, had there been a commandment among the ten to guide us in our dealings with the wild birds and mammals? Would the beautiful Carolina paroquet still be with us? Would we have spared a patch of southern primeval forest large enough for the survival of the ivory-billed woodpecker? Would the passenger pigeon, though in reduced flocks, still be one of the marvels of nature?

Maybe such a commandment would have read:

The Lord thy God hath placed upon the earth the wild creatures for thy pleasure to see. Thou shalt not molest them or disturb their homes. Thou shalt protect the forests and meadows and marshes of their dwelling places, and thou shalt not pollute the waters that are theirs. Thou shalt hold their lands inviolate against the encroachment of thy cities and thy roads, and shall in all ways see that their needs are met, so that each shall be able to perpetuate its own kind, and none shall be exterminated from the face of the earth.

Thoughtless as has been man's attitude toward the wild creatures, there is a brighter side, for the preservation of wildlife habitats in parks, sanctuaries and refuges is tangible proof of human spiritual growth. The same is not true of efforts designed merely to produce live targets.

Civilization is rapidly advancing into the last outposts of unreserved wild lands on this continent, and is so drastically altering those lands that their use by wildlife is becoming ever more impossible. Prompt action is required, if we are to save even a little of what is left. But there can be no success in any effort to preserve our native birds and mammals unless human apathy, greed and ignorance are overcome. Increased public esthetic appreciation and enlightenment on wildlife problems are essential to the fruitful outcome of any program for the preservation and protection of North America's wildlife heritage. To bring this about, is one of the pressing duties of informed people everywhere today.

Washington, D. C. — THE AUTHOR
July, 1955

ACKNOWLEDGMENTS

This book was made possible by the cooperation of many people and organizations, to all of whom the author wishes to express gratitude. They include the author's many friends in the Bureau of Sport Fisheries and Wildlife of the U. S. Fish and Wildlife Service, Department of the Interior. Among them are former assistant director of the Service Clarence Cottam, now director, Welder Wildlife Foundation, Sinton, Texas; J. Clark Salyer, II, staff specialist, Division of Wildlife; Philip A. DuMont, biologist, Branch of Wildlife Refuges, who rendered invaluable service in helping to bring this edition up to date; and Rex Gary Schmidt, now assigned to the Office of the Secretary, Department of the Interior.

The refuge managers and other refuge staff members helped the author see and photograph the areas and their wildlife. With these dedicated officials, he traveled many miles in the refuges.

The National Audubon Society, the Massachusetts Audubon Society and other organizations and individuals helped by opening their files to the author in a nation-wide search for the finest wildlife photographs available. Space does not permit naming all, but the author is no less grateful to each who contributed time and energy toward making this the best popular book on our wildlife refuges.

Author's note: Since publication of the first edition of this book, in 1955, the U. S. Fish and Wildlife Service has been divided into two bureaus—the Bureau of Sport Fisheries and Wildlife, a principal duty of which is the establishment and care of the national wildlife refuge system, and the Bureau of Commercial Fisheries. Wherever the name "U. S. Fish and Wildlife Service" appears in the text of this edition, therefore, it usually refers to the Bureau of Sport Fisheries and Wildlife.

Since 1955, too, the American Ornithologists' Union issued the FIFTH CHECK-LIST OF BIRDS (1957), which contains numerous changes in species names. Because of the extensive, costly alterations that would be required to make these adjustments throughout, it has seemed best to keep such changes to a minimum in this edition.

CONTENTS

INTRODUCTION

The national wildlife refuges need to be better known and appreciated by the public. In them are preserved precious samples of our country's rich heritage of plant and animal life. As our population increases and we make ever more intensive use of our land, it is only in areas like these refuges that many forms of wildlife can hope to survive. We must never forget that each plant and animal species we have today represents the end product of two and a half billion years of evolution. To the scientist each species is a precious "biological element." Mankind may as yet not have found any particular use for many of them, but the forward-looking biologist believes that eventually many will be found to have unique values and uses. Thus, our wildlife refuges and parks should be regarded as storehouses of biological treasures that, once destroyed, can never be replaced.

For Mr. Butcher, the problem is even more fundamental. He feels that we have a moral obligation to make sure that our activities do not make it impossible for the other forms of life with which we share the earth to survive. In his abhorrence of needless killing, he comes close to Albert Schweitzer's reverence for life concept. It may take a long time to convert western man to a feeling of kinship with all life, but the history of civilization indicates that this view will ultimately triumph. The teachings of St. Francis—one of Catholicism's most appealing saints—and the great religions of the East all reveal a respect for the world's lesser creatures. We have already outgrown such cruel sports as bear baiting and dog fighting, and it seems likely that some day we will renounce hunting as a form of amusement.

Mr. Butcher justly emphasizes the point that the future of wildlife is dependent on our leaving its homes undisturbed. Many forms of wildlife have highly specialized habitat requirements and, if areas that provide these requirements are not preserved, the species that live in them are doomed to extinction. We are today in the process of establishing land use patterns that, once set, are not easily changed—patterns that will presumably persist for generations to come. In any case, once an area has been disturbed and its original plant-animal community destroyed, it is seldom possible to restore it.

Our present system of national wildlife refuges represents a good start, but we are badly in need of many more refuges, especially in our lowlands where drainage continues to destroy marshes and swamps. Only if we preserve these wetlands will it be possible for our water birds to continue to move north and south across the continent with the changing seasons. Development is proceeding at such a pace in many areas that we must earmark as soon as possible all the remaining lands of high wildlife value and see to it that they are made refuges or parks. We must also insist that, once these areas have been set aside as refuges, they be regarded as inviolate. They can be truthfully said to be the most valuable lands in America, as their long-range values to both wildlife and mankind transcend such trivial matters as temporary economic benefits for some local community or a few members of our generation. As economic and local pressure for more land to exploit grows, the defense of these areas will become increasingly difficult. It therefore behooves every American of good will to know our national wildlife refuges and their importance to us. Only if this is done will we have an informed citizenry in a position to stand up and fight effectively the selfish groups who have already started to assail our refuge system.

Fortunately, as we enjoy an ever-increasing amount of leisure, with longer weekends and longer vacations, Americans are turning to the outdoors in greater numbers. Here we are finding the peace and healthy relaxation that is needed in today's world of intense activity. Up to now we have been centering our attention on the national parks, to the detriment and overcrowding of the parks. It is high time the public realizes it owns many other kinds of wild lands, including the vast national forests; but for those who enjoy wildlife, no areas can surpass the national wildlife refuges, to which this book provides such a splendid introduction.

Pelham, N. Y.
June, 1955

RICHARD H. POUGH
The Natural Areas Council, Inc.

You Are the Guest of Wildlife

● The national wildlife refuges have been established to help prevent extinction of our native birds and mammals. They are havens of safety in which the creatures live their natural lives unmolested by man, and they provide limitless opportunity for our delight in watching wildlife in natural settings. Parents, teachers and youth leaders find the refuges ideal for showing young people how birds and mammals respond to protection. In the wild, beautiful grasslands and woodlands of the refuges, in their weird cypress swamps and vast marshes, on their blue lakes and winding waterways, more successfully than in museums and zoos, all may become acquainted with the creatures with which we are sharing the earth; learn to distinguish one species from another; study their habits; discover the pleasure of observing wildlife; and experience the fun of using binoculars and field guides.

● At almost any time of year on any refuge, many kinds of birds or mammals may be seen; but it is during the spring and autumn migrations of birds that the greatest numbers are present in most areas. The mammals, particularly the furbearers, are often difficult to find, and are less in evidence. It may require several visits before one is rewarded with a glimpse of some of the rarer species; but merely to be on a refuge—to experience the solitude and beauty of its wild landscape—is a pleasure, and quiet waiting and watching enhances the enjoyment.

● Before starting a trip to a refuge, visitors would do well to write to the manager for information about seeing the refuge, on road conditions leading to it, and on whether there is a nearby town where suitable overnight accommodations and meals are available. Many refuges are situated along highways and are near cities. Others are far from towns and are reached over rough roads. Some can be reached or seen only by boat. (It may be advisable not to attempt to visit refuges having no resident manager. Most of these are difficult of access.)

● The Bureau of Sport Fisheries and Wildlife suggests going first to headquarters to find out what part of the refuge is open to visitors, and to obtain the Bureau's free pamphlet about the area. (Literature is now available for most of the larger refuges.) The Bureau asks visitors not to molest the birds and mammals, and not to approach too closely to bird nesting colonies. Firearms are prohibited at all times, except on areas where present regulations permit opening certain locations to shooting in season.

● The Bureau of Sport Fisheries and Wildlife asks that visitors leave no refuse—cans, bottles, papers and so forth—along refuge roadways; and it requests that extreme care be used to prevent woods and grass fires, which could cause serious harm to the wildlife and its habitat. The Bureau suggests using the ashtray in your car while driving; and when on trails, crush your cigarettes out on rock or sand.

The author

Canada geese.—Along the rivers and across the bays; over the lakes and through the valleys, ever southward they come.

THE PRIMITIVE LAND

YOU AND I—many people, perhaps—try to visualize primitive North America. The continent everywhere was a picture of unblemished natural beauty, alive with birds and mammals. It knew such purity and orderliness as only nature could design. Let us roll back the pages of the past:

IT IS AUTUMN. The scene is viewed from atop a bluff—a west bank escarpment of the upper Mississippi. Across the river, an unbroken forest of bright fall color stretches eastward to the horizon. The bluff overlooking the river, slopes gently down on its west side. It is covered with grass marred only by a small burned spot where, for generations, primitive men have lighted their signal fires. Down the slope, where the grass ends, the forest begins. At the foot of the bluff along the margin of the river, a belt of woodland grows; but even the tops of the tallest trees are far below the summit. Southward, through a gap in the escarpment, a stream flows, joining the river below. The stream valley widens toward the west, and an opening in the forest shows a beaver pond, with marsh and meadow beyond.

The river scene is one of animation, with hordes of migrating waterfowl. Down from the shores of the Arctic islands; down from bleak sea coasts and tundra; south along the rivers and across the bays; over the lakes and through the valleys; past the mountains and across the prairies, ever southward they come. Snow geese and Canadas, redheads and canvasbacks, teal, widgeons and shovelers, and with them the wood duck of brighter hues, the mallard, the scaup and the pintail. Rafted waterfowl blanket the river, up stream and down, as far as the eye can see. Their calls are incessant. For days they have come, weaving across the autumnal sky. Some fly high and others low. Some pass by and some descend and settle on the water to rest and feed.

Now the sun sets. Through the din of waterfowl, calls of a new kind are heard. Vigorous, resonant, the notes come from far overhead. The white cranes are flying, journeying to southern marshes. Magnificent creatures, they, pink-tinged in the sun's last light.

Elk and deer feed in the meadow. A skunk, white markings distinct in the twilight, hunts crickets and mice. A rabbit, pursued by a fox, runs frantically, and a barred owl calls and is answered by one of its kind.

Winter has come to the bluff. Tonight it is cold and the air still. The river is frozen and the snow deep. Stars are brilliant and the moon is full. On the escarpment northward, a wolf calls. Its voice rises clearly, gently, slowly, to a high sad note, then descends and fades in tones so low it can hardly be heard.

Again and again it sings to the moon, voice rising and falling, in the instinctive, urgent longing for a mate. It calls, nearer now, and an answering voice drifts up from the forest. There on the bluff the wolf approaches, handsome in winter coat. It looks across the river, then turns to the west; lifts its head and calls again. It watches the forest at the meadow's edge. Another comes slowly, stops, comes on again, turns, retreats and disappears. The male trots down and vanishes from sight, following her trail in the snowy forest.

Trees stand far apart in this forest, with limbs spread widely, where each woodland giant has won its place. When an old tree dies, a hundred spring up, and the struggle for dominance begins again.

Snow-coated ice covers the beavers' pond, and a white mound is the beavers' house. Smaller mounds of muskrat homes dot the marsh beyond.

From up the slope, two wolves descend, bounding through the moonlit snow. Onto the pond they come frolicking. With the female leading, they dash away, puffs of snow flying at each bound.

Dawn is breaking. In a meadow up-stream deer are yarded, where they browse on tender twigs of shrubs. A wolf stands hidden from the herd by trees. Another trots by, all eyes on him. The first moves slowly, keeping behind trees. Her job will be easy if the deer are calm. Now she crouches. The snow is deep and she is hidden. In a burst of speed she takes a deer. The male lopes over, and the feast begins. Thus the deer population is held to safe numbers.

Snow still clings to northerly slopes, but warm winds blow from the south. Spring is here, and the river ice is broken. It floats downstream, angular cakes grinding. All night a gentle rain has fallen, but a band of blue now brightens the sky. The clouds drift away and the sun comes out. Geese in wedge wing north. Faintly their calls come down.

To the south, a dark cloud hovers. The pigeons are coming! A sound like far-away thunder grows louder. The flocks approach, and their rumbling seems mingled with the tinkle of bells. The unbroken front follows the river, passing over in three levels.

All day the pigeons fly, their streams merging or parting in confluent lines, stretching across the sky and darkening the sun. Hawks follow the flocks. One climbs aloft, higher, higher, drifting above the pigeons. It strikes. Pigeons plunge frantically. One bird is taken and brought to earth. The others that dove rise again to the column. The flock curves left and then to the right, forming an S in the sky. The flocks diminish, but thousands of birds still come, flashing in the evening sun. Lower now, they skim the grass, swarm into the forest and settle to roost in the trees. Branches snap and fall with their weight. The night is turbulent with restless sound.

Lush green of summer covers the land. Waterfowl have gone again to their

The author

Skunk mothers lead their miniature young in search of beetles and grubs.

breeding grounds. Warblers have swarmed with vireos, thrushes and buntings. Broods raised in the valley are now on the wing and second broods are in nests. Doves call from woodlands and nests of orioles sway on pendulous twigs over river banks. Swallows that live in secret crevices of the bluff dart and swoop, now up now down, on hissing wings, their iridescent feathers shining in the sun.

Atop the bluff, the meadow is green—a playground for many young. Does wander here in the dawn light accompanied by spotted fawns. The little ones run and prance, while sedate mothers rest and chew their cuds. The meadow is a schoolroom, too, for here in the evening, fox mothers teach offspring to stalk and pounce on mice. And while foxes romp, skunk mothers lead their miniature young in search of beetles and grubs.

A group of bison makes its way along the river's sand bars, seeking firm ground into deep water to cross to the other side. Spring floods change old bars and channels, and each year new crossings must be found. A bull sinks deep and withdraws hurriedly—quicksands are dreaded. A cow finds firm

C. C. Pace, Soil Conservation Service

Does wander here in the dawn light.

ground and wades in deeper. She swims away. Another steps in and all follow. Shaggy heads bob as they swim in the current.

In the fern-grown, mossy stream valley tracks of raccoons, otters, and minks pattern the mud. Beside the stream winds an ancient forest trail—a path well worn by the hoofs of bison, elk and deer, by the soundless pads of panthers and bobcats, by the trotting paws of wolves and coyotes, and the pattering feet of foxes. It leads to a ledge at the base of the bluff, and drops to the river through vine-festooned woodlands.

Deer drink on the river's far bank. Up-stream a way, two bark canoes come. One carries four men; the other three. These are not primitive men. On they paddle, their canoes gleaming white in the midday sun. One man lifts a rod-like implement, holding it up with head pressed against it. A report echoes and a deer falls. The white man has come.*

---

* Historians say that Marquette, Joliet and five companions, late in June, 1673, traveled down the Mississippi for a thousand miles and were the first white men to see this part of the river.

Ebb and Flow and Ebb Again

THE PRIMITIVE CONTINENT is no more. The white man has come with his ax, trap and gun. Before the days of cities, before the building of roads and cutting of forests, before marshes and pot holes and lakes were drained, before the crack of firearms was heard, and lethal poisons strewn, all of this pristine land knew nature's peace and plenty.

There remain now only remnants of the once magnificent wilderness and some of the creatures that lived in it. Gone are the passenger pigeons that darkened the sun as their seemingly endless numbers flowed across the sky; and gone are the great auk, heath hen, the Carolina paroquet and the ivory-billed woodpecker. Whooping cranes, Eskimo curlew, the California condor and at least two of the kites hang on the brink of extinction. The prairie chicken and some of the grouse are at their lowest ebb. Few now remember the former abundance of waterfowl—the ducks, geese and swans.

Although legislation was enacted in 1962 to protect the golden eagle and give better protection to the bald eagle, both species are endangered by irresponsible gunners and by poisons. Some ranchers decorate fences with the carcasses of trapped, shot, or poisoned coyotes and bobcats. The otter, the mink, the fox, the fisher, the wolverine and others with coats of fur know the grip of steel jaws; and the antelope and the deer, the seal, the mountain lion, the elk and the moose know the sting of lead. In the words of John C. VanDyke, in *The Desert,* "Every bird and beast and creeping thing—the wolf in the forest, the antelope on the plain, and the wild fowl in the sedge—fly from man's approach. They know his civilization means their destruction. Even the grizzly, secure in the chaparral of his mountain home, flinches as he crosses the white man's trail. The boot mark in the dust smells of blood and iron. The great annihilator has come, and fear travels with him."

The first indication that Congress recognized wildlife as of concern to the federal government occurred with the passage of the congressional Act of February 9, 1871, which established the Commission of Fish and Fisheries (later the Bureau of Fisheries of the Department of Commerce). Then a few years later came the Act of June 30, 1886, which established the Division of Economic Ornithology and Mammalogy (later the Biological Survey of the Department of Agriculture). Neither of these Acts gave authority to protect wildlife, their objective being research only. Regulatory and management functions with respect to fisheries and wildlife were added gradually through the years by the Congress, or by the President under his inherent powers.

During the last years of the 19th century, market hunting nearly exterminated many species. Waterfowl and shorebirds were slaughtered by every possible means and were shipped to market. The *Lacey Act,* passed by Congress in 1900, helped to end this practice.

In 1918, the *Migratory Bird Treaty Act* was passed. It implemented the treaty between Great Britain and the United States, ratified in 1916, to protect birds migrating between Canada and the United States. A similar treaty with the United States of Mexico was ratified in 1937. Scope of the *Treaty Act* was wide. It prescribed limits to the open season for shooting, and it authorized the making of regulations to meet changing conditions.

By 1929, public interest in the preservation and conservation of waterfowl resulted in the first real federal legislative authority for a broad program of refuge acquisition and development. It was based upon the *Migratory Bird Treaty* with Great Britain, signed in 1916. The new legislation was known as the *Norbeck-Andresen Migratory Bird Conservation Act.*

To carry out the acquisition of lands in a business-like fashion, and to insure close cooperation between the executive and legislative branches of the government, this Act established the Migratory Bird Conservation Commission, composed of the secretaries of Agriculture, Commerce, and Interior, and two members each from the Senate and the House. The Commission has since that time passed upon all purchases of land made under the provisions of the Act. The Biological Survey, one of the predecessor agencies of the present Fish and Wildlife Service, immediately started surveys of areas throughout the forty-eight states in an effort to locate lands suitable for purchase under the newly acquired authority of the Conservation Act.

During the next year, Congress passed a special bill which authorized $250,000 for the purchase of the Cheyenne Bottoms Refuge in Kansas, a project which incidentally never was completed by the federal government because of a subsequent inflation in land prices due to an oil boom. There also followed shortly the purchase of St. Marks Refuge in Florida, Salton Sea in California, Swanquarter in North Carolina, and Crescent Lake in Nebraska. By 1932, several other areas were added to the system; some by purchase, some by withdrawal of public lands, and one by gift.

In 1934, came the *Migratory Bird Hunting Stamp Act* requiring all shooters

The 1950-51 duck stamp, painted by Walter A. Weber, depicted a pair of trumpeter swans.

Courtesy the Fish and Wildlife Service

of migratory birds to buy a one dollar stamp each year, receipts from sales to go into a special fund for acquisition, development, and management of inviolate waterfowl sanctuaries, for law enforcement, and for study and research in waterfowl management. During the first few years the revenue from sale of these stamps amounted to about a half-million dollars, gradually increasing to more than a million each year.

The next step was taken in 1939, when under Reorganization Plan No. II (53 Stat. 1433), the Biological Survey was transferred from the Department of Agriculture, and Fisheries from the Department of Commerce, to the Department of the Interior. Then in 1940, under Reorganization Plan No. III, the two bureaus were combined to form the Fish and Wildlife Service. Further reorganization occurred in 1956. An Act (70 Stat. 1119) created the United States Fish and Wildlife Service to be administered by a commissioner and to be comprised of two bureaus: a Bureau of Sport Fisheries and Wildlife for sport fisheries and wild birds and mammals (except whales, seals and sea lions), and a Bureau of Commercial Fisheries.

The 1940 *Convention on Nature Protection and Wildlife Preservation in the Western Hemisphere,* an outgrowth of the *Migratory Bird Treaty,* dealt not alone with the protection of nature on this continent, but on both American continents. As expressed in the preamble, its purpose was "to protect and preserve representatives of all species of native flora and fauna, including migratory birds, in sufficient numbers and over areas extensive enough to assure them from becoming extinct."

The *Pittman-Robertson Federal Aid in Wildlife Restoration Act,* passed in 1937, called for a ten (later increased to eleven) percent federal excise tax on sporting arms and ammunition to be placed in a special fund in the U. S. Treasury and appropriated by Congress to the states each year to help them establish various wildlife projects. The states pay one quarter and the federal government three quarters of the cost of projects. By 1960, the federal portion of this fund was about 12.8 million dollars annually.

In 1948, the *Migratory Bird Hunting Stamp Act* came up for amendment to raise the price of the stamp to two dollars. Appended to the bill was a provision to authorize the director, Bureau of Sport Fisheries and Wildlife, at the discretion of the Secretary of the Interior, to open to public shooting any waterfowl refuge, but not to exceed twenty-five percent of the area, when the waterfowl population justified it. Opposition of nature protection groups prevented this; but in 1949 another attempt succeeded.

In 1958, the Act again was amended, raising the price of the stamps to three dollars, and increasing the shooting area to forty percent. This time the bill was slipped through so quietly that there was no opportunity to block the shooting provision. All who value wildlife for its own sake should write their senators and representatives, Washington 25, D. C., and ask that the *Migratory Bird*

Wesley F. Kubichek

The refuge boundary marker of the Bureau of Sport Fisheries and Wildlife is a familiar sight in many parts of our country.

Hunting Stamp Act be amended to keep our national refuges closed to shooting and safe for wildlife.

In the early 1930's, waterfowl populations reached a new low because of overshooting and because of drought in the breeding areas of the continent. A closed season should have been declared in the interest of waterfowl. The rescue of the ducks came through a rider attached to the 1934 *Migratory Bird Hunting Stamp Act*, by which $6,000,000 was to be transferred from any unexpended balance left over from the previous year's relief funds and made immediately available to the emergency duck rescue program. This program took the form of a large expansion of the refuge system.

Our national wildlife refuge system today comprises nearly 290 areas. In the care of the U. S. Fish and Wildlife Service, it constitutes the most intensively managed system of reservations for the protection of wildlife in the world. The refuges vary from a few acres to more than 4000 square miles in area. When the waterfowl and other migrants come south in the fall, they find food and protection in refuges generally located no more than 200 miles apart along the four principal flyways—along both coasts and through the interior. The first refuge, Pelican Island, Florida, established in 1903, was for the protection of a nesting colony of brown pelicans. In the next few years many other reserves of this kind were established along both coasts and in Alaska. More than forty of these are for colonial nesting birds. Over a dozen other refuges provide habitat for large mammals, including the bison, elk, antelope, deer and bighorn sheep. The more than 216 waterfowl refuges are of three principal kinds; those in the north for nesting, those along the flyways for resting and feeding, and the wintering grounds in the south.

Most of the areas that are refuges today represent restorations of unsuccessful drainage projects or the development of new marshes by the construction of low dams and water-control structures. Management practices include the growing of food-producing vegetation, control of disease, and the reduction of predatory species such as snakes, turtles, and other nest destroyers.

The waterfowl refuges are aiding the survival of such notable species as the blue and snow geese and the whistling swan today. Without them the birds would become rare or extinct. The breeding grounds of these geese, swans and some others are on the islands beyond Hudson Bay and along the Arctic Sea coasts of Alaska and Yukon Territory and elsewhere. As yet, we have not shown much concern about these breeding areas because they have seemed safe from interference by man. But already exploitive activities are reaching above the Arctic Circle. The time may be approaching when we and the Canadians will have to establish additional patrolled breeding ground sanctuaries for the far north breeders, if these species are to continue as members of our continental fauna.

The idea that certain refuges should be given up by the Fish and Wildlife Service is sometimes expressed, and this is heard particularly with regard to the refuges established to preserve the endangered large mammals—elk, antelope and bighorn sheep. Our federal government has no greater responsibility than to preserve for the enjoyment of ourselves and future generations those species which are threatened with extinction, both birds and mammals. As the years go by, and civilization continues to spread, the need for more and larger refuges becomes increasingly urgent. Any proposal to abandon refuges, whether from within the Service itself or elsewhere, deserves careful scrutiny.

The central office of the Fish and Wildlife Service is in the Department of the Interior, Washington, D. C., and six regional offices are located at Portland, Oregon; Albuquerque, New Mexico; Minneapolis, Minnesota; Atlanta, Georgia; Boston, Massachusetts; and Juneau, Alaska. Field personnel reside on more than a hundred and forty of the refuges.

The Service today is highly responsive to the wishes of the gunning fraternity. Laws and regulations governing the killing of wildlife, and often governing the actions of the Service itself, are influenced by the gunners. This is because the funds for all new wildlife refuge lands and waters are contributed through purchase of duck stamps by this group. The refuges have been especially successful in benefitting mallards and Canada geese, two of the many species the shooters like to kill. But the gunning fraternity often hampers or defeats federal authorities in efforts to reduce bag limits or shorten the open season, and it is aided in its legislative aspirations by hardware dealers, sporting goods manufacturers, hunting camp operators, sportsmen's magazines and, above all, the arms and ammunition makers. These interests constitute a force to which state and federal legislators are sensitive; all seek profit through the spilled blood of wildlife.

The sportsmen boast that they support a six billion dollar a year business; but those who enjoy nature for its own sake, support an even greater business. Whereas 15,000,000 men and boys take pleasure in killing, more than 30,000,000 people go yearly to see the wonders of the national parks and monuments. Countless other millions visit state parks, wilderness areas and refuges. In this regard, the Bureau of Sport Fisheries and Wildlife reported that observation of wildlife, picnicking, swimming and photography were the most popular uses of the refuges in 1961. Nearly 7,500,000 visitors, or about sixty-seven percent of the total, sought enjoyment of these activities. Fishing accounted for about twenty-nine percent, or 3,500,000 persons; while shooting was pursued by 302,427 persons, or three and a half to four and a half percent, on ninety refuges.

J. Clark Salyer II, chief of the Branch of Wildlife Refuges in 1955, had something to say about this at a meeting of the Service's regional directors in that year. Speaking about visitors other than fishermen and gunners, he said, "It must be emphasized that they . . . are the most potent and vocal supporters we have. When the chips are down, it is always this group which has resolved the nation's great conservation crises, and they have been the most steadfast supporters of the refuge program."

The refuge system offers a measure of hope for the future of wildlife, but as constituted today, its areas are neither large enough nor numerous enough to justify our complacency. Much more needs to be done to preserve additional wildlife habitat before the safe future of endangered species is assured. Although the system is inadequate to fully meet the needs of our vanishing wildlife, it is under constant attack by private interests seeking to exploit it. Real estate developers, road builders, oil and gas companies and mining interests are among these. Certain government agencies also seek to utilize the refuges for such devastating purposes as dam building, gunnery practice and artillery ranges. Whether justified or not, and often it is not, such use, when permitted, reduces or eliminates their value to wildlife. Actually, the refuges are contributing to local economic welfare. The Fish and Wildlife Service encourages activities on them such as cooperative farming for the production of food for man and wildlife, and grazing and haying when these will reduce fire hazards. These operations returned more than $1,946,000 to the U. S. Treasury in a single year (1960), of which twenty-five percent was paid to the counties in which the refuges are located, in lieu of taxes.

In 1961, Congress passed a bill to accelerate the acquisition of wetlands. The bill called for federal loans for land purchase, the money to be paid back to the federal treasury with funds from the sale of duck stamps. In 1962, two other pieces of legislation were enacted affecting the refuge system. One authorized an increase of refuge use for recreation. The other halted payment of federal subsidies to drain wetlands which the Bureau of Sport Fisheries and Wildlife considered important for waterfowl.

The 1961 law, if Congress appropriates sufficient money, will preserve some rapidly vanishing habitat. The bill halting subsidy payments for wetlands drainage is equally important. The use of refuges for recreation has dangerous implications. Parts of some refuges should be made accessible to those wishing to observe wildlife, but if public use goes much beyond this, the value of the areas to birds and mammals is likely to be reduced.

Under these and other laws, the Bureau of Sport Fisheries and Wildlife is pursuing certain objectives, among which are these: To develop fully the existing refuges and those acquired for habitat improvement; to maintain adequately both existing and newly acquired areas, providing upkeep, protection, and proper land management; to provide operating funds and field staffs required to develop, manage, and maintain the areas and their resources; to facilitate research to safeguard wildlife populations; and to provide for enjoyment and use of wildlife resources consistent with the objectives of the refuge program.

Killing for Fun

I WISH now to speak in defense of the defenseless—the innocent, beautiful creatures of the wild against whom man wages a needless, relentless, pitiless war —a war in which he uses every conceivable trick to entice harmless creatures to come within gun range, or to lure them into traps; a war in which he hides to await the unsuspecting, and greets them with a hail of lead; a war in which he uses hounds to tree the hunted, and at close range blasts it to death; a war in which there is no sympathy or justice for the hunted, but in which the hunter becomes an idol to his community and a hero to his children.

An October, 1960, release of the Fish and Wildlife Service says that, for the preceding year, hunting license sales continued an upward trend to an all-time high of almost 18,500,000. This does not include landowners shooting on their own properties and men of the armed services who, in some states, are not required to buy licenses. By glamorizing the chase and the kill, the gunning fraternity is attracting thousands of new recruits each year; while soldiers, having learned to handle firearms, are adding to the increase.

What we most need is a new attitude toward wildlife. Dismal indeed is the viewpoint that the wild creatures are of no value unless they serve as targets. Those who appreciate wildlife for its own sake cannot accept the fanatical idea that there is or can be fun in killing. It seems incredible in these enlightened days that great numbers of men should seek pleasure in making sport of the lives of innocent creatures. More and more people are coming to realize that to do so is wrong, and to teach youngsters to do so is doubly wrong. Any man who thinks this matter through, if honest, should reach this conclusion.

If the present pressure for killing is not soon drastically reduced, additional species seem fated to vanish. To kill a beautiful creature that has the same right to life as we is a moral obliquity. To force a creature to give up its life merely to prove oneself a marksman, or to bolster a down-trodden ego, is indefensible.

Sport shooting exercises primeval instinct—an instinct that enlightened society is striving to subdue. Why is it, then, that society does not frown on pleasure killing? Probably because it is not a spectator sport. The great mass of our people who might otherwise bring influence against it, never come close enough to it to discover its true nature. In his book, *Our Vanishing Wildlife*, Dr. William T. Hornaday said, "The number of armed men and boys who annually take the field in the United States in pursuit of birds and quadrupeds is enormous. People who do not shoot have no conception of it; and neither do they comprehend the mechanical perfection and fearful deadliness of the weapons used. This feature of the situation can hardly be realized until some aspect of it is actually seen."

The gunning fraternity is motivated by the thought that shooting wildlife is wholesome and manly. Boys are taught this, often before they develop the ability to think independently. Although some advertisements and magazine articles

Waterfowl shooters in California hide behind these piles of hay and wait for the ducks and geese to fly over from nearby marshes.

The author

would have you believe so, gun-toting and killing do not make a man more of a man than he is, or put a single drop of redder blood in his veins.

Motion picture shorts depict sport shooting with bows and arrows, rifles and shotguns, and occasionally with the aid of hounds and other means. Producers, aware of audience resistance to such films, carefully word the commentary to win sympathy and approval. In the case of a bear hunt, the pursued animal is described as a ruthless, blood-thirsty killer. Life and limb of human beings and livestock are said to be in danger as long as the animal remains at large. The hunter is regarded, therefore, as doing a public service in ridding the countryside of the "marauder." Thus, to the audience, the bear is made out to be the devil incarnate, and the hunter an avenging angel. Pictures like this, and lurid articles of a similar nature appearing in national magazines of almost every kind, distort the truth and create prejudice, fear and hatred toward animals. In contrast to these, the beautiful productions of the Walt Disney Studios, the *True Life Adventure Series*, are stimulating public appreciation and understanding of the wild creatures.

There is nothing praiseworthy about becoming callous to the sight of blood and suffering. In war, men must harden to these; but even now, the time when war will be outlawed may be closer than we think. To end the merciless, relentless aggression against wildlife might well hasten the day when nation will cease to fight nation.

The gunner knows the wrong inherent in his sport, and he, better than anyone, knows the weakness of his position. He dreads criticism, and is ever ready to defend himself. He tells you that he will give up shooting the wild creatures when you give up eating beef; but we know that killing for fun and the raising of livestock for food have nothing in common. Livestock slaughter, furthermore, is carried on under humane laws.

The gunner tells you that to pursue and kill wild animals is to obey a primitive instinct, and that it is character building. It may be true that he is bowing to a primitive instinct, but the idea that by doing so he improves his character is absurd. Such reasoning shows a troubled conscience.

Attempting to justify sport shooting, the gunner often refers to Biblical passages. A favorite is Genesis 1: 26, "Let us make man in our image, after our likeness; and let them have dominion over the fish of the sea, and over the fowl of the air . . . and over all the earth." This salves his conscience because he misinterprets the meaning of the phrase "have dominion over." It does not imply the right to kill, but to govern, and bears with it responsibility for the welfare of the governed. The gunner is endowed with no divine authority to kill needlessly. If he were, the verse would contain a contradiction, for there hardly could be anything more unlike divine perfection than a human being who kills God's creatures for fun. There is a commandment that says, "Thou shalt not kill."

Some gunners seem satisfied that they are doing their duty to wildlife, and are compensating for killing, by purchasing the annual duck stamp and through payment of the tax on arms and ammunition, which goes to the Bureau of Sport Fisheries and Wildlife; and many believe that wildlife protection is made possible solely through their own activities, while they accuse the non-gunner of doing nothing at all for wildlife. The Bureau receives approximately $63,000,-000 annually to carry on its work. Of this amount, about $20,000,000 comes from the arms tax and the duck stamp, and nearly $30,000,000 from the tax-paying public, through the federal treasury. Almost $13,000,000 derives from other sources, including more than $6,000,000 from a tax on fishing tackle. These figures make it plain that the gunners are not alone in supporting the work of the Fish and Wildlife Service. It should be said, too, that many people who have an interest in wildlife for its own sake can always be counted on to defend it and the refuge system in times of emergency.

The gunner will tell you that hunting was the oldest necessity, and that a sport based on it is as natural as breathing. It *was* a necessity in primitive and pioneer times. Today there is no longer any valid reason to eat wild meat, and the contention that to secure it is a primary reason for going afield with a gun seems a poor excuse. For most people, food is more easily and more economically obtained by other means than shooting wild creatures. Killing is the primary reason that most men go afield, and many in the fraternity admit this. Improvement of marksmanship with rifle and shotgun is also a principal motive, but living creatures are not legitimate targets.

Bow and arrow shooting is becoming popular in some parts of our country. Many who are enticed to participate do not fully understand the added brutality of a weapon that may fail to strike a vital spot without killing, and may dangle for days, festering and paining with every move, until death finally comes.

The gunner tries to vindicate himself by saying that those who would save the birds and mammals from being shot are motivated by sentimentality, as though sentimentality were undesirable. Let him call it by whatever name he will; the fact is that it is much the same motive that prompts the saving of anything of beauty—the great works of nature such as the Grand Canyon and Crater Lake, or the great works of art and architecture. That is not sentimentality, but sentiment, and it is a worthy emotion, for a great deal of good has been accomplished by it. By such an argument, the gunner shows again he is the victim of his conscience.

The gunner is often heard to say that if it were not for "hunting" he would have no excuse to go into the country. Positive enjoyment of the outdoors cannot be experienced by approaching the wild creatures as targets and causing them to fall bleeding and dead at one's feet. There are many thrilling, healthful ways to enjoy the outdoors without killing the creatures that add interest to the country and make their homes there.

In discussing with the gunner the pros and cons of his sport, it is best not to engage in argument, or to try to convert him. It is not you, but his friends, his relations and his community who can accomplish the most. Therefore, do whatever you can to promote right thinking among them. The gunner does not *want* to be regarded by his fellows as being motivated by brute instinct.

Deplorable as are the actions of the law-abiding gunner, the activities of the commercial duck shooters must be regarded as despicable. Catering to restauranteurs in the cities, these men may slaughter hundreds of baited ducks in a single night. To apprehend these violators of the *Migratory Bird Treaty Act*, law enforcement officers—The Fish and Wildlife Service's "G men"—are kept busy day and night. America's wildlife is not for sale!

A thoughtful, humane person cultivates a sense of justice toward all life. There is nothing fair in the unequal contest between a helpless creature and a man armed with a modern high-powered, long-range rifle or shotgun. The increasing efficiency of firearms requires less and less skill on the part of the shooter. To take a good photograph of a wild bird or mammal calls for infinitely more skill, and the trophy is lasting and may give pleasure to many. After being "shot" by a camera, the animal continues to live its natural happy life, to raise its young, and to give enjoyment to other people who see it. If you must shoot, do it with a camera.

It is true that, under the artificial conditions which civilization has produced, it is sometimes necessary for man to take a hand in preserving the balance of nature by removing individuals of a species that locally has become too abundant. There will always be men ready to do this remorseful, necessary job; but never let it be said that *you* are one of them. Collecting for museums, if not carried too far; killing in the wilderness to prevent oneself from starving; or killing in self-defense—these, too, may be legitimate reasons for taking life. But to reduce or exterminate the so-called predators, as some farmers and gunners advocate, often brings a plague of rodents that spells doom for farm crops. Furthermore, the predators have high esthetic appeal. To see a mountain lion or a coyote in the wild may give a far greater thrill than seeing a herd of deer; and to glimpse a fox may be more rewarding than to see a covey of quail. Some gunners take the view that all meat-eating mammals and birds should be wiped out because they compete for the "game" the gunner likes to shoot. To one who values wildlife for the pleasure of seeing it and having it around, all creatures have their rightful place in the panorama of life, and he does not speak of some species as "game," "predators," "vermin" or "varmints." * When unmolested, all the wild creatures lead clean, orderly, beautiful lives as designed by nature.

---

* The word "game" is used by gunners to designate the species they like to kill, but it finds no place in the vocabulary of those who do not shoot. Instead, terms such as "wildlife," "furbearers," "larger mammals," and "upland birds" are used.

Lamentable as man's treatment of wildlife has been, the leaders and organizations of the gunning fraternity (whose primary objective is to maintain an adequate supply of live targets) have done and are doing a great deal for wildlife. They promote wildlife legislation (sometimes not in the best interest of wildlife) and keep in touch with the law-makers. They join forces with others when threats to the national parks and similar wild lands occur. They have a keen sense of the esthetic value of such lands and the wildlife on them, and there is fine cooperation between all groups interested in the outdoors on such occasions. Even the gun clubs sometimes preserve valuable wildlife habitat. In addition, the gunning fraternity has sponsored a great deal of wildlife research through studies carried on all over the continent. As a result, important information has been learned and published, and this has made scientific wildlife management possible. The Wildlife Management Institute, Washington, D. C., is responsible for many outstanding projects. One of these is the Delta Waterfowl Research Station in Manitoba, of which Harold Titus said, in *Field and Stream*, "Here is the lone spot in the continent's vast duck producing area where a competent staff on a typical site with sufficient equipment has been established for a truly long-pull investigation of all those factors which govern waterfowl abundance." Restoration of the pronghorn antelope in many areas of the West is another example of work well done.

In the ranks of the gunning fraternity there are many fine people, but there is not one who would not be better by putting his gun aside for more constructive pastimes. Dr. Hornaday has said, "Every man who still shoots game is a soldier in the army of destruction! There is no blinking that fact. Such men do not stand on the summit with the men who now protect the game and do not shoot at all."

Catering to the Whims of Fashion

IN ALL HISTORY, the mind of man has not conceived an implement of greater cruelty than the steel trap. Never before has a device caused such widespread suffering. Every year, literally millions of innocent, harmless furbearing animals endure pain, freezing, thirst and slow death because of this trap. Why? Merely to satisfy the whims of fashion.

The cruelty of the steel trap is not realized by the general public. As with pleasure killing, it is an activity without spectators. Articles that might bring the horrors of trapping to the magazine-reading public do not find their way into print because most magazines, particularly those read by women, derive income from the advertising of fur merchants. Trapping differs in one respect from sport shooting, in that usually it is not done for fun, except occasionally by boys who are encouraged to do it as a "healthy outdoor occupation."

Victims of the trap may remain alive for hours, sometimes for days, until they die of exposure, or until the trapper makes his rounds. Not infrequently a trapped animal becomes the prey of another animal. There is perhaps no more pitiful sight than a fox, a beautiful, intelligent creature, frozen to unconsciousness, still having life in its body. One can only try to imagine the suffering it endured. A raccoon, trapped and exposed to rain and wind for long hours or even several days and nights, must feel the most intense suffering before the trapper comes to end its misery. Animals, no more than we, can endure prolonged exposure to inclement weather and excessive temperatures.

For many years efforts have been made to encourage the designing of a humane trap—one that will cause instantaneous death, or that will not inflict pain. Some quick-killing traps are in use today, but they are generally too costly for practical use, and are designed only for particular kinds of animals. Some believe that a thoroughly humane trap, priced to permit its being used as widely as the present-day steel trap, is beyond possibility. Perhaps that is so. But even if an economically priced humane trap were invented, the fact would still remain that fear—the fear an animal feels when suddenly held—is a phase of its suffering. Occasionally one dies in the trap from fear alone, for almost all wild furbearing animals rely on their ability to run to avoid harm.

The desire of trapped animals to free themselves is seen in dreadful testimony, where all too frequently a paw is left behind, with bone broken and flesh torn. The ground and vegetation all around may be torn and chewed in the frantic struggle.

A trap does not select its prey. In many parts of our country, there are no laws to prohibit trapping during periods of motherhood. The trapping of pregnant females or of a mother away from her young is multiple killing, cruel and wasteful in the extreme.

One of the heartless phases of trapping is a method used to secure scent from live animals to lure more animals to the trap. Because this is so utterly repulsive and the plight of the creatures used for this purpose is so pitiful, it is perhaps better not described here.

It would be difficult to imagine anything more inhumane than the steel trap; yet, because of the mental attitude that accompanies them, certain kinds of exhibitions are cruel to the point of revulsion. *Life*, a few years ago, published a picture story entitled "Ohio Circle Fox Hunt," which concluded with a little child cheered by its elders, beating a tired fox to death. It was not the fact that a local fox population needed reduction, but the way in which the reduction was made that prompted scorn from coast to coast. More recently, *Look* published a picture story entitled "Greyhounds vs. Coyote," in which two ranchers in an automobile chased a coyote to exhaustion, then released three lean greyhounds to the attack. Before the hounds had completed the job, one of the ranchers swung the coyote aloft by the tail, and brought it down with a "skull cracking" blow. Exhibitions such as these, as well as pastimes like "coon-on-a-log" and the "goose pull," show the depths to which some human minds are capable of sinking. They emphasize the necessity for right-thinking people everywhere to encourage greater public understanding and sympathy toward wildlife.

An eloquent plea for the wild furbearers by the great actress Minnie Maddern Fiske appeared some years ago as a foreword to a booklet, *From Thumbscrew to Steel Trap,* by Henry Salt, published by the Society for the Prevention of Cruelty to Animals. It was one of the most poignant articles ever written on the subject. Mrs. Fiske wrote: "It is only in work connected with the protection of dumb animals that anything is learned of the crimes of human society —our crimes—against the lower animals. These crimes are unnecessary; they persist because they are hidden from our view. It is beyond imagination that an intelligent Christian woman would wear furs if she witnessed the animals in the agonies of the trap. Once the truth is brought home, it will be impossible for right-thinking women to escape the question 'shall the steel trap go or stay?' It is women, most of them unconsciously, who support the most stupendous concern in organized cruelty on the face of the earth—trapping.

"Trapping means the unbelievable torture of vast numbers of animals every year. It means the excruciating anguish of the clutch, fever, sickness, thirst, starvation—almost every agony conceivable to the living body. These creatures are as sensitive to torture and torment as we.

"How true are the words, addressed to women, in a southern newspaper: 'As you lie comfortable in bed at night, remember that through the long hours, millions of creatures are groaning and tearing themselves to pieces that you may wrap yourself in their skins. And there are countless mothers of the wild among these panting things. There are acts of amazing heroism—the trapped mother bear or fox, who will somehow reach her hungry little ones, dragging her trap with her for days. If you mothers have imagination, you can imagine that mother enduring the torture of the clutch, and at the same time suckling her young.' "

Edwin Markham asks, "Ladies, are the furs you wear worth the hell of this despair?"

The American Humane Association has asked, "Shall we be permitted to achieve success or shall we continue to ignore an opportunity to effect reform in a business that owes its existence to frightful cruelty? The answer rests with the women of America."

Some say that cruel trapping will never end. Women, they say, will not give up wearing furs as long as there are furbearers to be trapped. But there are others who point to the response of women to the near extinction of egrets and other birds in the early part of this century. Plume hunters catering to the millinery trade were killing these beautiful birds in our southern swamps during the nesting season in order to take their nuptial plumes for women's hats. Killing the adult birds meant death for the young. When the women learned the story, the demand for egret feathers ended.

Already many women are giving up wearing wild furs, and are buying ranch-raised furs or the beautiful synthetic furs that are now on the market. An organization called Defenders of Wildlife, established in the 1940's, successor to the Anti Steel Trap League, is bringing to nation-wide attention the cruelty of the steel trap, and is meeting with a success that proves the innate humanity of our people. In addition to a quarterly bulletin and a junior bulletin for children ages six through fourteen, the organization rents wildlife films and distributes free educational aids to teachers, students, and Boy and Girl Scout groups, as well as to individuals, clubs and societies upon request. Most women who see the films become ardent defenders of the wildlings, and are determined never again to buy wild furs. Further information about the organization may be obtained by writing to Defenders of Wildlife, 809 Dupont Circle Building, 1346 Connecticut Avenue, N. W., Washington 6, D. C.

MANY species of wildlife are rapidly disappearing. Only a change in men's minds can stay the decline. There must be a trend away from thinking of the living creatures as targets or enemies or as a source of profit from pelts, toward kindness and a sense of kinship with them. There is need for less thought of destroying, and more of trying to protect them; less hostility, and more friendliness and appreciation of their beauty and wonder. It requires men and women of high moral courage and with a keen sense of justice to work for universal recognition of the rights of these harmless, helpless, flesh-and-blood creatures; to end their needless suffering and death; to abolish the pitiless, shameful tearing of flesh, shattering of bone and infliction of pain in the name of sport and fashion. It is time to stop thinking of the gunner as a hero and of his sport as wholesome.

Let us hold to the truth that it is wrong to kill for fun or to cause needless suffering. Let us bring about reform of the practicing gunner and trapper by promoting proper public opinion. When those closest to the gunner and the trapper—their relations, friends and community—recognize pleasure killing and needless infliction of pain for what they are, the gunner no longer will take pride in his trophies, or the trapper in his pelts. To bring this about, let us resort to every means at our command—the press, the radio, the schools and the churches.

Let us begin by encouraging our youngsters to feel sympathy and kindness toward animals; by stimulating within them love for the animals and a desire to learn about their interesting life habits; by showing them that pleasure from wildlife comes not from killing, but from observing it. Junior membership in Defenders of Wildlife and membership in the Junior Audubon Clubs are ideal means for developing in our children a humane attitude toward the creatures of the wild.

Let us avoid literature and broadcast programs that glorify the gunner and glamorize the chase and the kill; avoid motion pictures whose alleged purposes are to teach youngsters "good sportsmanship" and "to handle firearms safely," but which actually are designed to win new recruits to the gunning fraternity and to stimulate the sale of firearms; and let us no longer resort to the purchase of toy firearms for youthful amusement. John Muir once wrote, "Under proper training even the most savage boy will rise above the bloody flesh and sport business. . . . God-like sympathy grows and thrives and spreads far beyond the teachings of churches and schools, where too often the mean, blinding, loveless doctrine is taught that animals have neither mind nor soul, have no rights that we are bound to respect, and were made only for man, to be . . . slaughtered or enslaved."

To strive to eliminate suffering and misery among the wildlings is an urgent responsibility of thinking people everywhere. It rests largely with parents, educators and church leaders. We are truly humane when we practice the Golden Rule, not alone toward our own kind, but toward all the beautiful and interesting birds and mammals with which we are sharing the earth.

The trap jaws clanked and held him fast
    None marked his fright, none heard his cries.
His struggles ceased; he lay at last
    With wide uncomprehending eyes
And watched the sky grow dark above
    And watched the sunset turn to gray;
And quaked in anguish while he strove
    To gnaw the prisoned leg away.

Then day came rosy from the east,
    But still those steel jaws kept their hold;
And no one watched the prisoned beast
    But fear and hunger, thirst and cold.
Oppressed by pain his dread grew numb.
    Fright no more stirred his flagging breath.
He longed in vain to see him come,
    The cruel biped, bringing death.
Then through the gloom that night came one
    Who set the timid spirit free:
"I know thine anguish, little son—
    So once men trapped and tortured me."

—F. F. Van de Water.

We are weary of witnessing the greed, selfishness and cruelty of "civilized" men toward the wild creatures of the earth. We are sick of tales of slaughter and pictures of carnage. It is time for a sweeping reformation; and that is precisely what we now demand.—William T. Hornaday.

NATIONAL WILDLIFE REFUGES

ARANSAS NATIONAL WILDLIFE REFUGE, established in 1937, is seventy-four square miles in area, and is situated on the Blackjack Peninsula between Aransas and San Antonio bays, on the Texas coast. It consists of salt marshes along the outer fringes, while the peninsula itself is sandy, with gently undulating higher ground, in places supporting low forests of post, live and blackjack oaks that are picturesquely shaped along the eastward bluffs by prevailing winds from the Gulf of Mexico. The Fish and Wildlife Service has cleared extensive tracts for wildlife species needing grasslands. A number of fresh water ponds occupy openings in the wooded areas.

The sky was gray and a cool wind blew from the gulf. We went out to the Intracoastal Waterway, where that wide, man-made canal cuts through the marshes. While there is nothing extraordinary or unique about these marshes, they have the distinction of being the wintering ground of the rarest bird in North America—the big white whooping crane. This was late April. Perhaps the last of the cranes had already flown north. For years we had clung to the hope that someday we might see this magnificent bird. Had we come earlier in the season, there would have been little doubt about seeing it. We had traveled many hundreds of miles to get here, so it might be now or never. As the boat made its way through the choppy, leaden water, with spray dashing over the bow, we kept our binoculars trained on the level line of marsh ahead. Suddenly, there it was, a speck of white, far away but distinct, and then another! As we drew nearer, we feared they might take off before we had a really good look. We soon reached our nearest possible point, and still they fed quietly. Now even the red on their heads was visible through the binoculars. We lingered; and after the great birds had wandered some distance, now on the grassy mud of the marsh, now wading in pools of open water, and back to the mud again, their increasing restlessness indicated they might fly. First one, then the other, launched itself into the air and, with long legs and necks extended, flew to another part of the refuge. We were particularly fortunate, because this part of the crane wintering ground has since been closed to visitors.

The whooping crane stands five feet tall and has a wing-spread of seven and a half to nine feet. Aransas is the bird's natural wintering ground. In spring it takes off for its breeding range in northern Canada, returning to Aransas again in the autumn. On

Once there may have been over a thousand whooping cranes, but shooting has reduced them to about three dozen wild birds.

Wesley F. Kubichek, Fish and Wildlife Service

Allan D. Cruickshank, from National Audubon Society

Five feet tall with a wing-spread of seven and a half feet, the whooping crane is North America's largest migratory bird.

The author

With their long necks and legs extended, whooping cranes in flight are thrilling to see.

these migratory flights, the crane is subjected to natural hazards, and to the guns of uninformed, thoughtless men who would consider so large a bird a good target. Robert P. Allen, in *The Whooping Crane*, Research Report No. 3, page 83, National Audubon Society, 1952, says, "It is my belief that the original population of *Grus americana*, in recent times, and down to 1860, or possibly 1870, totalled between 1300 and 1400 individuals." Today the whooping crane is reduced to about three dozen wild individuals.

When a species, such as the whooping crane, has been so drastically reduced, its continued existence becomes precarious. The crane's present population could be wiped out over night, and once gone, it would be extinct forever. The Fish and Wildlife Service, the National Audubon Society and many other nature protection groups, as well as authorities in Canada, are united in an effort to save this bird, and, if possible, to restore it to safe numbers. What the results of these efforts will be, only the future can tell. If success is to be achieved, one thing is certain—that people everywhere must learn about the plight of the crane and its threatened extinction. This applies particularly to people living in North and South Dakota, Nebraska, Kansas, Oklahoma and Texas, and in the Canadian provinces through which the crane migrates. With wide-spread public sympathy and appreciation, it may yet be possible to bring the whooping crane back in sufficient abundance so that more and more people will be able to enjoy seeing it.

The gray sandhill crane, only a little smaller than the whooping, and the Rio Grande turkey, inhabit the refuge, and many of the latter have been trapped to restock other areas. Sennett's white-tailed hawk and Audubon's caracara nest here, with the mottled duck, which has a range naturally limited to the coasts of Texas and Louisiana. The duck is only one of many species of waterfowl that winter in or migrate through the refuge, for during the cooler months, pintails, mallards, shovelers, widgeons, cinnamon, blue-winged and green-winged teal, canvasbacks, redheads, ring-necked ducks, lesser scaups, buffleheads, gadwalls, ruddy and fulvous tree ducks, and Canada, lesser Canada, blue, lesser snow and white-fronted geese can be seen at the refuge.

Shorebirds of numerous species stop here by the thousands during migration, many remaining to winter, and they can be seen easily in the marshy areas and around the shallow margins of ponds. Here are sandpipers, dowitchers, curlews, stilts, black-bellied, ringed, mountain, thick-billed, snowy, upland and piping plovers, killdeers and the sora, king and clapper rails. Among the larger wading birds are the beautiful roseate spoonbills, the reddish, American and snowy egrets, and several species of herons. The Cassin's sparrow also is a resident of the refuge.

Along the Texas coast, nature stages one of her grandest songbird shows. This occurs in April, when thrushes, buntings, tanagers, vireos, warblers and dozens of other species are migrating. The songsters literally swarm through here, following the coastline as they come from South and Central America and Mexico on their way north and northeastward across our country. Many of them go on to Canada. At times they are so numerous that the trees and shrubs appear to be blossoming with animated flowers.

Besides the avian population, there are also many kinds of mammals that make their homes at Aransas. The nine-banded armadillo is one that visitors are interested to see. Covered in scaly armor, and measuring about two and a half feet from the tip of its long nose to the tip of its tapering tail, this odd little creature lives in burrows and thrives on insects, spiders and scorpions. It usually raises four young, all of the same sex. It is inclined to be overtrusting, but if approached too closely will set off at a rapid run. Raccoon, opossum, squirrel, whitetail deer, skunk, and swamp and jack rabbits inhabit the refuge, and here, too, dwells the little wild pig called the collared peccary or javelina. Unlike the razor-backed hog of the southern Appalachian Mountains, the peccary, less than two feet tall at the shoulder, is not a domesticated animal gone wild.

Almost everywhere needlessly hunted and killed, the peccary or javelina finds Aransas a haven of safety.

The author

The author

Oaks along the east side of Aransas are picturesquely shaped by gales from the Gulf of Mexico.

It is a native American. Needlessly persecuted in the name of "sport" its former range, as far north as southwestern Arkansas, has been reduced to southern Texas, Arizona and New Mexico. A peculiarity of the animal is the musk gland on the back, just forward of the tail. When alarmed, scent is given off by this gland, probably to warn other peccaries of danger. The peccary usually bears twins, which are able to stand and run about a few hours after birth. This little animal is nowhere abundant, and it deserves all the protection we can give it.

When Aransas was established, there was a pre-existing mineral lease on the area. Today the refuge has been invaded by a number of gas wells that have been drilled along its west side. Great barges powered by tugs, as well as yachts and other craft are constantly plying the Intracoastal Waterway, and promiscuous shooting from the decks of boats sometimes occurs, resulting in the loss of cranes and other protected birds. These intrusions make the protection of wildlife and the management of the refuge extremely difficult. To entice the cranes to places of greater safety, the Fish and Wildlife Service is developing pools elsewhere in the refuge, with food supplies identical to those along the waterway. The canal right-of-way had been acquired before the refuge was established, and prior to construction, the route was moved to do as little harm as possible to the area. Already most of our vast land area is being used for our needs. Wildlife, too, must have land for its needs, if it is to continue to exist and give pleasure to those who want to see it.

Headquarters is in the refuge, and the address is Austwell, Texas. The area is reached southwest from Galveston and Houston, over State Route 35 to Tivoli, then east a few miles over a paved road to Austwell and the refuge. There are shell-surfaced roads through parts of the refuge that enable visitors to see the area and its wildlife. Overnight accommodations are available at Rockport, on State Route 35, thirty miles southwest of Tivoli.

BEAR RIVER MIGRATORY BIRD REFUGE, 101 square miles in area, is located on the delta marshes where the Bear River empties into Great Salt Lake, Utah. It was established by an Act of Congress, in 1928, to provide a protected habitat for waterfowl and many other birds. This refuge is one of the showplaces of the Fish and Wildlife Service, for not only is it a concentration spot during migration for literally millions of ducks and geese, but the area has a scenic quality, its great diked pools reflecting the blue wall of the Promontory Mountains on the west and the snow-streaked crests of the towering Wasatch Range on the east. These magnificent mountains form backgrounds for the flying, soaring feathered hordes.

Bear River lies between the central and Pacific flyways, some of its waterfowl in autumn going southeast toward the Texas coast, and some going west to join the birds that migrate through or winter in the interior valleys of California. The refuge provides breeding habitat for about sixty of the nearly 200 species of birds that have been recorded in the area. Excepting perhaps in mid-winter, there is superb wildlife activity to be seen here. In spring, waterfowl are moving north, and, although they do not remain as long as on the autumn migration, their numbers at any one time are impressive. At this season, Canada geese, mallards, widgeons, pintails, cinnamon, green-winged and blue-winged teal, shovelers, redheads, scaups and ruddy ducks are on the refuge, as well as American bitterns, great blue and black-crowned night herons, four species of grebes—western, eared, horned and pied-billed—and Virginia and sora rails, snowy plovers, long-billed curlews and Forster's and black terns. Four species of gulls are common on the refuge—Franklin's and California nest here, Bonaparte's and ring-billed migrate through, and the herring gull is a common migrant. The short-eared owl

The Promontory Mountains provide a spectacular background for the flying hordes at Bear River.

Wesley F. Kubichek, Fish and Wildlife Service

Allan D. Cruickshank, from Nat'l Audubon Society

The redhead is one of many kinds of waterfowl to be seen at Bear River.

is common, while the burrowing, horned and long-eared owls are seen less frequently. The black-billed magpie and the beautiful yellow-headed blackbird, are among the many breeding birds of the refuge. The visitor may see white-faced glossy ibises feeding in pools close to the dikes, and with them the handsome avocets sweeping the shallow water with their long up-curved bills. Black-necked stilts, too, wade through the shallows on tall, slender pink legs, their sharply pointed black wings and white throats and breasts strikingly handsome.

In summer white pelicans come to the refuge by thousands. These huge birds, with their black wing tips appear clumsy, but on the wing they present a pleasing picture of grace and beauty. They may be seen streaming across the landscape in long lines or in V-formation, going to or returning from the nesting islands forty miles or more away in the middle of Great Salt Lake. On occasion circling flocks of pelicans rise on motionless wings into the blue sky on up-drafts of warm air. A humming sound, created by wind in their wings, is plainly audible. Sometimes they go up almost beyond the reach of vision.

The white pelican now survives in a few limited colonies. Its range, over which it once thrived in vast numbers, extends from southern Canada to its wintering grounds in southern California, the Gulf of Mexico and in Everglades National Park in southern Florida. It has a wing-spread of between eight and nine feet, and its size makes it a living target that some gunners cannot resist. Such men attempt to justify their action on the grounds that the pelican eats fish that fishermen want, yet scientific investigation has shown that the bird eats small mullet, carp and suckers and rarely blue-gilled sunfish, which have little commercial value. Public enlightenment can save the pelican from needless persecution.

For the grand show, autumn is the best season to visit Bear River. It is then that hundreds of thousands of waterfowl and shorebirds, as well as swallows and other land birds come to the area. The waters are blackened by swimming ducks and geese, the air streaked with their flying formations, and there is the babble of bird calls day and night. The big white whistling swans, most graceful of all waterfowl, are present in great numbers, swimming or flying in lines, their white wings and bodies flashing in the sun, backed by the blue mountains. Here are the Canada, the lesser snow, the diminutive cackling, white-fronted and Ross's geese; and among the ducks there are widgeons, canvas-backs, lesser and greater scaups, ring-necks, American golden-eyes, buffleheads and American and red-breasted mergansers. More rarely seen are Barrow's golden-eyes, old-squaws, white-winged and surf scoters and hooded mergansers. Shorebirds include solitary, pectoral, Baird's, least, red-backed and western sandpipers, greater and lesser yellowlegs snipes, long-billed curlews, dowitchers, black-bellied plovers, killdeers, marbled godwits and sanderlings.

Some of the mammals of the refuge are muskrats, weasels, skunks, marmots, ground squirrels, cottontail and jack rabbits, beavers and coyotes, and a number of rodents.

To one familiar with the history of America's waterfowl from the time when countless millions darkened the sky over inland and coastal waters of the continent, it seems a wonder that there are any left today, so ruthless has been the destruction of the birds and their habitat by man. Civilization has moved in on waterfowl habitat—marshes and lakes and pot holes by the thousands have been drained, and rivers and streams polluted with sewage and industrial waste, and these forms of habitat destruction still continue at a serious rate. Although the loss of some habitat has been inevitable, a great

The southern limits of the green-winged teal's breeding range includes Bear River Refuge.

The author

The black-necked stilt inhabits Bear River, and its loud cries announce the presence of its nest when one approaches too close.

Photographs
by the author

The stilt, with its striking black and white plumage, is well named for its exceptionally long pink legs.

Allan D. Cruickshank
from Nat'l Audubon Society

During the breeding season the yellow-headed blackbird is a truly handsome songster, glossy black body, wings and tail contrasting with gleaming yellow head.

The avocet, belonging to the same family as the stilt, but larger, has cinnamon coloring on head and neck, and a distinctly up-curved bill.

Hugo H. Schroder

Ralph E. Lawrence, courtesy Mass. Audubon Society

A black band around yellow bill identifies this graceful bird as the ring-billed gull.

The author

A duck hospital at Bear River has saved the lives of countless thousands of waterfowl stricken with botulism.

deal could have been and can be avoided. Another preventable cause of waterfowl decline has been shooting. So great is the urge to kill on the part of some men, that protection of waterfowl is constantly hampered by pressures brought by those who do the killing. On the Bear River marshes alone, in the words of the Fish and Wildlife Service, "200,000 ducks were killed annually for eastern markets between 1877 and 1900." And thousands of ducks died from botulism, a disease in the West caused by polluted water. This was first given serious study at Bear River, about 1910, by Dr. Alexander Wetmore, former secretary of the Smithsonian Institution. Dr. Wetmore said, "Following the reduction of water levels and the crowding of great concentrations of birds into smaller areas, losses from botulism were first noted about 1900. More and more ducks sickened as the epidemic spread over the stagnant waters of the shallow alkali flats, and in 1910, and again in 1913, upward of a million died around the mouth of the Bear River." In 1932, the last year of catastrophic loss, nearly half a million birds succumbed to the malady.

The Fish and Wildlife Service is constantly combatting the menace of botulism in its many waterfowl refuges. This is done by careful regulation of water levels. While research on methods of preventing and controlling this disease has been under way for many years, there still are periodic outbreaks which take a heavy toll of ducks throughout the West. In order to save ducks with mild infection or when first attacked, a hospital

The author

The large white pelicans are numerous at Bear River, sometimes rising high into the sky in milling flocks.

has been established on this refuge. Here thousands of birds have been treated with an antitoxin injection, and have been banded and released after recovery.

Banding is done to learn more about migration and as an aid in developing principles of sound management. A small aluminum band, bearing a number and the request to mail it to the Fish and Wildlife Service, Washington, D. C., is placed around a bird's leg. In this way, if the bird is recovered, the finder sends the band in, and states the date and where it was found. While a few banded birds have been recovered thousands of miles from their places of banding, the majority follow well defined flyways or migration routes. As a result of this program, which is carried on not only by the Fish and Wildlife Service, but by organizations and individuals all across the country—all of them using the Service's bands—a great mass of information has been obtained. An outstanding case was the discovery of the winter home of the chimney swift. A mystery to ornithologists for many years, during which time a quarter million of the swifts were banded, suddenly the question was answered when thirteen bands were returned to Washington from the jungles of Peru, South America.

To those who enjoy wildlife for the sheer pleasure of seeing it, it is not pleasant to realize that the State of Utah, in granting its assent to federal purchase of the Bear River Marshes, imposed a requirement in the law that not to exceed forty percent of the area must be open to public shooting each autumn.

The refuge is threatened with impairment by a Bureau of Reclamation scheme to dam the Bear River. There must be constant vigilance by nature protection groups to see that the value of this important area is not reduced. Already the refuge water is being polluted by industrial waste which is dumped into the Bear River.

Headquarters is in the refuge, and the address is Brigham City, Utah. The area is reached on a paved road about fifteen miles west from Brigham City. The dikes of the refuge contain narrow roads, and some of these are open to the public. There are a picnic area and an observation tower near headquarters. Overnight accommodations are available at Brigham City.

BLACKWATER NATIONAL WILDLIFE REFUGE is situated in eastern Maryland at the junction of the Little and Big Blackwater rivers. An Atlantic waterfowl flyway refuge, it was established in 1933, under the *Migratory Bird Conservation Act* of 1929, to provide resting and feeding grounds for ducks and geese, and to serve as a study area for the development and management of commercial muskrat marshes.

Covering seventeen square miles of croplands, winding waterways, tidal marshes, many ponds, diked pools, low, sandy, wooded ridges and uplands, the refuge is picturesque, especially where dark stands of loblolly pine rise abruptly along the borders of the level marshes. Wooded tracts standing at varying distances lend perspective, and, reflected in the mirroring pools, add great beauty and charm. Interspersed with sweet gum and red maple, the woodlands make a grand show of color in autumn, the season when waterfowl visit the refuge in large numbers. Although much of the area can be explored by driving along the winding dirt roads, the visitor should not fail to do some of his wandering on foot. Dike trails lead to scenes that are especially beautiful in the calm of early morning—the time when both songsters and waterfowl are most active. Canada geese, flying in flocks of thousands, move from water areas to refuge croplands and back again. Ducks, too, are on the wing, flying in graceful formations or resting on the ponds. Black ducks, widgeons, and blue-winged and green-winged teal are the most

The Canada goose, most abundant of its kind in North America, is resident at nearly all waterfowl refuges during at least part of the year, as is the widgeon.

The author

Allan D. Cruickshank, from Nat'l Audubon Society

Quite rare throughout its range, the hooded merganser is one of the handsomest of our ducks.

numerous; while pintails, mallards, gadwalls, shovelers and the handsome hooded merganser are winter residents. Present all year are the little downy woodpecker and big black and white pileated woodpecker, with its flaming red crest, its loud call echoing through the forest, and the diminutive brown-headed nuthatch, whose nasal call can be heard among the loblollys. High overhead soars the huge bald eagle, dark with white head and tail. In spring, the wooded areas are alive with twenty or more species of migrating warblers. Among the earliest to arrive are the yellow-throated and the pine warblers, which remain to nest. The clear calls of the bobwhite may be heard from field and woodland border. King, Virginia and sora rails and the Florida gallinule nest in the refuge.

The Canada goose is one of Blackwater's most abundant autumn and winter species. Compared with that of other geese, its summer range is vast; for it breeds from Newfoundland west across Labrador, around Hudson Bay, and from the northern Rocky Mountains and prairie provinces of Canada south, in suitable spots, to California, Nevada, northern Utah, Colorado and Nebraska; while the winter range extends along both coasts and across the country. Striking in appearance, with brown body, wings and tail, jet black neck and head, and distinctive white cheek patch, this big bird flies at night as well as during the day, on its long migration journeys. Its clear honking calls coming down to earth from the hazy blue, draw attention to a V-formation moving across the

Allan D. Cruickshank
from Nat'l Audubon Society

The downy woodpecker is a permanent resident of Blackwater's woodlands.

The brown thrasher's song sounds along woodland borders in spring at Blackwater.

Allan D. Cruickshank
courtesy Mass.
Audubon Society

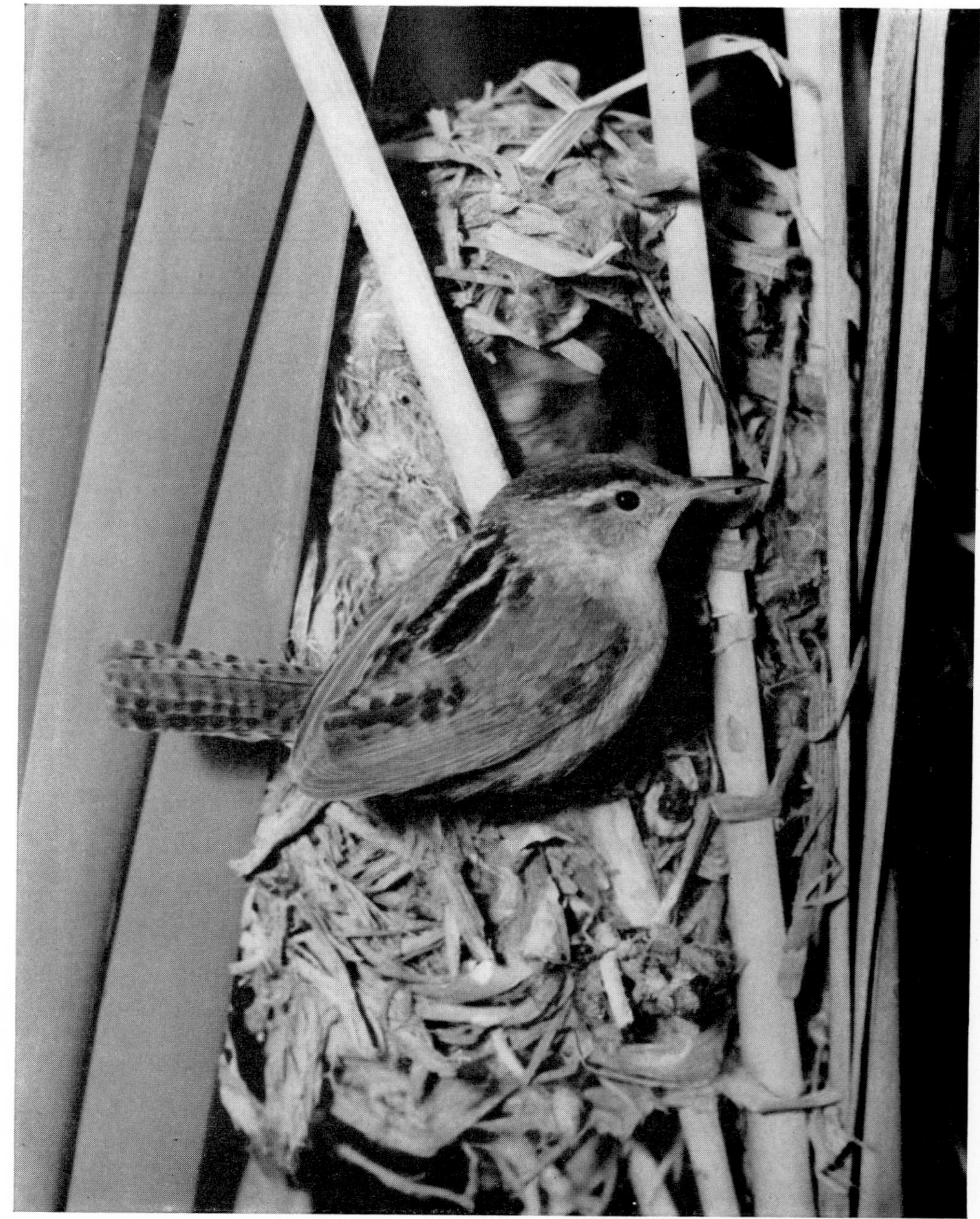

Allan D. Cruickshank, from Nat'l Audubon Society

Cattail marshes are the nesting grounds of the long-billed marsh wren, where the twittering song of these feathered mites sound from deep in the greenery.

Hugo H. Schroder, courtesy Nature Magazine

Gadwalls are among the several species of ducks that spend the winter at Blackwater where they feed on the mirror-like pools.

The author

sky. In the words of the ornithologist Arthur Cleveland Bent, set forth in his *Life Histories of North American Birds,* "It is only when traveling long distances that they fly high in the air in the well-known V-shaped flocks which experience has taught them is the easiest and most convenient for rapid and protracted flight. In this formation the leader, cleaving the air in advance, has the hardest work to perform . . . the others follow along in the diverging lines at regular intervals, so spaced that each has room enough to work his wings freely, to see clearly ahead, and to save resistance in the wake of the bird ahead of him. As the wingbeats are not always in perfect unison, the line seems to have an undulatory motion, especially noticeable when near at hand; but often the flock seems to move along in perfect step. Flight is not always maintained in the stereotyped wedge formation; sometimes a single, long, sloping line is formed or more rarely they progress in Indian file." Characteristics of this goose are its courtship antics, its loyalty to a life-long mate, and its keen ability to distinguish sounds that foretell the approach of an enemy. There is perhaps no more thrilling combat among wild creatures than the onslaught

Canada geese make silhouettes in flight.

The author

William H. Lawrence, courtesy Mass. Audubon Society

The mockingbird is well-known in our southern states from the Pacific to the Atlantic, and it inhabits numerous refuges.

of one male Canada goose upon another during the courting period. When a bird is shot and wounded and is unable to rise with the flock, its mate, wheeling back to earth, attempts to launch the wounded bird, and, failing, remains with it.

One of the big problems in the protection and management of ducks and geese is to prevent them from doing damage to crops on farms near the refuges. To help prevent this, the Fish and Wildlife Service, at Blackwater and at many other waterfowl refuges, raises grain crops of various kinds, both for green browse and to supplement the supply of aquatic plants for the birds. Dry-land crops are generally grown on a share basis—the actual work of planting, cultivating and harvesting being done on refuge land by nearby farmers who leave a part of the grain for the birds.

Blackwater Refuge headquarters is in the area, and the address is Route 1, Cambridge, Maryland. It is reached south from Cambridge on State Route 16, six miles to Church Creek and the junction of State Route 335 to the left, thence four miles to a refuge sign, and two miles to a right-hand fork and on to the refuge entrance on the right. Overnight accommodations are available at Cambridge.

CAPE ROMAIN NATIONAL WILDLIFE REFUGE, on the South Carolina coast, includes a large area of salt marsh, the wide expanse of Bulls Bay and three barrier islands, including beautiful Bulls Island. It is an Atlantic flyway refuge of fifty-four square miles, established in 1932 primarily for black ducks, teal and shorebirds.

The marshes, broken into numerous islands by winding waterways, are the permanent habitat of clapper rails, and the wintering ground of some Canada geese and many species of ducks. The gem spot of the refuge is Bulls Island. Its beauty alone attracts visitors. It is a densely forested sea island, six miles long, with a broad sandy beach on the ocean side. Dominant trees are loblolly pine, holly, large-flowered magnolia, live and water oaks, red bay, wax myrtle, sweet gum and cabbage palm, the latter forming pure stands around ponds and inlets. Cassina, an abundant evergreen shrub, is loaded with bright red berries in winter. Vegetation behind the dunes is stunted and windswept by Atlantic gales, and the forest at the north end of the island is rapidly being destroyed, for here the ocean is washing the land away, and the beach is a graveyard of gaunt gray trunks and limbs pounded by the surf.

Raccoons, otters, whitetail deer and the introduced fox squirrel inhabit the island. Loggerhead turtles come to the sandy beaches at night in May and June to lay their

Royal terns nest in colonies on the beach at Cape Romain.

Wesley F. Kubichek, Fish and Wildlife Service

The author

The shoal tidal flats in Bulls Bay are the feeding grounds of oystercatchers.

eggs, and alligators sun themselves along the banks of sloughs and ponds. Mud flats are the habitat of the little fiddler crab, so named because the left claw is large and gives it the appearance of holding a fiddle.

Fresh water ponds have been developed on the island, and these are swarming in winter with widgeons, pintails, black ducks, scaups, ring-necks and ruddy ducks, gadwalls, redheads, canvasbacks, golden-eyes, mergansers, shovelers, green-winged and blue-winged teal, buffleheads and mallards, the latter adding a brilliant touch with their shining green heads. White-winged scoters and other sea ducks can be seen in the surf beyond the beach in winter. Bald eagles and an introduced pure strain of turkeys raise their young on the island. Common and red-throated loons, horned grebes, and green, great blue and Louisiana herons, American and snowy egrets and the handsome white wood ibis are also present, the ibis coming only in summer. Caspian and Forster's terns are present in winter, while royal, Cabot's, gull-billed and least are summer residents. The latter, smallest of its group, is only slightly larger than a swallow. Gliding low over the waters of the bay, black skimmers feed. Large black and white birds with red and black bills, they are an impressive and unforgettable sight as they travel in flocks, their long lower mandibles lowered to scoop food particles from the water's surface.

The mud flats and sand bars between island and mainland, especially at low tide, are covered with shorebirds—dowitchers, marbled godwits, Husonian curlews, western, least and red-backed sandpipers, black-bellied and ringed plovers, ruddy turnstones, oystercatchers and many others. The oystercatchers are of special interest to visitors. They are a characteristic bird of the area, and it was particularly for them that the refuge was established. Herring and laughing gulls and brown pelicans can be seen along the outer beach, the pelicans gliding in undulating lines just above the breakers. The osprey or fish hawk adds further interest to the refuge. Shell collectors find the beach a fertile hunting ground, since razor clams, sand dollars, whelks, sea urchins, corallines and many other beautiful species are abundant.

Inhabiting the tall dark moss-draped forest are numerous song and insectivorous birds—many of the 231 species recorded in the refuge remaining as year-round residents. Several woodpeckers may be seen, including the large and spectacular pileated.

The bald eagle formerly resident over most of North America, particularly the coasts, is the largest bird of the refuge, and one nest has been built in the top of a tall pine on the island. With its brown-black wings and body and its gleaming white head and

Green herons live in the marshes and along the margins of pools at Cape Romain.

Allan D. Cruickshank, from Nat'l Audubon Society

Allan D. Cruickshank, from Nat'l Audubon Society

Laughing gulls, named for their laugh-like calls, add beauty to our Atlantic and gulf coasts as they travel in small flocks.

tail, it adds a majestic touch to the landscape when it soars overhead or rests on a snag beside the Intracoastal Waterway, which runs along the west side of the refuge. The bald eagle is our national emblem, its majestic form appearing on coins; but even though protected by a special federal law in the United States, it is frequently shot, for it offers a big target to the irresponsible gunner. Although often erroneously regarded as a dangerous predator, it lives mostly on fish that are of little value. The eagle is not a good fisherman, but the osprey is, and frequently the eagle will force the osprey to surrender its catch while in flight. Such attacks are thrilling aerial battles to watch.

Because the adjacent fresh and brackish Santee delta supported a rich growth of marsh plants, the northern end of the Cape Romain Refuge formerly was a paradise for wintering waterfowl. But that has now been wiped out by man's interference. In the 1940's the water of the Santee was diverted by a canal and two dams into the channel of the Cooper River for hydroelectric development. The promoters of this project, as is sometimes the case, were not much concerned about the feasibility of the project. To them, the incentive was to win public approval and build up pressure to get construction started, and in this they succeeded. Besides the partial destruction of the waterfowl area,

Allan D. Cruickshank, courtesy Nature Magazine

Bonaparte's, smallest North American gull, breeds in northwestern Canada, but migrates through the eastern states as far as the Gulf of Mexico. Black skimmers, large black and white birds with red bills, fly in flocks over Bulls Bay, skimming the water with their elongated lower mandibles.

The author

Allan D. Cruickshank, from Nat'l Audubon Society

For sheer grace, few birds can match the terns, and the least tern, smallest of all, is only a little larger than a barn swallow, which it fairly imitates in form and flight.

one of the most magnificent primeval stands of cypress in the country—in the lower bottomlands of the Santee—was dried up and has since been logged; 180,000 acres of giant virgin cypress, gum and oak in Santee Lake alone were inundated; silt, flowing down the Cooper and emptying into Charleston harbor, requires the City of Charleston to pay an additional sum each year to keep the harbor dredged for shipping; industries, which were enticed to the area through promises of low cost electricity, are not having their electrical needs adequately met by the power plant, and the power company has been forced to construct a supplementary steam plant. What price power!

Visitors to Bulls Island are amazed at the superb beauty of this area. All of our southern coast once was equally beautiful, but real estate development and other human activity—some of it justified, but much of it not necessary—have reduced most of the shore to a landscape marred by resorts, logging and industry. Not only has natural beauty suffered, but wildlife is disappearing. Viewed in this light, the work of the Fish and Wildlife Service takes on added significance, for only through protection of the refuges in its care can we hope to retain these wonders and beauties of nature. The Service deserves widespread public support and encouragement in carrying on its work,

Allan D. Cruickshank
from Nat'l Audubon Society

The bald eagle is an inspiring sight as it soars over Cape Romain.

This majestic eagle, our national emblem, raises its young high in the tops of loblolly pines on Bulls Island.

Arthur H. Fisher
courtesy Nature Magazine

to ensure that Bulls Island and other important wildlife habitats and beauty spots shall not be destroyed.

Cape Romain headquarters is on the mainland edge of the refuge, and the address is McClellanville, South Carolina. Those intending to visit Bulls Island should write to the refuge manager for information. The island may be explored on foot over an excellent system of trails. Overnight accommodations are available at Dominick House on the Island, and at nearby Awendaw on U. S. Highway 17, twenty-nine miles north of Charleston. The refuge is reached from north or south over U. S. Highway 17.

The ancient forests of Bulls Island have a tropical air with their understory of cabbage palms.

The author

CHINCOTEAGUE NATIONAL WILDLIFE REFUGE, established in 1943, includes the southern third of Assateague Island. An ocean barrier island on Maryland's and Virginia's eastern shore, the refuge comprises thirteen and a half square miles of marshes, sand dunes, wide sandy beaches, woodlands and diked pools. After crossing Chincoteague Inlet, the boat brings the visitor to the landing on Assateague Island near the lighthouse. Here a forest of tall, picturesquely shaped loblolly pines covers the low sand hills on this part of the island. Northward, the pines become much smaller, being scattered over the sunny sides of the White Hills, but standing tall and straight on the cooler westward-facing slopes. The understory trees of the forest are holly, oak, myrtle, with wild rose, sumac and tangles of greenbrier. Along the marshes there are thick stands of bay, and over wide stretches the forests give way to grassy marshes behind the high outer dunes. On the clean, wild beach huge Atlantic swells rise into great green walls that plunge landward in seething masses of white foam.

Chincoteague lies strategically on the lanes of migrating geese. Atlantic brant, greater snow and Canada geese find the area a haven. Pintails, widgeons, mallards, gadwalls, ruddies, blacks, wood and ring-necked ducks seek the sheltered marshy pools. Greater and lesser scaups, redheads, canvasbacks, golden-eyes, buffleheads and old-squaws prefer the bay areas. Rafts of black, surf and white-winged scoters ride the swells just beyond the line of breakers, and gleaming white whistling swans sometimes appear on their way to more southerly feeding grounds.

Shorebirds are abundant in migration—piping, killdeer, ringed, Wilson's and black-bellied plovers, oystercatchers, Hudsonian curlews, semipalmated, spotted, red-backed, western, Baird's, buff-breasted, white-rumped, stilt and least sandpipers, marbled godwits, sanderlings, greater and lesser yellowlegs, dowitchers, knots, willets and the handsomely

Walls of green water rise and plunge in churning foam on the beach at Chincoteague.

The author

Jack Dermid, from Nat'l Audubon Society

Mourning doves live in Chincoteague's pinelands, and in many other refuges.

marked and colorful ruddy turnstones. Some of these species nest on the refuge, in addition to clapper rails, laughing gulls, least terns, American bitterns and black skimmers. After the breeding period each summer, several thousand herons and egrets visit the refuge. They include ten species, with American and snowy egrets and little blue herons predominating. Seaside, Ipswich and white-throated sparrows, catbirds, red-breasted and brown-headed nuthatches, mourning doves and long-billed marsh wrens are a few of the area's numerous songbirds, migrant and permanent. The myrtle warbler occurs in great numbers on the island in winter; while the prairie warbler is probably the most abundant small bird there during June.

Concerning the Atlantic flyway, Fish and Wildlife Service biologists tell us that "Chincoteague Refuge is an important waystation. It is located where several lanes of waterfowl traffic converge. One of these routes begins at the top of the world—the summer home of the greater snow goose and the Atlantic brant in northern Greenland and the islands of the Arctic Sea. In the latitude of the Delaware and Chesapeake bays, the Atlantic coast route receives an important tributary from the west. It has its beginnings in the prairie provinces of Canada, the Mackenzie Delta, eastern Alaska, Ontario and the states bordering the Great Lakes. For many of the birds that follow these routes, Chincoteague is the first refuge encountered on their long autumnal journey."

There is an interesting story conerning the food of the Atlantic brant. The biologists say: "Eelgrass has always been the chief winter food of the brant. Heavy growths of the ribbon-like plant formerly covered the tidal flats from North Carolina to Nova Scotia. About 1930, a blight struck the eelgrass all along the coast. Within the space of a year or two, most of it had disappeared. This had an immediate and very nearly disastrous effect on the brant, and its population rapidly declined." However, the brant turned to other foods, such as sea lettuce, and, as eelgrass has slowly come back in some areas, the brant is gradually increasing.

Gay yellowthroats wearing distinctive masks, sing in the thickets of Chincoteague Refuge.

Photographs by Allan D. Cruickshank from Nat'l Audubon Society

Tangles of greenbrier and bay are the summer haunt of the gray-feathered catbirds.

Allan D. Cruickshank
from Nat'l Audubon
Society

The wild, clear call of the greater yellowlegs can be heard at Chincoteague during migration. The lesser yellowlegs, too, visit this area.

The American bittern, shown here on its nest, is safe in its protective coloration of stripes and mottling in brown.

C. J. Henry
Fish and Wildlife Service

Photographs by the author

A far north breeder, the greater snow goose winters from Chincoteague south to Cape Romain. The lesser snow goose also breeds in the far north, but winters in California and on the coast of the Gulf of Mexico. Chincoteague light stands high amid the tall old loblolly pines on Assateague Island.

Howard H. Cleaves, from Nat'l Audubon Society

Wilson's petrels skim swallow-like over the open ocean. Antarctic breeders, they sometimes come close to our Atlantic coast from May to September.

The Atlantic brant closely resembles the black brant of the Pacific coast, the main difference being the much lighter underparts of the Atlantic. They are small by comparison with most other geese, being only a little larger than a good sized mallard.

The ranges of the two brant do not overlap except perhaps slightly in the northern breeding grounds. Rarely a straggler invades the winter range of the other. The Atlantic brant breeds along the shore of northwestern Greenland and on the islands west of there, and winters on the Atlantic coast from North Carolina to southern New England; while the black brant breeds on the Arctic coast of Alaska, Northwest Territories and eastern Siberia, wintering on our Pacific coast from southern British Columbia to Lower California and, on the west side of the Pacific, south to Japan. F. H. Kortright in his book *The Ducks, Geese and Swans of North America,* quotes Allan Brooks: "No other ducks or geese can compare with brant in sheer beauty of movement. On the water they sit as lightly as gulls, the tail upraised and the neat little head poised

Courtesy Nature Magazine

Allan D. Cruickshank, from Nat'l Audubon Society

The ringed plover, left, and the larger Hudsonian curlew, breed in far northern Canada, but migrate along our shores. Gannets nest on islands in the Gulf of St. Lawrence, notably Bonaventure Island, and winter at sea off our Atlantic coast. Occasionally they may be seen off Chincoteague and other coastal refuges.

Hugh M. Halliday, from Nat'l Audubon Society

M. H. Oldham, from Nat'l Audubon Society

Dolphins, also called porpoises, large mammals of the ocean, make leaps clear of the water as they travel. Their wanderings often bring them close to shore.

on the graceful neck. Seeking their food, they pick daintily at the water and pivot swiftly to do so. On the wing they are at their best."

Mammals of the refuge include raccoons, muskrats, red foxes and whitetailed deer. Porpoises are common off shore. The natural beauty of Chincoteague Refuge is such that prior to its establishment as a refuge, it was considered for inclusion in the system of magnificent areas under the care of the National Park Service. Like beautiful Bulls Island, in Cape Romain National Wildlife Refuge, it is one of the few sea islands of our Atlantic coast still largely undisturbed. In the wildlife management program of the Fish and Wildlife Service, utmost care is taken to ensure that the island's land and vegetation retain their charm.

Headquarters is at the village of Chincoteague, Virginia, on nearby Chincoteague Island. The refuge is reached south from Salisbury, Maryland, on U. S. Highway 13 to State Route 175 east to Chincoteague; and north from Norfolk, Virginia, by the Cape Charles Ferry to Cape Charles, Virginia, and north on U. S. Highway 13 to State Route 175. Information about boat transportation to the refuge can be obtained by writing to the refuge manager.

DESERT, KOFA and CABEZA PRIETA GAME RANGES have been established as inviolate sanctuaries for the rare desert bighorn sheep. All three contain spectacular mountainous desert, the first in southern Nevada, and the others in southwestern Arizona, and all are inhabited by the fascinating plants and animals typical of our arid Southwest.

The Desert Game Range, 3419 square miles, is the third largest area under the Bureau of Sport Fisheries and Wildlife. Established in 1936, it is about a quarter the size of the Arctic National Wildlife Range in the northeastern corner of Alaska. It gives protection to the Nelson's bighorn. Typical of our southwest desert country, it is crossed by long ridges of high, splintered mountains with broad alluvial gravel fans spreading gently downward from their bases. Sheep Mountain, 9706 feet in elevation, in the southeastern part of the refuge, bears a fine conifer forest along its summits. This range is preferred by the sheep more than any other part of the refuge. To the southwest of this ridge, clearly visible across an intervening valley, rises Charleston Peak, 11,910 feet in elevation, with an even more extensive forest covering its crests. Northward, range after range breaks the skyline as far as the eye can see.

It may seem surprising that there can be a tall conifer forest anywhere in this land of aridity; yet the trees in these mountains include species common at lower elevations in parts of northern California, Oregon and Washington. Among them are ponderosa, limber, foxtail and piñon pines, western juniper and lowland white and Douglas firs. In winter snow falls deep in these forests.

The surrounding desert is burning hot in summer, although on a winter night the temperature may drop to well below freezing. The sparse desert vegetation consists of various kinds of cacti—golden cholla, beavertail, niggerhead and diamond—and such shrubs as four-winged saltbrush, rabbitbrush, bottlebrush, creosote bush, mesquite, Apache plume and cliff rose. Here also are century plant, Mojave and banana yucca, as well as the tree-size yucca—the Joshua tree, *Yucca brevifolia* var. *jaegeriana*—one of

The mountainous landscape of the Desert Game Range is typical of our Southwest. Habitat of the bighorn, it is grown in places with stands of Joshua trees, a few of which are shown here.

The author

E. P. Haddon, Fish and Wildlife Service

Avidly sought by gunners, the bighorn today depends on refuges for its survival, but gunners want parts or all of three of the four bighorn areas removed from Fish and Wildlife Service protection and opened to shooting. Only an alert public can prevent this.

the most striking floral features of this desert. It forms vast open forests, covering thousands of acres in parts of the refuge, the finest stand of the short-leaved Joshua tree to be found anywhere. Another variety of the Joshua tree, *Yucca brevifolia,* which has larger leaves, is protected in Joshua Tree National Monument, California. The stand in the Desert Game Range is much more extensive than the one in the monument. Botanically, this weird tree is important, and it deserves the protection it is being given in these two reservations.

The Desert Game Range is the home of over sixty mammals besides the bighorn. They include antelopes, mule deer, jack rabbits, coyotes, gray and kit foxes, spotted skunks, porcupines, badgers, golden-mantled and antelope ground squirrels, chipmunks, desert kangaroo rats, and, in the Spring Mountains, a small introduced band of elk.

Bighorn sheep of a number of species and races inhabit North America from Alaska to northern Mexico. The most northerly is the handsome white Dall sheep of Alaska.

The Stone or black bighorn occurs in Yukon and British Columbia. The Rocky Mountain bighorn ranges from Alberta through Montana, Colorado and southward through the deserts to Mexico. The Nelson's bighorn is a subspecies of the Rocky Mountain, as is also the Gaillard bighorn of the Kofa and Cabeza Prieta game ranges of Arizona. The Audubon bighorn, which inhabited parts of the northern great plains, is now extinct.

The bighorn is a dweller of the wilderness and does not tolerate civilization. In the wilds of Alaska and Canada it still finds suitable wilderness country, but settlement of the West has driven the bighorn from much of its former winter range on the grassy slopes of the mountains. Serious causes of its depletion since the coming of the white man have been disease and shooting. On occasions it has been killed for meat; but more often, these days, merely as a trophy, for many so-called "sportsmen" cannot resist taking a head with its great spread of horns. To kill so rare and beautiful a creature for this purpose is unjustifiable. It has been reported recently that the headless bodies of sheep have been found at desert water holes, where the animals have been ambushed by trophy hunters. Says former Park Service Biologist Victor H. Cahalane, in his *Mammals of North America,* "Building a little rock blind overlooking a spring or seep, a poacher may wait days for the desert sheep to come to drink, as they must eventually. Whether he kills for his own trophy, or to sell the head for money, the poacher of a rare bighorn is one of the meanest of outlaws."

Another detriment to bighorn survival in unprotected areas is competition with domestic sheep for feed. Where sheep are raised in the West, the flocks usually are driven into the high, verdant mountain meadows for the summer months, where they consume the food plants of the wild sheep. Fortunately there are no domestic sheep on the Desert Game Range.

Duelling between rams during the mating season has won renown for the bighorn. Usually a duel begins with two rams standing side by side, facing in opposite directions. In this position they strike each other with rapid thrusts of their sharp front hoofs.

The gray fox, living as happily in the deserts of Southwest as in the green lands of the East, is one of the interesting mammals of the Desert Game Range.

Charles W. Schwartz

Laurence M. Huey, courtesy Nature Magazine

The kit fox is smaller and less cautious than the gray, and although a few may still live on the Desert Game Range, it has been destroyed by trap and poison over wide areas, and needs protection to prevent extinction.

After a few minutes they walk apart about twenty-five feet, turn and face each other, rear up on their hind legs and bound forward on all fours in a furious charge. The impact of horns resounds through the crags, and sometimes it momentarily stuns the contestants. They back off and repeat the charge again and again, and battles have been known to last up to two hours.

The ewes select an isolated spot or almost inaccessible ledge to give birth, which usually occurs from March to May at the Desert Game Range. The lambs are able to stand soon after birth, and in a week or so, are able to follow their mothers. Cahalane (*ibid.*), describing a lamb nursery, says that when the ewes go off to feed, one ewe is chosen to guard the young. He says that like human children, the lambs enjoy each other's company; they play tag, follow the leader over the rough terrain, and sometimes a pair will wage a butting contest to try out the tiny horns that are just beginning to grow. The ewe is dignified during the games, but occasionally she will condescend to play with the lambs.

Poaching on the Desert Game Range is a problem to the refuge staff, which is much too small to do an adequate patrolling job. At least one man should be on constant patrol; but this is not possible because Congress does not appropriate enough money. As though insufficient funds to protect these wonderful animals were not trouble enough, the Air Force has used a sizeable part of the range for gunnery purposes. During such use, all personnel are excluded. Part of the activity is covered by an agreement, and an

The handsome head of the bighorn is the prize of headhunters who sometimes poach on the Desert, Kofa and Cabeza Prieta game ranges to obtain it. The Fish and Wildlife Service could prevent this poaching if Congress would appropriate sufficient money to enable the hiring of more men to patrol the refuges.

Guy E. Mitchell
courtesy Nature Magazine

additional use privilege is being negotiated. Yucca Flat atomic proving ground is not inside the game range, but is adjacent to its northwest corner. We can only hope that this is far enough away from the sheep so as to cause the animals no harm.

Local gunners forced opening of the Desert Game Range to public shooting of bighorns and deer, and requests have been made to use parts of it for ranching. Worse still is the idea that the Fish and Wildlife Service abandon all of its refuges except the most important of the waterfowl areas. All such pressures must be carefully watched and vigorously resisted, for the survival of many of North America's finest wildlife forms are at stake. The Desert Game Range, like other federally administered lands, is the property of all the people of the nation, and not exclusively of the local communities.

The name of this refuge appears unfortunate. The word "game" seems to imply that only the gunners have an interest in the bighorn. A more appropriate name might be National Desert Bighorn Range. Similar adjustments in the names of the Kofa and Cabeza Prieta game ranges would seem equally fitting. The suggested change would conform to names of other Fish and Wildlife Service refuges such as the National Bison Range.

Headquarters is in the Federal Building at Las Vegas, Nevada, and two subheadquarters are in the refuge. U. S. Highway 95 runs across the southern end of the refuge. The road to the Corn Creek sub-headquarters branches east from Highway 95, nineteen miles north of Las Vegas. Overnight accommodations are available at Las Vegas.

Kofa and Cabeza Prieta game ranges are the only other places where the desert or Gaillard bighorn is being protected by the Fish and Wildlife Service.

Kofa, situated in southwestern Arizona, was established in 1939. It consists of 1031 square miles of desert lying along the east side of State Route 95, northeast of Yuma. It embraces the Castle Dome Mountains, which rise in striking spires and domes, and the Kofa Range, standing in a grand and splintered escarpment cut by numerous deep canyons. High in a cleft on the north wall of Kofa's Palm Canyon is a small grove of the Washingtonia palm, *Washingtonia fillifera,* the only natural location of this species in Arizona. Along with the bighorns, it deserves strict protection. Both Kofa and Cabeza Prieta are rich in botanical species. They contain habitat of the giant saguaro cactus, the palo verde, mahogany and many other desert plants.

The Army has a huge proving ground just south of Kofa, and has coveted the refuge land for an extension of its activities.

Cabeza Prieta, also established in 1939, is a magnificent stretch of desert, embracing 1034 square miles, and is situated east of Yuma on the Mexican border. It adjoins Organ Pipe Cactus National Monument on the east, and the two areas constitute the only remaining range of the Sonora antelope still found in a pure form in the United

The author

The Kofa Mountains typify the magnificent landscapes of the three bighorn refuges. Kofa and Cabeza Prieta, botanic gardens of desert plant life, are grown with the giant cactus or saguaro, the cholla and the ocotillo and dozens of bright-flowering species. And here, too, dwell the vermillion flycatcher, lower left, the Gila woodpecker and a long list of other birds of the desert.

Allan D. Cruickshank, from Nat'l Audubon Society

The author

George McClellan Bradt

Burrowing owls are dwellers of the deserts and grasslands of the West.

Wm. M. Rush
U. S. Forest Service

Rimrock caves in our southwestern mountains are the home of the ringtail. Having a gentle nature, large dark eyes and handsome tail, it is exceptionally appealing to one fortunate enough to make its acquaintance.

The spotted skunk, resident throughout our country excepting the east coast states, is a friend of farmers and ranchers, catching more mice than a cat. A spritely animal, it does handstands in play or when annoyed.

H. H. Sheldon
courtesy Nature Magazine

Wm. L. and Irene Finley courtesy Nature Magazine

Wright M. Pierce from Nat'l Audubon Society

The glossy black phainopepla, upper left, with its crested head and white wing-patches, and the Arizona hooded oriole with black throat and brilliant orange "hood," inhabit Cabeza Prieta Game Range, as does the nocturnal kangaroo rat named for its ability to hop like a kangaroo.

E. R. Kalmbach, Fish and Wildlife Service

States. Cabeza Prieta is inhabited by many desert dwellers such as the glossy black phainopepla, the dazzling red Arizona cardinal, the Palmer's thrasher, a foremost avain songster, the canyon wren whose descending trill echoes among canyon walls, the cactus wren which nests amid the bristling spines of the chollas, and whose rasping, wavering monotone song seems the embodiment of the desert's searing heat. Here, too, are the white-winged dove and the scaled quail.

Many western mountain ranges like the Kofa and Castle Domes are the habitat of the handsome violet-green swallow and the white-throated swift. Least earth-bound of creatures is the swift. An aerial acrobat of the first order, zooming into space from over the rim of a towering canyon wall, it plunges like a winged bullet into the dim depths, then on quivering wings it climbs, zigzags with unbelievable speed, glides, approaches the sheer face of an escarpment to disappear into a tiny nesting crevice. Free of the mundane problems of other creatures—too small and too fast to entice the hawk, not needing to come to earth for food, but taking insects on the wing, and wise enough to place its nest in the face of an inaccessible cliff, what enemies can it have? Little wonder this carefree creature seems bursting with the sheer joy of being alive. Sociable during the mating and nesting period, the white-throats are seen in numbers about the canyons of our western mountains, where they fill the sunshine with ceaseless merry twitterings and the swish of speed. Black, with white on throat, breast and sides of rump, the swift is readily distinguishable from the violet-greens,

The Gambel's quail is sociable, traveling and feeding in groups. Its clear call and quiet chatter notes are characteristic of our Southwest deserts and semi-arid lands.

Karl H. Maslowski, from Nat'l Audubon Society

Paul J. Fair, from Nat'l Audubon Society

The scaled quail is a desert dweller recognized by its pale gray body and white crest.

which have iridescent backs and wings and snow white under parts. The small gray Vaux swift, also a westerner, has a more northerly breeding range; while the gray chimney swift is strictly an easterner.

The Air Force has been using almost the entire area of Cabeza Prieta for gunnery practice. During the time the Air Force uses the area, even the refuge manager is excluded from entry. In his *Wildlife Refuges*, Dr. Ira N. Gabrielson says: "Of all the refuges in the federal system, these two (Cabeza Prieta and Kofa) are the driest. The landscape is characterized by numerous low but exceedingly rugged mountain ranges. Yet, in these sun-baked ranges the desert bighorns find conditions so suitable that, if human poaching can be controlled, good herds of these remarkable desert dwellers may again travel their arid slopes."

Under the circumstances, a working agreement has been made between the Bureau of Sport Fisheries and Wildlife and the Air Force allowing the refuge staff to use the area on week ends and providing a closer liaison than formerly, to avoid disturbance of the area and infraction of regulations by military personnel.

Headquarters for Kofa and Cabeza Prieta is at Yuma, where there are motels.

GREAT WHITE HERON NATIONAL WILDLIFE REFUGE consists of a number of mangrove-covered keys lying mostly east of Key West, Florida. A group of similar keys west of that town, known as Key West National Wildlife Refuge, serves the same function—to protect the nesting habitat of the great white heron—so that the two are logically treated together. The Great White Heron Refuge, established in 1938 and formerly guarded by the National Audubon Society, is 2151 acres in area, while the Key West Refuge, established in 1908, is 2019 acres. Together they total a little over four and a half square miles.

The breeding range of the great white heron in the United States is confined almost exclusively to these few small islands. The bird occurs also in Cuba, Jamaica and Yucatan. Of snow white plumage, greenish yellow legs and yellow bill, this heron is as large as the great blue heron. It is an inspiringly magnificent creature of the most superb beauty, deserving the best protection we can give it. Although the bird raises its young in nests built in the tops of the low mangroves of the refuge keys only, it ranges across the shoal waters of Florida Bay and along the fringe of the mainland shore, where it receives protection in Everglades National Park.

To see the great white heron standing in the shallow bay, its form reflected in the blue water, is an unforgetable sight. Here it associates with great blue herons, roseate

The brown noddy tern, with rounded tail and white cap, breeds in the Dry Tortugas Islands west of Key West, Florida, and in the Hawaiian Islands, but nowhere else under the American flag. The name is derived from the bird's habit of nodding during courtship and when meeting another of its kind.

Hugo H. Schroder

Allan D. Cruickshank, from Nat'l Audubon Society

Rarest of our herons is the great white, which is confined to the Florida keys and the Florida Bay area.

spoonbills and other waders, including the smaller American egret, with which it is often confused. In addition to size, a distinguishing feature between this egret and the white heron is the color of the legs—the egret having black legs. The snowy egret, still smaller, has black bill and legs, but yellow feet, referred to by some as "golden slippers."

The survival of any bird or mammal with a range as limited as that of the great white heron, whose population probably does not number much over 1000 individuals, is precarious, especially where man has entered the scene with his exploitive activities. The great white heron is subject to the devastating effects of tropical hurricanes that sometimes sweep across the keys.

The islands also protect nesting white-crowned pigeons, which migrate here probably from the Bahama Islands, remaining on these and other nearby keys, but nowhere else in the United States, for about five months of the year—May to September. These pigeons occur also in the Greater and Lesser Antilles, Yucatan and the Caribbean coast of Honduras. This handsome bird is slaty gray, with a distinct white crown, the back of the head purplish chestnut, and back of neck irridescent green.

Another bird that visits the keys of the two Great White Heron Refuge areas is the frigate-bird, a large fantastic creature of glossy black, with an orange-red sac on the throat of the male, which is inflated during the breeding season. The female is brown-tinged and has a white breast; while the immature birds are similar to the female, but with head and neck white. The forked tail and the long, narrow, sharply angled wings are striking features as the birds soar effortlessly over the keys. The young birds, because of their white heads, may be confused with the swallow-tailed kite; but the kite has white under the wings. The frigate-bird breeds in the Bahama Islands, coming to Florida in winter, where it can be seen almost anywhere along the keys. Brown

Narrow, angular, sharply-tipped wings and long forked tail are marks of the frigate-bird. It is a tropical bird that nests nowhere in the United States, but comes to the Florida keys and the gulf coast in its wanderings. The beauty of its effortless flight makes it a joy to watch.

Hugo H. Schroder

Wm. Z. Harmon, courtesy Nature Magazine

In all of our country, the only place where the white-crowned pigeon can be seen is along the Florida keys. It also inhabits the islands around the Caribbean Sea.

pelicans are abundant among the keys, as well as various gulls, terns, kingfishers, ospreys and black skimmers. Mangrove cuckoos come to the keys in summer.

It is not always possible to visit the refuge keys, because of their inaccessibility. Fortunately, the great white heron may be seen on other more accessible islands, as well as on the mainland shore in Everglades National Park. Visitors may occasionally see the big pale-colored Wurdeman's heron, a rare hybrid between the great blue and the great white.

The refuges are under the supervision of the Fish and Wildlife Service manager at Tavernier, on Key Largo. Overnight accommodations are available at numerous places along the keys, including Key West. U. S. Highway 1 traverses the chain of keys, reaching the first of them—Key Largo—fifty-one miles south of Miami. An ideal way to enjoy the birds of the keys, Florida Bay and Everglades National Park is to join the tours of the National Audubon Society, whose office is at 311 East Flagler Street, Miami 32.

HART MOUNTAIN NATIONAL ANTELOPE REFUGE, located in south-central Oregon, comprises an area of high, sage-covered plateau on the east slope of Hart Mountain, 8020 feet in elevation. The west face of the mountain is a towering escarpment of lava that rises 4000 feet from the lake-strewn floor of Warner Valley. Established in 1936, the refuge is 376 square miles in extent. Its chief purpose is to provide a safe summer range and kidding grounds for the pronghorn antelope. Also in 1936, the Sheldon National Antelope Refuge and the adjoining Sheldon Antelope Range were established for the same purpose. These two tracts, located mostly in the northwestern corner of Nevada, are about twenty miles as the crow flies, due south of Hart Mountain. They lie in a vast region that, in past years, was the natural habitat of the pronghorn. The two refuges and the range form a well-rounded project for pronghorn protection, because they contain winter and summer ranges of the animal—the Sheldon Refuge

Swift and graceful, the pronghorn antelope is at home in the western sage. Once it may have been as abundant as the bison, but when the white man came with his gun, it disappeared from wide regions.

Ernest J. Greenwalt, Fish and Wildlife Service

and Hart Mountain area contributing summer habitat, and the Sheldon Range winter.

Sage is the dominant and almost everpresent plant of Hart Mountain, and it is the most important browse species of the antelope. It clothes the rolling plateau in a nearly unbroken carpet of gray-green. In sheltered draws, grass covers the slopes, and groves of aspen find sustenance in the moist, protected canyons. Mountain mahogany occurs in places, and there is a small stand of ponderosa pine in one valley.

Besides the antelope, many other mammals find safety in the protected environment of Hart Mountain. Some of these are the mule deer, porcupine, coyote, jack rabbit and harvest mouse. The coyote deserves a more friendly attitude on the part of man. Any harm it does is often far outweighed by its ceaseless work in controlling rodents—ground squirrels, jack rabbits and gophers. It is a highly intelligent animal and an interesting one to watch in the wild. A glimpse of a coyote trotting off through the sage gives many people a greater thrill than seeing an entire herd of deer. Over large parts of our West, the coyote has been extirpated in response to the cries of livestock raisers,

One need only see the enthusiasm with which the so-called sportsman greets the open season on pronghorns to realize the importance of Hart Mountain and the Sheldon refuges to this magnificent animal.

The author

National Park Service

Hart Mountain and a number of other western refuges provide sanctuary for mule deer, which range over most of the West. Outside the refuges it becomes the target of gunners.

and in these sections his call, symbol of the wild west, has been silenced. In 1953, a large number of Colorado ranchers, who realized that their range lands were being overrun and harmed by rodents, banded together and posted their lands against further poisoning and trapping of the coyote. This was such an unexpected reversal of action, that a number of national magazines in the nature protection field published announcements and articles about it under the title "Coyote Sanctuary."

In the high country of Hart Mountain, the sage hen is perhaps the most conspicuous bird. Other avian inhabitants are the barn swallow, marsh hawk, meadowlark,

J. C. Allen, courtesy Nature Magazine

Jack rabbits are fairly abundant and occur on most western refuges. Whenever ranchers interfere with the natural controls on their population, the rabbits become overabundant.

horned lark, rock wren, red-breasted and white-breasted nuthatches, black-chinned hummingbird and golden eagle. Some of the lakes of the Warner Valley lie within the northwestern corner of the refuge, where Canada geese, western grebe, white pelican and several kinds of ducks may be seen. It is fortunate that part of the lakes area is in the refuge, because it enables migrating birds to find a place of safety from the ordeal of autumn shooting. The valley also is a waterfowl breeding habitat. The whole area of the blue lakes, reflecting the escarpment of black lava, which stands along their southeastern shores is a region of startling beauty. The full impact of it is perhaps most strongly felt if one sees it first from the escarpment rim on the road that winds down through a break in the wall. At each bend the view widens, with more and more lakes appearing, and the horizon stretching far away to the northwest.

The pronghorn antelope is one of the handsomest of North American ungulates. Its bright tawny coat, white beneath, two broad dark bands on under side of neck, conspicuously white rump patch and black horns give it a striking appearance. It has won renown for its speed. Undoubtedly the swiftest of our mammals, it has been clocked at sixty miles an hour. Alert and sensitive to the approach of danger, the antelope is always on the lookout, posting sentinels to guard the band. Occasionally coyotes, two or more acting as a team, will drive an antelope to exhaustion; but while coyotes may take some toll of antelope fawns, they are not a serious threat to adult animals, since other prey is much more easily obtained.

The rutting season is in September and October, and the young begin to appear in May. The does bear one fawn the first year, and usually two thereafter. Fawns develop rapidly, and are able to run more than twenty miles an hour a day or two after birth. When about a week old, they are led by their mothers to the band, where they join with their contemporaries in play. The little animals race with one another, have butting

Ranchers are showing more tolerance of the coyote, recognizing that it works daily, holidays included, to keep rodent populations down, thus saving the ranchers the time and expense of doing the job themselves.

David de L. Condon, National Park Service

Olaus J. Murie

The sage grouse is one of the more conspicuous birds of Hart Mountain. Here and in the Sheldon refuges it receives needed protection, for almost everywhere else it is declining as a result of shooting.

The male sage grouse puts on an amazing courtship display, with tail spread, air sacs inflated, and ruff enveloping the head. Local gunners are urging Hart Mountain and the Sheldon refuges be abandoned and opened to shooting.

Joe Van Wormer
from Nat'l Audubon Society

The author

Hart Mountain, along its northwestern side, rises hundreds of feet in a sheer wall of basalt that towers above the beautiful lake-strewn Warner Valley.

bouts, and, while the does are resting or chewing the cud, bound onto their mothers' backs in a game that suggests "king of the castle."

The antelope has no relatives on this continent, and is not closely related to the antelopes of other continents. It once was extremely abundant, some authorities believing that it may have been as numerous as the bison, numbering in the millions. With the coming of the white man and his use of the land, the antelope was greatly reduced, and entirely extirpated over vast areas of its former range. In recent years, protection has brought it back in areas like Hart Mountain, and from these sanctuaries animals have been taken to restock other parts of the country. The western sage-covered plains, from southern Saskatchewan and Alberta, in Canada, south to northern Mexico, and from central Nebraska and Texas west to central Oregon, western Nevada and the Sacramento and San Joaquin valleys of California, were its original range. Through restocking, it has made a favorable recovery in parts of this range in many western states.

Hart Mountain-Sheldon antelope refuges and the Charles Sheldon Antelope Range are administered jointly. Headquarters is at Lakeview, Oregon, Box 111. Subheadquarters also are maintained on the areas. Hart Mountain is in the wilderness, far from paved roads, and although it may be reached by a rough road west from Frenchglen near Malheur National Wildlife Refuge, a much better approach is east from U. S. Highway 395 four miles north of Lakeview to a dirt road right, to a junction at Adel, and north to the refuge; or south from Burns on the same highway, nineteen miles south of Valley Falls to the same dirt road to the left. It can also be reached over another unpaved road that branches east from U. S. Highway 395 about nineteen miles north of Valley Falls and about ninety-eight miles south of Burns. This is the road that crosses the beautiful Warner Valley and climbs up the Hart Mountain escarpment. Overnight accommodations are available at Burns, Lakeview and Frenchglen. No accommodations or supplies of any kind, including gasoline, are available in the refuge.

KENTUCKY WOODLANDS NATIONAL WILDLIFE REFUGE is a tract of ninety-nine square miles of rolling wooded country, in western Kentucky, lying between the Cumberland River on the east and the Tennessee on the west. It is a sanctuary for wild turkey, whitetail deer, a few ruffed grouse and, more recently, waterfowl. The fallow deer and the European red deer were introduced years ago when the land was privately owned. They still exist on the refuge. The introduction of exotic species usually is not considered advisable by most wildlife authorities, because they often compete with native species, may transmit diseases and disturb the natural biological conditions. These two deer fortunately are not increasing here.

In the early days a number of iron ore deposits in the area were worked commercially. Most of the woodlands were cut for charcoal to smelt the ore, but good second growth now covers the hills. The forests consist of deciduous hardwoods, including shagbark hickory, dogwood, redbud, blackjack, southern red and post oaks, box-elder, maple and elm. The handsome evergreen mountain laurel adds its spring floral display to that of the dogwood and redbud. Mostly an upland area, Kentucky Woodlands is unlike nearly all of the other national wildlife refuges in its general appearance.

Kentucky Lake bounds the refuge on the west. This was formed when the Tennessee Valley Authority built the Gilbertsville Dam. It created a number of shallow water areas

The woodchuck or groundhog is an interesting member of North America's fauna, and deserves protection.

B. W. Muir, U. S. Forest Service

Allan D. Cruickshank, from Nat'l Audubon Society

Radford, Soil Conservation Service

Screech owls occur in two color phases—red and gray—irrespective of sex. Like other owls, they work nightly for the farmer keeping white-footed mice and other small rodents in check.

in protected coves and bays where waterfowl now come during migration. Many small farm fields have been joined into large fields by removal of intervening fences, and these areas provide ideal feeding grounds for geese. On this flat alluvial flood plain of the Cumberland, the Service raises crops suitable for waterfowl, and in this part of the refuge there are four small artificial lakes used by ducks and geese. Thus, an area that prior to its establishment as a refuge was of little or no value to waterfowl, it is now attracting birds by thousands each year, particularly Canada geese, with some blue and snow geese, as well as most species of ducks and herons.

A few years ago the TVA proposed to build two dams on the Cumberland down stream from the refuge. These would do no harm to the refuge. More recently, the Corps of Army Engineers has proposed one large dam be built instead. This dam, scheduled for completion in 1963, will create the Barkley Reservoir. The lake will inundate all of the cropland and four small lakes. However, under authority of the *Fish and Wildlife Coordination Act* of 1934, as amended in 1958, the Corps is buying replacement croplands, and a new headquarters access road has been built.

The eastern turkey is one of the interesting species of Kentucky Woodlands. Several hundred here are descendants of an original remnant stock of wild birds, and are,

John H. Gerard
from Nat'l Audubon Society

The eastern bluebird, with brilliant blue on head, back, wings and tail, and chestnut breast, is one of the most loved of our songbirds. Two close relatives are the western and mountain bluebirds of our western states.

The black-billed cuckoo flies noiselessly through eastern woodlands in summer, uttering a call that sounds like knocking on wood. The yellow-billed cuckoo is quite similar, and both winter in South America. The mangrove cuckoo lives in Florida's mangrove jungles.

H. H. Pittman
courtesy Nature Magazine

C. C. Pace, Soil Conservation Service

In spring the drumming of the ruffed grouse, above, sounds in Kentucky Woodlands. At the break of dawn the loud gobbling of the native wild turkeys can be heard among the wooded hills of the refuge.

B. F. McMurry, Fish and Wildlife Service

Charles W. Schwartz

Some show hostility toward the weasels, yet no creature is more courageous and none offers better rodent control. The long-tailed weasel is shown here.

therefore, pure blooded native birds. Some of them are used to restock other areas of suitable turkey habitat to help perpetuate the race. In most other places where there are wild turkeys today, the birds have interbred with domestic turkeys, and have lost their racial integrity. The eastern turkey once inhabited North America from southern Maine to Florida, west to eastern Texas and southern Ontario. The Merriam turkey occurs from southwestern Texas, New Mexico, Arizona and southern Colorado, and the Rio Grande turkey inhabits south Texas, including Aransas National Wildlife Refuge. Shooting and the destruction of habitat have removed this handsome bird from all but a few areas, although restocking is helping to bring it back in a number of places. Turkeys range in small flocks, except during the breeding season, when they pair, or when a male will sometimes select a small harem. They roost at night in trees, and at the first suggestion of dawn, they utter their loud gobbling call which can be heard for long distances through the forest. They run swiftly, and at the approach of danger, take off and are quickly out of sight. During the mating season, the males strut before the females, spreading their tails and scraping the tips of their primary wing feathers along the ground.

During the spring migration, when the drumming of the ruffed grouse can be heard in the woodlands, the trees swarm with warblers, scarlet and summer tanagers, vireos and other songsters, while the clear notes of the wood thrush sound from the valleys and hillsides.

Headquarters is in the refuge, and the address is Route 1, Golden Pond, Kentucky. The area is reached west from Bowling Green, Kentucky, on U. S. Highway 68, ninety-four miles to the junction with State Route 289 right, nine miles to headquarters; and east from Paducah, Kentucky, on U. S. Highway 68, forty-eight miles to the same state route junction. The best times to visit the refuge are during the spring migration and in November and December, when the waterfowl are present.

LACASSINE and SABINE NATIONAL WILDLIFE REFUGES are only a few miles apart, in the Louisiana coastal marshes. Both protect ancestral waterfowl wintering grounds, particularly of blue and lesser snow geese.

Lacassine is forty-nine square miles in area, and was established in 1937. Most of the refuge is occupied by a diked pool of about twenty-five square miles, the Intracoastal Waterway forming its southern boundary. The pool, principal management area of the refuge, supports a thick growth of waterfowl food plants. There are almost no trees except for an unusually fine cypress head near the southwest corner of the pool. This small stand of tall cypresses provides nest sites for egrets, herons and anhingas. During the spring breeding period, the grove is a veritable bird city, the trees loaded with nests. Besides the blue and snow geese, other distinctive birds of the refuge are Canada and white-fronted geese, Florida gallinules, glossy ibises and various songbirds, as well as lesser scaups, mallards, gadwalls, pintails, teal, and fulvous tree, ring-necked and mottled ducks.

Muskrats, raccoons, mink, otters, alligators and armadillos live here. Of these the armadillo is likely to arouse the most interest on the part of the average visitor. It lives on the levees of the pool, and because it is a burrowing animal, it may be necessary for the Fish and Wildlife Service to control its numbers from time to time, to prevent injury to the levees. The armadillo presents a strange sight. About two and a half feet from nose to tip of tail, it trots and roots about in the small shrubs and grass. Clad in its scaly armor plating, it is unafraid unless approached too closely, when it takes off on the run, seeking safety in a burrow or in the dense vegetation. It has poor

During the breeding period, Lacassine's beautiful cypress grove becomes a bird city, loaded with the nests of herons, egrets and other large water birds.

The author

sight and not too good a sense of smell, but seems keenly sensitive to ground vibration. It mates in summer, and the young, miniature replicas of the adults, are born from February to April, and are able to wander about with their mother a few hours after birth. They eat ants and other insects, as well as berries, and frequently travel in groups while foraging. To reach insects a foot or two above the ground in vegetation, they stand on their hindlegs, bracing themselves with their tails. They also assume this pose to sniff the air when danger threatens. The armadillo is a gentle, tolerant animal, and occasionally shares its underground nest with a cotton rat, opossum or cottontail rabbit.

During autumn and winter, the blue goose is one of Lacassine's residents. This handsome bird, with white head and neck, pink bill, blue-gray body and wings, breeds in the stormy tundra islands north of Hudson Bay. It migrates 3000 miles to reach Lacassine, and begins its southward journey congregating at the south end of Hudson Bay or James Bay. The flight from there may cross Wisconsin or Michigan, depending on winds, and stops en route to Louisiana are being made more and more, as national refuges provide attractive feeding grounds. The northward route in spring is about 600 miles longer, following the Missouri Valley to Winnipeg. After feeding in the vicinity of Winnipeg for a month or more, the birds move northward to Southampton Island and Baffin Island. The long journey is one to stir the imagination. It is an outstanding example of the marvel of bird migration. One asks, as he must ever do, when contemplating the migration of birds, what causes the urge to migrate? What is the guiding power that keeps the birds on their course?

In an article, *Wild Goose Rendezvous*, published in the *Canadian Geographical Journal*, May, 1941, J. Dewey Soper describes seeing the blue geese passing through Manitoba: "When this feathered tide sweeps in, it is as though some great torrent has been unleashed. A deluge pours into Manitoba—flock after flock, composed of myriads of individuals. With what eagerness they come, filled with an unconquerable urge to push northward! Accompanying this bold advance is a deafening clamour of wild voices thrilling with buoyant determination and high adventure. The movement continues day and night once momentum is gained, it never slackens until finally it comes to a temporary halt as the last of the multitude rest and feed on the appointed meeting grounds. This great gathering of the clans of the plains, chiefly west and northwest of Winnipeg, continues for two or three weeks, or sometimes a month, according to season; then another stirring event takes place as the vast flocks, in successive groups, leave for the Arctic."

Lacassine headquarters is in the eastern end of the refuge, and the address is Lake Arthur, Louisiana. The refuge is not easy to reach or to explore. Prospective visitors may drive from U. S. Highway 90 at Jennings, south on State Route 25, ten miles to Lake Arthur. Here, directions to headquarters should be obtained. The time to see the large concentration of waterfowl is during the winter.

Sabine is more than four times as large as Lacassine—223 square miles. It is in two separate sections, and part of its south boundary almost touches the shore of the gulf. The smaller east section comprises the drainage of Grand Bayou, a marsh that today is still in its primeval condition. The Fish and Wildlife Service hopes to preserve natural conditions here, and this can be done if activities of land owners outside the refuge boundaries do not interfere. Calcasieu Lake lies between this part of the refuge and the larger western section, which extends twenty-nine miles to the shore of Sabine Lake. This once was a commercially operated muskrat marsh owned by the Orange-Cameron Land Company, which constructed canals and dikes that cross the area. At the junction of two canals, the company built houses, a club house and a skinning plant. Here, at "the four corners," are a few trees, the principal place where trees grow inside the refuge, although a clump or two stand elsewhere in the vastness of the pool. During the spring songbird migration, the four corners trees are a gathering place for many colorful species. Cooper's tanagers, indigo buntings, boat-tailed

Allan D. Cruickshank
from Nat'l Audubon Society

Named for its spoon-like bill, the shoveler is one of many kinds of waterfowl that winter at Lacassine and other southern refuges.

Lacassine and Sabine are noted for their wintering blue geese. To these areas and the National Audubon Society's Rainey Sanctuary, they come by thousands every autumn.

The author

The author

Oddest of North America's mammals is the armadillo.

grackles, red-winged blackbirds, yellow-throats, prothonotary warblers and dozens of other birds may be seen at this junction. The endless marshes protect king rails, wood, white and white-faced glossy ibises, snowy and American egrets, green, Louisiana and great blue herons, roseate spoonbills, Florida and purple gallinules, coots, American and least bitterns, black-necked stilts, Wilson's snipes and greater and lesser yellowlegs. The rare mottled duck reaches the northern and eastern limits of its narrow range here. To enjoy the winter sunshine and warmth of this southern area come blue, lesser snow, white-fronted and Canada geese, blue-winged and green-winged teal, shovelers and mallards. Alligators and armadillos inhabit the area, and muskrats are numerous.

The lesser snow goose has a wider range than the blue, for it winters not only on the Louisiana and Texas coasts, but in California and elsewhere, and its breeding grounds extend from the north coast of Alaska east to southern Baffinland. It is larger than the rare Ross's goose, and both of these and the greater snow goose of the east coast are pure white with black wing-tips. F. H. Kortright, in his book *The Ducks, Geese and Swans of North America*, quotes George Bird Grinnell: "The spectacle of a flock of these white geese flying is a very beautiful one. Sometimes they perform remarkable evolutions on the wing, and if seen at a distance look like so many snow flakes being whirled hither and thither by the wind. Scarcely less beautiful is the sight which may often be seen in the Rocky Mountain region during the migration. As one rides along under the October sun, he may have his attention attracted by sweet, faint, distant sounds, interrupted at first, and then gradually coming nearer and clearer, yet still only a murmur; the rider hears it from above, before, behind and all around, faintly sweet and musically discordant, always softened by distance, like the sound of far-off harps, or sweet bells jangled, of the distant baying of mellow-voiced hounds. Looking up into the sky above him he sees the serene blue far on high flecked with tiny white moving shapes, which seem like snow flakes drifting lazily across the azure sky; and down to earth, falling, falling, falling, come the musical cries of the little wavies that are journeying toward the southland."

Sabine offers unusually good opportunities for bird-watching, especially along State Route 104, which runs through the refuge. Christmas bird counts conducted by the Audubon Society and others have been among the nation's outstanding ones. In 1953, the census was 151 species, the nation's second highest at that time.

At Lacassine and Sabine, as well as at other marsh refuges, the muskrat, which thrives on marsh plants, plays an important role. Biologists have found that by careful control of the muskrat population, vegetation can be kept at the density and abundance best suited for waterfowl. When muskrats are too few, vegetation clogs the water areas needed by the ducks and geese; and when over-numerous, they eat out too much, reducing the cover and food of the birds. To maintain the muskrat population at the proper level, trappers on a share basis are allowed to operate in the refuges. In refuges used as avian breeding grounds, muskrat houses, which are built of dried vegetation,

Muskrats are important at Lacassine and Sabine because they control cattail growth in waterfowl pools. Without them, the pools would become choked with vegetation.

Courtesy Nature Magazine

Below, F. C. Gillett

The author

The Louisiana heron, recognized by slaty blue above and white on belly, is one of several large wading birds at Lacassine and Sabine.

provide nesting sites for waterfowl, particularly Canada geese. These muskrat nesting sites have increased the use of some refuges by waterfowl.

Sabine headquarters is in the refuge, and the address is Sulphur, Louisiana. It is reached south from U. S. Highway 90 at Sulphur, eighteen miles to Hackberry on State Route 104, and from there a short distance to the refuge. Overnight accommodations are available at Sulphur and Lake Charles, Louisiana.

LAGUNA ATASCOSA and SANTA ANA NATIONAL WILDLIFE REFUGES are in south Texas, and are the habitat of many kinds of birds that are not to be seen anywhere else in our country. For this reason they are of unusual interest to bird enthusiasts. A group of bird-watchers saw 245 species of birds in one day in both refuges. Visitors intending to see one of these areas should plan to see both, for they are only sixty miles apart by road.

Laguna Atascosa, located near Port Isabel on the Texas coast, is an area of mesquite, cactus, yucca and grassland encompassing a brackish water lagoon and man-made fresh water impoundments. Sixty-five square miles in extent, it is hot in summer, but ideal for autumn, winter and spring bird-watching. Established in 1946, it provides protection for waterfowl, doves and hundreds of migrant song and wading birds.

Along the shallows and mud flats in spring, one may see roseate spoonbills, white ibises, reddish, snowy and American egrets, avocets, white pelicans, gull-billed terns, willets and Wilson's plovers, to name only a few. On the wind-swept grassy areas the long-billed curlews, with their amazingly long, downward-curving bills, are present all year, and Hudsonian curlews and black-bellied plovers are here in winter. Among the twenty-eight different species of waterfowl recorded for the refuge are the "big two" of the lower Texas coast—the pintail and redhead—which together total over a million ducks using the refuge at one time. Less abundant ducks are shovelers, widgeons, mottled ducks, teal and scaups.

In the chaparral areas are the roadrunner, verdin, Couch's kingbird, derby flycatcher, hooded oriole, Sennett's thrasher, curve-billed thrasher, golden-fronted wood-

Laguna Atascosa protects white pelicans in winter.

The author

G. B. Saunders, Fish and Wildlife Service

Besides the white-winged dove, there are mourning, Mexican ground, white-fronted and Inca doves at Santa Ana.

pecker, blue grosbeak, Bewick's and cactus wrens, and Texas and black-throated sparrows. Overhead against the blue sky, Harris' and Sennett's white-tailed hawks can sometimes be seen, the latter an unusually handsome bird, especially when soaring with its gleaming white tail spread fan-like, showing the band of black near the edge.

In February and March, the yuccas display their large clusters of white blossoms, the mesquite and huisache send out their small fragrant yellow flowers, and several kinds of cacti bloom—the Englemann prickly pear with bright yellow and orange rose-like flowers, being the most showy and abundant.

Mammals of the area include deer, raccoons, peccaries, coyotes, bobcats, bridled

Photographs by the author

In the view above, the bird-watcher's dream comes true, for here at Laguna Atascosa are five roseate spoonbills, six avocets, a white ibis, a glossy ibis, a long-billed curlew and a gull-billed tern. The scene below shows a picturesque stand of yuccas overlooking the lagoon.

The white-faced glossy ibis is a winter resident at Santa Ana. It migrates north in summer and is present at Bear River, in Utah. The eastern glossy lives in south Florida.

Photographs by
Allan D. Cruikshank
from Nat'l Audubon Society

With black wing-tips, pink legs, and pink face and bill, the white ibis is more abundant than the glossy. It often travels in single file in long, undulating lines.

Photographs by the author

Willets winter along the gulf coast, and sometimes occur in huge flocks. The scene below, looking down stream, was taken at Santa Ana where the refuge borders the Rio Grande. The vegetation on the bluff is the Texas brush, famous as wildlife habitat. It has been destroyed almost everywhere except in this refuge.

Kate Peel Anderson, courtesy Nature Magazine

The green jay is one of a number of birds that reach the northern limits of their ranges in the Santa Ana and Laguna Atascosa region.

weasels and packrats. Huge nests of the latter may be seen standing three or more feet tall among the chaparral.

Santa Ana National Wildlife Refuge, consisting of three square miles of the original south Texas brush and native hardwoods, is located on the bank of the Rio Grande. Agriculture and urban deveolpment have almost completely wiped out this unique jungle-like brush that formerly bordered the river for miles—one of the richest bird and mammal habitats to be found anywhere. This little refuge is a museum piece, a sample of the kind of vegetation that once covered wide areas on both sides of the Rio Grande. It is inhabited by many species of birds and mammals native to Mexico, which reach the northern limits of their ranges here in the lower Rio Grande Valley.

Visitors to Santa Ana may expect to see white-fronted, mourning and Mexican ground doves, and occasionally the Inca dove. The refuge is also the summer home of many white-winged doves and the large red-billed pigeons. Other birds to be seen are the green jays, Sennett's thrashers, Texas sparrows, Lomita wrens, Rio Grande vireos, Audubon's, hooded, Scott's and Bullock's orioles, Texas and golden-fronted woodpeckers, Merrill's pauraques, vermilion, beardless and Mexican crested flycatchers and the groove-billed ani. Among the many spring migrants may be seen the strikingly beautiful indigo and painted buntings, sometimes together in the same shrub. In two small marshes on the refuge, snowy and American egrets, white-faced glossy ibises, great blue herons and other wading birds may be seen. In these marsh areas can often be found least grebes, derby flycatchers and anhingas. Black-bellied tree ducks, rose-throated becards and Sennett's warblers, rare birds in the United States, also nest on the refuge. Mammals include the handsome spotted ocelot cat, jaguarundi, coyote, bobcat, bridled weasel and raccoon.

Ebony trees grow in the area, two specimens being of exceptional girth, and mesquites here reach tree size. Other interesting native trees are the retama, guayacan, tepeguaje, anaqua and chapote. Englemann prickly pear and pencil cactus are abundant.

Both refuges are under the same management. Headquarters is in the Post Office Building at San Benito, Texas. Laguna Atascosa is reached east from San Benito, and Santa Ana is reached south from Alamo. Detailed directions may be obtained from headquarters. Good overnight accommodations are available in the nearby towns of Harlingen, San Benito, Pharr, McAllen and Westlaco.

LOWER SOURIS, UPPER SOURIS and DES LACS NATIONAL WILDLIFE REFUGES are on the Souris River watershed in North Dakota, the two Souris refuges being on the Souris River itself, while Des Lacs is on a tributary of that name. All three are narrow areas extending miles along the valleys. They were established in 1935 to provide

A pair of greater prairie chickens dispute over a courtship ground. The Souris refuges are helping to preserve this species. The lesser prairie chicken, paler and smaller, ranges from Kansas to New Mexico, and is in equal need of protection.

Charles W. Schwartz

Frank N. Wilson, courtesy Nature Magazine

The upland plover once was thought to be on the verge of extinction, but recently it has shown an increase. Its decline was caused by shooting.

not only resting, breeding and feeding grounds for waterfowl, but also sanctuary for prairie chickens and sharp-tailed grouse. This is the heart of the favored duck breeding ground of North America, and stories are recounted of the millions of birds seen here by early explorers. The market hunters of the 1890's seemed to take it for granted that the vast numbers of ducks could never be depleted. They slaughtered without restraint and shipped the birds to city markets. Next came the agriculturalists. The wide marshes of the Souris were to them useless wastelands that should be drained to produce crops; but all too late, after planting, it was found that drainage was inadequate. In 1935, the Fish and Wildlife Service acquired the three areas, built dams and dikes and restored the marshes, and now the birds are back in countless thousands.

The water control structures of the two upper refuges, particularly Lake Darling in Upper Souris, serve to control floods and to provide the town of Minot and other communities with a continuous source of fresh, clean water. The impoundments also supply irrigation water for many acres of hay.

In a contest for the most beautiful bird song, a thrush might win, yet the bobolink must rank a close second. Although lacking the dreamy quality of the thrushes, the bobolink's spirited almost metallic tinkle, uttered on the wing, holds the listener spell-bound.

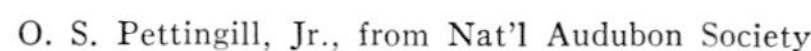

O. S. Pettingill, Jr., from Nat'l Audubon Society

C. J. Henry, former Lower Souris manager, writing in *Audubon Magazine* for July-August 1948, under title of *Summer on the Souris Marsh*, says, "The fame of man as the spoiler is often loud acclaimed. But here, like a gleaming jewel, slumbers the vast marsh, mirrored in the glories of the prairie sunset, an example that man can and has lifted a hand to restore what he had once destroyed."

The Souris River, which has its source in Canada, winds down into North Dakota, then bends north and enters Canada again, its waters eventually flowing into Hudson Bay. The river lies in the northern Great Plains, an endless rolling expanse of short grass prairie, where thousands of glacial pot holes and lakes add to the available waterfowl nesting habitat beyond refuge boundaries. But man seems not to learn from experience, for today the farmers are hard at work operating under government subsidy, draining the pot holes to make room for more crops. Soil conservation authorities say that not all of the pot holes can be drained; yet a great deal of habitat is being wiped out.

Lower Souris is ninety-two square miles in area, and is about a half mile wide, extending for seventy miles along the river. Upper Souris and Des Lacs are fifty and thirty square miles in area respectively.

Summer visitors to Lower Souris will see more than a dozen different species of ducks that breed here. They will see most of North America's grebes—red-necked, pied-billed, eared, horned and western. Here, too, are ring-billed and Franklin's gulls, white pelicans, double-crested cormorants, coots, common terns, great blue and black-crowned

The killdeer makes its presence known by its loud call which seems to say its own name.

Ray C. Erickson, Fish and Wildlife Service

Allan D. Cruickshank, from Nat'l Audubon Society

A white facial crescent identifies the male blue-winged teal, a breeding bird of the Souris refuges and northward into Canada. It winters as far south as Brazil and Chile.

night herons, avocets, killdeers, upland plovers, Wilson's phalaropes and such typical marsh dwellers as yellow-headed and red-winged blackbirds. Five species of sparrows—Leconte's, Nelson's, grasshopper, Baird's and clay-colored—together with Sprague's pipits and chestnut-collared longspurs, all are sought by bird students. At night the deep-toned hooting of the horned owl sounds across the marshes, as well as the delicate trill of the little screech owl. In all, nearly 270 species of birds have been recorded for the Souris loop refuges.

The upland plover was nearly brought to extinction by the gunners, but in recent

Fish and Wildlife Service

The author

The female Wilson's phalarope and the females of the other two phalaropes—northern and red—are the only birds that have more brightly colored spring plumage than their males. The pied-billed, right, is one of five grebes inhabiting the Souris refuges.

years it has slowly recovered under protection afforded it through the *Migratory Bird Treaty Act*.

Another of the many feathered beauties that come to the refuge in spring to raise their young is the bobolink. Southerners call it the reedbird or ricebird because of its fondness for rice. Unfortunately the ripening of the rice crop coincides with the southward migration of the bobolink. When flocks of bobolinks feed on the rice, they are sometimes shot by thousands. In its nesting range, the species suffers another setback during the hay-mowing season, for it nests in fields, and countless thousands of eggs and young are destroyed every year, crushed by the wheels of harvesting machinery. Formerly much more abundant in our northeastern states than it is today, the bobolink appears to have shifted its breeding range to the westward. The tinkling notes of the male, as the bird flutters up from the grass on quivering wings, are of such magic quality as to merit this bird a place among the finest songsters of the avian world, and it deserves all the protection we can give it. Like many of the songbirds that give us pleasure in spring and summer, the bobolink spends its winters in South America—in southern Brazil, Bolivia and Paraguay.

Lower Souris headquarters is on the refuge, and the address is Upham, North Dakota. It is reached from U. S. Highway 2, at Towner, northwest on State Route 14, twenty-three miles to Upham and the refuge. Upper Souris headquarters is on the refuge, and the address is Foxholm. It is reached northwest from Minot on U. S. Highway 52, nineteen miles to Foxholm, and three miles to the refuge. Thirty-four miles farther, on U. S. Highway 52, is Kenmare, the address for Des Lacs, and the refuge is nearby.

Wesley F. Kubichek, Fish and Wildlife Service

Western grebes, above, breed in colonies on inland marshes. Like other species of their kind, they have an amazing courtship performance in which a pair runs rapidly over the water together. This has been ably shown in the Disney *True Life Adventure Series* entitled *Water Birds.* The graceful pintail also breeds on the Souris marshes.

The author

LOXAHATCHEE NATIONAL WILDLIFE REFUGE established in 1951, is situated southwest of Palm Beach, Florida. It is a watery wilderness of 228 square miles broken by many small islands grown with shrubs and trees—white bay, myrtle, strangler fig and moss-draped cypress. Grass, water lilies, pond lilies and pickerel-weed grow in the shallows around the islands.

For several years, beginning in 1949, the Army Engineers constructed dikes here to conserve water for the nearby farms and ranches, and to prevent flooding of farmlands and coastal communities during heavy rains. The Fish and Wildlife Service recognized the potentiality of this diked reservoir—water conservation pool number 1—as a wildlife habitat, and, with the cooperation of the engineers, took steps to make the area attractive to waterfowl and other birds, as well as mammals.

Adjoining Loxahatchee Refuge on the south, another larger area has been diked, pool number 2, and a much larger one, pool number 3, is planned to adjoin this on the southwest. These two new areas will be administered for wildlife by the Florida Game and Fresh Water Fish Commission.

Loxahatchee is the southernmost wintering ground in this country for the waterfowl of the Atlantic flyway. Teal, pintails, lesser scaups, ringnecks, redheads, mallards and wood ducks thrive on the Egyptian wheat, sorghum, millet and rice planted here by the Fish and Wildlife Service. Bobcats, otters, raccoons and alligators also make their homes on the refuge.

The wide water areas of Loxahatchee are picturesquely broken into bays, ponds and narrow waterways by islands of low, dense vegetation.

The author

Rex Gary Schmidt, Fish and Wildlife Service

Brown, spotted with white, and a little larger than an ibis, the limpkin is one of the characteristic birds of Loxahatchee.

One of the most characteristic birds of Loxahatchee is the limpkin, a brown wading bird as large as a bittern, with long, downward-curving bill. On one of those brilliant days typical of winter in Florida, we visited Loxahatchee. At nearly every turn among the islands a limpkin flew from a thicket. The weird cries of this bird carried across the vast solitudes of the marshes. Long lines of white ibises flew across or soared against the blue sky adding a touch of indescribable beauty; while occasionally the clear, gleaming white of an American egret or a flock of little snowy egrets flew overhead to settle far beyond the irregular skyline of the island forests.

The largest bird of the refuge is the spectacular gray Florida crane; but the bird which many hope will benefit from protection in this area is the Everglade kite. Locally known as the snail hawk and hook-billed hawk, this handsome species is now close to extinction. Formerly it inhabited most of the fresh water marshes of the Florida Peninsula, and favorite places were the headwaters of the Saint Johns River, the Loxahatchee Marshes and the Lake Okeechobee country. Today, almost the only remaining habitat of this kite is along the southwest side of Lake Okeechobee, and the only breeding range is Redlight Reef on the southwest shore of the lake.

There are two principal reasons for the present serious plight of this bird. The fresh water snail, *Pomacea caliginosa,* which is the bird's only food, depends on permanent shallow bodies of water. Man has drained marsh after marsh, and when an area is once dried up, the snail perishes. Even though a marsh may again become covered with water, the snail remains absent (unless reintroduced artificially), so that the area no longer

The Everglade kite has been brought to the brink of extinction by gunners and by the drainage of its marsh habitat.

Hugo H. Schroder, courtesy Mass. Audubon Society

William H. Lawrence, courtesy Nature Magazine

Among the several waders of Loxahatchee is the yellow-crowned night heron.

Allan D. Cruickshank
from Nat'l Audubon Society

Plume hunters, during the latter part of the 19th century, nearly exterminated the snowy egret, left, and the American egret. Both are shown wearing nuptial plumes which were used to ornament hats.

The American egret, larger than the snowy, has been restored to safe numbers, together with the snowy, and they are giving pleasure to all who want to see them.

The author

The boat-tailed grackle, right, inhabits the Loxahatchee marshes throughout the year. Both the purple and bronzed grackles are more abundant on uplands, and the purple is perhaps the best known.

Photographs by
Allan D. Cruickshank
from Nat'l Audubon Society

With bright purple head and neck, red and yellow bill and yellow legs, the purple gallinule is one of the most gaudily colored birds of our southern marshes. Long toes enable it to walk on lily pads.

Hugo H. Schroder

North America's only stork is the wood ibis. Its broad black and white wings make it strikingly picturesque in flight.

serves as kite habitat. The second reason is shooting by gunners who fail to identify the bird. Because the kite is hawk-like in appearance, and since most gunners kill any hawk on sight, the kite has suffered severe decimation.

The male Everglade kite is dark gray or nearly black, with red legs and red at the base of the bill, and a wide white patch that goes completely around the base of the tail.

Allan D. Cruickshank, from Nat'l Audubon Society

Black-crowned night herons have a wide range and can be seen on most if not all our marsh refuges.

The author

The coot, with dark gray plumage, white bill and green lobed feet, so far has escaped any concerted attention of the gunners, and is more abundant in some areas than most of the ducks.

The female also has the white patch around the base of the tail, but the body and wings are buff, with dark streaking, and there is a white line over the eye. The white tail patch is a distinctive feature of the kite. The marsh hawk also has a white patch at the base of its tail—but only on top. However, this often causes a gunner to confuse the kite with the hawk. (The marsh hawk, too, is a protected species.) While the kite has wide wings, the marsh hawk's wings are comparatively narrow. The kite flies low and keeps a steady course, head tipped downward searching the vegetation for snails; while the hawk often dips from side to side, and alters its course frequently. The kite's bill, slender and sharply hooked, adapted to prying the snail from its shell, is another distinctive feature of the species.

Whether Loxahatchee Refuge will serve as a haven for the Everglade kite and help to restore it to safer numbers depends on whether the snail can be brought back in the area. Further success depends on a campaign of education about the kite in Florida. To enlighten the public and the gunners on the threatening extinction of this large, beautiful bird, the Florida Game and Fresh Water Fish Commission has been showing to duck shooters a film on the life of the kite, by Bayard Read, and urging them to refrain from shooting the bird. The fact that twenty-five percent of the refuge may be opened to public shooting in season can hardly be considered beneficial to the kite or any other species inhabiting the area.

Headquarters is on the refuge near Delray Beach. It is reached from West Palm Beach and from Fort Lauderdale. The best time of year to see waterfowl and other wildlife here is during the winter months.

MALHEUR NATIONAL WILDLIFE REFUGE is in southeastern Oregon, on the Pacific waterfowl flyway. It comprises 289 square miles of marsh, hills, rimrock, semi-arid plains, ponds, riverbottom and three lakes—Malheur, Mud and Harney—fed by streams flowing from the Steens Mountains to the south and the Blue Mountains to the north. The region for miles around shows signs of geologically recent volcanic activity, with cinder cones, lava flows and other weird formations.

In early times, the Malheur area was a wildlife paradise, where ducks, geese and marsh birds nested abundantly. In describing the history of the Malheur region, the Fish and Wildlife Service says that during the years of Indian uprisings, in the mid 1860's, the Army established Fort Harney about twenty miles north of Malheur Lake. With the first detachment of cavalry came a lieutenant, Charles E. Bendire, a young man keenly interested in wildlife, whose findings give us the first detailed account of the vast numbers of waterfowl and shorebirds of the Malheur Lake country. He wrote of great migrations of ducks, geese, swans and sandhill cranes; of colonies of nesting pelicans, grebes, cormorants, gulls and terns, and of myriads of waterfowl that raised their young here.

After Bendire's time, says the Service, the plume hunters came to slaughter the swans, grebes, egrets and other birds for the millinery trade. Their nefarious activities almost exterminated the egrets, and greatly reduced the tern colonies. Fur trappers likewise reaped harvests of beaver, otter, mink and muskrat skins by thousands. The early settlers shot ducks, geese and swans for their feathers or for food. As more people settled in the region, dams were built on the streams flowing into the lakes to impound water for irrigating hay fields. As a result, the marshes gradually dried up and the waterfowl feeding and nesting grounds disappeared.

Malheur's Blitzen Valley provides shelter and browse for mule deer.

Ray C. Erickson, Fish and Wildlife Service

In 1908, Lake Malheur Reservation, a part of the present refuge, was set aside to protect this vital breeding area; but the continuing waterfowl decline, drainage of the marshes for agriculture, and the cycle of drought, caused such drastic changes that by 1930 the birds no longer nested here in important numbers. A ranch in the adjoining Blitzen Valley was purchased by the federal government in 1935, and added to the lake to comprise the Malheur National Wildlife Refuge. In 1941, another large ranch north and west of Harney Lake was acquired, completing the present sanctuary. Water was restored, vegetation recovered, and again Malheur is a major breeding area.

A dozen species of ducks, as well as Canada geese, raise their broods here in spring, as does the big gray sandhill crane. During this season and in early summer, visitors see, besides the waterfowl, graceful black-necked stilts, avocets, willets, killdeers, Wilson's phalaropes, long-billed curlews, Wilson's snipes, white-faced glossy ibises, American egrets, American bitterns, great blue herons, western grebes, coots, white pelicans, ring-billed and California gulls, black and Forster's terns, sage hen, California valley quail, the strikingly handsome black-billed magpies, western kingbirds, marsh and rock wrens, California shrikes and Brewer's, red-winged and yellow-headed blackbirds. The trees and flower beds at refuge headquarters are thronged with robins, yellow and MacGillivray's

In early times, colonies of terns thrived on the Malheur marshes. These and most other birds were nearly wiped out in this area, but today the refuge is one of the Fish and Wildlife Service's show places. Both the Forster's tern shown here, and the handsome black tern, can be seen on the refuge.

E. R. Kalmbach, Fish and Wildlife Service

Ray C. Erickson, Fish and Wildlife Service

The long-billed curlew, a bird of startling appearance because of the length of its bill, is one of several shore birds that thrive on Malheur in summer.

The author

The depth of water in the Malheur marshes is carefully adjusted, as in other waterfowl refuges, to suit the needs of wildlife. Cottontail rabbits, below, and other small mammals, find sanctuary on drier areas of the refuge.

Wilford L. Miller, from Nat'l Audubon Society

Alfred M. Bailey, R. J. Niedrach, courtesy Am. Forestry Ass'n

Golden eagles nest in the vicinity of Harney Lake on Malheur's west side.

warblers, red-breasted and white-breasted nuthatches and rufous, black-chinned and broad-tailed hummingbirds. The beautiful lazuli bunting and six kinds of swallows—violet-green, rough-winged, bank, barn, cliff and tree—nest in the area. Swainson's, rough-legged, marsh and sparrow hawks, peregrine and prairie falcons and ravens, as well as horned and short-eared owls, inhabit the refuge. In all, nearly 230 species of birds have been recorded here.

Antelopes, jack and cottontail rabbits and chipmunks live in the sage flats and rocky outcrops; while mink, muskrats and beavers thrive in the marsh and riverbottoms, and mule deer find shelter among the willows along the Blitzen.

Taking the road to Harney Lake, which passes the foot of a towering basaltic escarpment, one may see golden eagles, which nest high in the crags. Inhabiting most of North America, particularly the West, the golden eagle, feathered in brown, with golden tinge on head and shoulders, today is considered a relatively rare species. Its huge size, its wing-spread of six and a half to seven and a half feet, and its superb ability to soar on motionless wings, make it a stirring sight to watch. Gliding swiftly on the wind, or circling up on rising currents of warm air, no living creature can more thoroughly capture the

Allan D. Cruickshank, from Nat'l Audubon Society

The barn swallow, as well as the violet-green, rough-winged, bank, cliff and tree, adds life and beauty to the refuge scene.

imagination or arouse the envy of the earth-bound observer. Great master of air travel, the golden eagle is truly a wonder of the bird world.

In 1962, Congress amended the bald eagle protective law to include the golden eagle. Previously, the golden had been unprotected and was shot or poisoned over its entire North American range, particularly in twenty counties of southern Texas. In these coun-

Clifford H. Atkins

Rugged canyons are the favorite habitat of canyon wrens whose musical descending trills ring along the escarpments and in the defiles. Here, too, dwells the spritely, diminutive western chipmunk.

National Park Service

R. Dale Sanders, U. S. Forest Service

Beavers find habitat to their liking in the valley of the Blitzen River, which in places is hemmed in by sheer walls of volcanic rock.

The author

National Park Service

When the beavers take over a stream for home territory, they build substantially. A beaver house is shown, above, and a beaver dam, below, forms a pond in which the house is built. During warm months, the beaver transports twigs and branches with edible bark to the pond bottom for winter food.

Joseph S. Dixon

Courtesy Nature Magazine

The ferruginous rough-legged hawk, a westerner, is one of the large, handsome, soaring buteos. White leg-feathers show this to be a young bird.

ties, predatory mammals had been wiped out by livestock interests so that rabbits and ground squirrels multiplied, providing abundant food for the eagles. Therefore the eagles wintered here in exceptionally large numbers. Stockmen blamed the eagles for the death of any of their animals, and employed aviator gunners to shoot the birds down. One gunner boasted about killing more than 1,000 eagles. The golden eagle amendment is weak in that the Secretary of the Interior must allow killing on state request. The bald eagle, which has been declining because of breeding failure, benefits from the amendment—immature bald eagles in flight are hardly distinguishable from the golden, and many were being shot.

For many years, ornithologists doubted whether the golden eagle could rightfully be counted among the birds of eastern United States. It was not until after the establishment of Hawk Mountain Sanctuary, on Kittatinny Ridge in eastern Pennsylvania, that ample evidence was obtained to show that the golden eagle does indeed range over the eastern part of our country in considerable numbers. The nesting range of these golden eagles extends northward into Canada from northern New York and northern New England. More are seen at Hawk Mountain than elsewhere, possibly because of the number of observers there, but a small number may winter at isolated places from Maine to the Carolinas. The author had the privilege of making the first sight record of the golden eagle at Brigantine National Wildlife Refuge, on the New Jersey coast, in December, 1951.

Malheur headquarters is on the refuge, and the address is Burns, Oregon. The area is reached from U. S. Highways 20 and 395 at Burns, south thirty-five miles on State Route 205. The best time to visit the area is from spring through autumn. Overnight accommodations are available at Burns, and at Frenchglen south of the refuge. Hart Mountain National Wildlife Refuge is a hundred miles southwest of Malheur.

White-necked ravens, birds of the arid and semi-arid Southwest, do not come as far north as Malheur, although the American raven lives in this region. The name refers to the white feathers at the base of the neck, which are invisible unless blown by the wind.

E. R. Kalmbach, Fish and Wildlife Service

MATTAMUSKEET and SWANQUARTER NATIONAL WILDLIFE REFUGES, in eastern North Carolina, are two large areas established for migrating waterfowl. They are only twelve miles apart by road, so that visitors can plan to see both of them.

Mattamuskeet is seventy-eight square miles in area embracing Lake Mattamuskeet. The lake itself is fourteen miles long and six miles wide, and is bounded by marshes and woodlands of gum and loblolly pine on its south and west sides. In a few places picturesque stands of cypress trees grow in the water close to shore. In 1914 a propect was started to drain this shallow lake and turn the area into farmland. Although the soil was fertile for

The large white whistling swans come to Mattamuskeet every autumn, flying from the Arctic regions where they raise their young.

Fish and Wildlife Service

The author

Canada geese continue to be fairly abundant because of the protection given them on the refuges.

the most part, the attempts of more than one company to make a success of the project resulted in failure. It was abandoned only after millions of dollars had been spent in construction of a system of canals and dikes, and the installation of a pumping station.

In 1934 the area was purchased by the federal government and placed in the care of the Fish and Wildlife Service to be administered for migratory waterfowl.

Mattamuskeet is one of the largest of the east coast refuges; Santee, Okefenokee and Loxahatchee being considerably larger. During the fall and winter, the refuge feeds the greatest concentration of both Canada geese and whistling swans on the Atlantic coast.

The breeding range of the swan extends west from the islands north of Hudson Bay and along the Arctic and Bering Sea coasts of Alaska, and it spends the winter from Oregon to Lower California on the Pacific coast, and from Chesapeake Bay to North Carolina on the Atlantic coast. This pure white bird, with black legs and bill, has a wing-spread of six to seven feet. It is our second largest waterfowl, the rare trumpeter swan exceeding it in wing-spread by very little. For sheer grace and beauty, the swan has almost no equal. Flying in diagonal line or wedge formation, long necks extended and huge wings fanning in slow rhythm, flashing in brilliant sunshine against a blue sky, it is one of the most inspiring sights in the entire world of nature. Swans fly high, sometimes above the clouds. They require five or six years to reach maturity, and they mate for life. It is not many years ago that the whistling swan was so reduced in numbers through shooting, that it was thought to be well on its way to extinction. Under the *Migratory Bird Treaty*, ratified by the United States and Great Britain in 1916, and by Mexico in 1936, swan shooting became illegal. This brought about a recovery of the swan population. The bird has high esthetic value and should never be subjected to shooting; but in 1962, the Bureau of Sport Fisheries and Wildlife, with the approval of the Secretary of the Interior, recommended an "experimental hunt" and issued 1,000 permits, in Utah, allowing one swan per gunner during the open season from October 13 through December 26. The Department of the Interior deserved the criticism it received for this action.

Other waterfowl that make Mattamuskeet a lively and colorful scene in autumn are green and blue-winged teal, widgeons, mallards, wood and black ducks, shovelers, gadwalls and pintails, the latter being the most abundant. A few greater snow geese usually winter on the refuge, and rarely a few blues. Great blue, little blue, green and black-crowned night herons, American and least bitterns and, in summer, the big white American egret, wade through the marshes and along the lake shore. In winter the American pipit, cedar waxwing, ruby-crowned kinglet, myrtle warbler, horned lark, meadowlark and red-winged blackbird are present. The red-wings gather into flocks numbering in the thousands

Nothing is more entrancingly beautiful than the great white whistling swans fanning their wings against the blue sky. Even the least appreciative must marvel at the sight; yet to one whose eyes and ears are tuned to the wonders of nature, every moment in the wilds brings the refreshment and spiritual uplift that only contact with nature can give. To such a person, the needless death of any creature of beauty—for "sport" or mere proof of marksmanship—causes naught but the most profound regret.

The author

S. A. Grimes
from Mass. Audubon Society

Red-winged blackbirds assemble in vast flocks at Mattamuskeet in autumn and early winter, and during the warmer months they raise their young on nearly all of the waterfowl refuges.

The meadowlark, with bright yellow breast and black markings, might be designated the symbol of the national wildlife refuges, for either the eastern or western species is present on nearly every refuge in the system.

The author

The author

No one entering Swanquarter can have any doubt about the purpose of this refuge.

in autumn and winter and swarm on and close to the refuge.

Whitetail deer, raccoons, muskrats, foxes, mink, otters, opossums and gray squirrels are among the mammals living in the area. Alligators also may be seen here.

The best way for visitors to see Mattamuskeet is to stroll along the tree-grown dikes that run east and west from the old pumping station, which is now used as a lodge. Here mirror-like canals parallel the dikes. The canals would make an ideal place for canoeing, and no mode of transportation is better suited to seeing wildlife. At the west end of the refuge there is a stand of loblolly pines with an understory of holly. This appears to be in primeval condition, and deserves preservation. A tract of 250 acres, it has been designated a primitive area for permanent preservation, as have a number of other areas on the refuges. With the cutting of loblolly forests almost everywhere else, this stand will become more and more valuable as an esthetic attraction. Even now, there may no longer be another such stand of loblolly pine. Repeated efforts have been made by loggers to buy this tract or the trees on it for lumber.

One of the stipulations imposed by the state in approving purchase—state approval being required in the purchase of any national wildlife refuge—was that a part of the area be kept open to shooting during each gunning season. Without this agreement the state would not have permitted refuge establishment. This, of course, amounts to a reduction by about a fifth in the effectiveness of the refuge. Similar arrangements have been worked out in several other refuges, a situation which eventually should be improved in favor of the birds.

A serious by-product of any waterfowl shooting is the possibility of lead poisoning of waterfowl. Spent shot, which settles in the mud of lake bottoms where the waterfowl feed, is taken into the birds' digestive systems and often results in death. Studies have been made to discover a different material for shot, which either would disintegrate in the water or would not be poisonous to the waterfowl. So far, any substitute for lead has proved less satisfactory or much more expensive, and the poisoning of birds continues wherever shooting is done over the shallow water of feeding areas.

Headquarters is in the refuge, and the address is New Holland, North Carolina. The area is reached south from Norfolk, Virginia, on U. S. Highway 17 to the junction with State Route 37, twenty-four miles south of Elizabeth City. Thence twelve miles south on State Route 37, crossing Albemarle Sound to U. S. Highway 64, seventeen miles east to Columbia and the junction with State Route 94, which runs south across Mattamuskeet Lake to U. S. Highway 264. From here, go two miles left to New Holland where a sign points to headquarters and Mattamuskeet Lodge. From the south, the area is reached on U. S. Highway 17, north from Wilmington, North Carolina, to Washington, North Carolina, then east on U. S. Highway 264 to the refuge, a total distance of 194 miles. Meals and overnight accommodations are provided at the lodge. The greatest concentration of waterfowl is in autumn, before and during the gunning season; while the songbirds are most numerous in spring.

Whistling swans.

The author

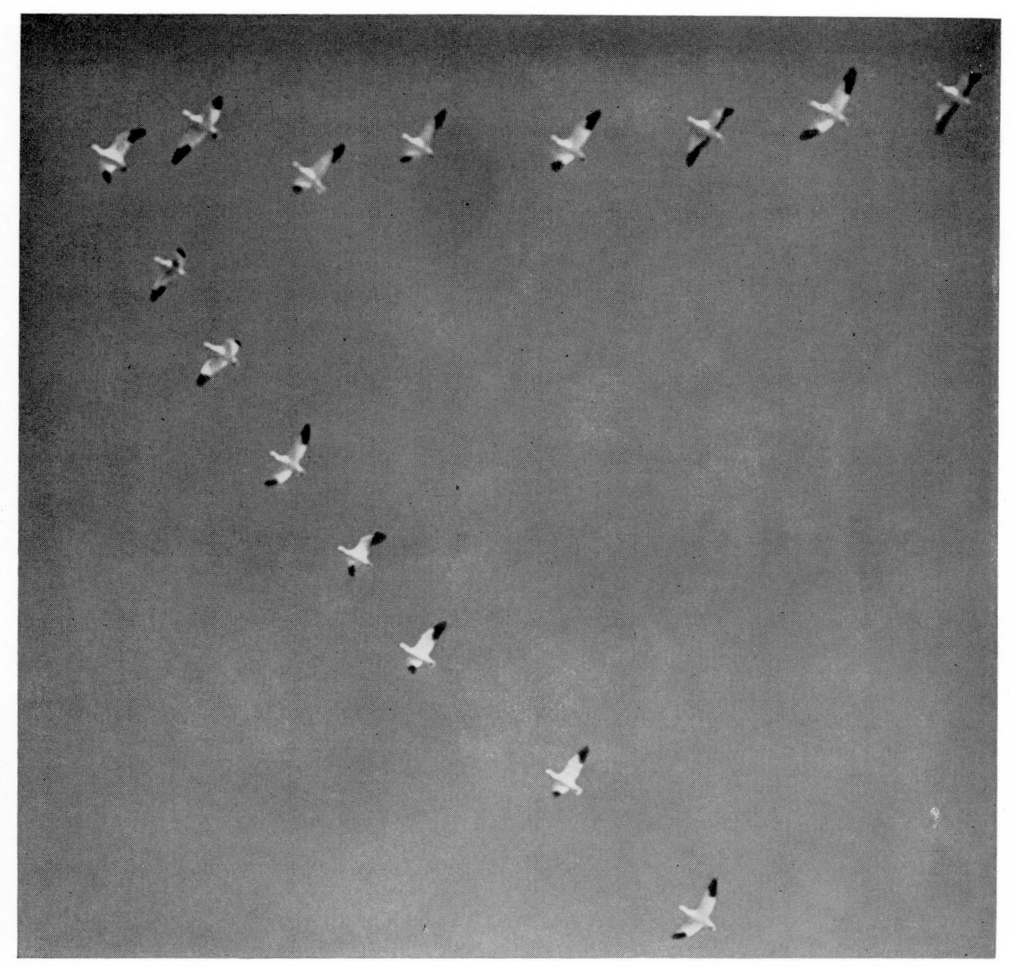

Wesley F. Kubichek, Fish and Wildlife Service

Snow geese.

Swanquarter National Wildlife Refuge is southwest of Mattamuskeet. It borders Pamlico Sound, and includes several hundred acres of the sound itself. In addition to a stand of loblolly pine, the land area contains an unusually beautiful hardwood swamp forest of many kinds of broad-leafed evergreen trees—the habitat of raccoons, otters, wood ducks and pileated woodpeckers. By cutting a loop trail through it, this forest could be made attractive and easily accessible for visitors to explore. To cross water areas, elevated wooden walks might be built wide enough for single-file hiking. Twenty-four square miles in extent, the refuge was established in 1932 to give protection to swans and a number of diving ducks such as the American golden-eye, redhead, bufflehead, canvas-back, lesser scaup and old-squaw, and several of the surface-feeding ducks—mallard, black, pintail and green-winged teal.

Swanquarter is under the supervision of the manager at Mattamuskeet. Mattamuskeet Lodge is convenient for visitors to both refuges.

MOOSEHORN NATIONAL WILDLIFE REFUGE is located in eastern Maine near the Canadian border. It was established in 1937 to protect a woodcock breeding area, as well as the habitat of spruce and ruffed grouse and waterfowl. The refuge, acquired originally by the Resettlement Administration as a submarginal land project, is in two separate parts totaling thirty-five square miles. The Moosehorn Unit, situated four miles west of Calais, is the larger. It consists of wooded hills, bogs, meadows, alder thickets, fresh water marshes, streams and lakes. Balsam firs, black, red and white spruces, white cedars, red and white pines, paper and gray birches, moosewood, big-tooth and trembling aspens, red oaks, larches and sugar and red maples are its dominant trees. The Edmunds Unit is thirty-six miles south of Calais. It lies along the shores of Broad and Burnt coves, in Cobscook Bay, which is salt tidal water, with the Whiting River winding through it. This unit is picturesque, with low, rocky hills grown with maples, red and white spruces, balsam firs, gray and paper birches, quaking aspens and white pines. Bunchberry, various mosses and club mosses grow in the woodlands, and sea lavender along the tidal margins. The tide here rises and falls about twenty feet.

There is an impressive population of mammals at Moosehorn—whitetail deer, black bears, skunks, raccoons, red foxes, woodchucks, beavers, mink, otters, weasel, bobcats, varying or snowshoe hares, chipmunks, flying, red and gray squirrels, porcupines, muskrats and rarely moose. Occasionally a lynx may wander in. A surprising assortment of small mammals also has been recorded in the refuge—hairy-tailed and star-nosed moles, short-tailed, white-chinned water and masked shrews, little brown bats, red-backed, white-footed and meadow mice, and woodland and Hudson Bay jumping mice.

Ducks that use the area are ring-necks, blacks, American golden-eyes, mallards, pintails, blue-winged and green-winged teal, buffleheads, old-squaws, American eiders, surf, white-winged and black scoters, wood ducks and American, hooded and red-breasted mergansers, and Canada geese and Atlantic brant. A number of owls occur in the refuge—horned, screech, saw-whet and rarely the hawk owl, which breeds in northern Canada and winters in southern Canada, occasionally entering our northern states. Hawks of the refuge are sharp-shinned, red-tailed, broad-winged, marsh, pigeon, kestrel and peregrine falcon. A few songbirds recorded here are brown-capped and

Spruce-clad islands and rocky points make an interesting shore-line at the Edmunds Unit of Moosehorn.

The author

Peter J. Van Huizen, Fish and Wildlife Service

Moosehorn is important because it protects nesting habitat and singing grounds of the woodcock, as well as providing sanctuary for many other birds and mammals. Therefore it should remain in the care of the Fish and Wildlife Service.

Allan D. Cruickshank
from Nat'l Audubon
Society

Great black-backed gulls are present all year in the salt water coves of the Edmunds Unit.

Common loons feed and breed on Hobart Lake in the Edmunds Unit of Moosehorn.

Hugh M. Halliday
from National Audubon
Society

The white-breasted nuthatch is a permanent resident in Moosehorn woodlands where it often associates with chickadees and woodpeckers in winter.

Photographs by
Allan D. Cruickshank
from Nat'l Audubon Society

The red-breasted nuthatch, dweller of conifer forests, may be present at Moosehorn, although its population fluctuates from year to year.

L. K. Couch, Fish and Wildlife Service

Going quietly about his business with intent to harm no one, the porcupine has an ever-ready defense against any who threaten him.

black-capped chickadees, golden-crowned kinglets, red-breasted and white-breasted nuthatches, kingbirds, blue jays, slate-colored juncos, veerys, olive-backed and hermit thrushes, cedar waxwings, red-eyed and blue-headed vireos, numerous warblers, evening and pine grosbeaks, pine siskins, goldfinches, eastern snow buntings, redpolls and white-winged crossbills. The gentle song of the white-throated sparrow, which seems to say "Oh, sweet Canada, Canada, Canada," sounds along forest margins during early summer.

The woodcock, for whose protection Moosehorn was established primarily, is an odd appearing fellow, with an extraordinary walk, for besides its chunky body and comparatively short, broad, rounded wings, it has a large head, an extremely long bill for its size, and its unusually large eyes seem placed too high. Its markings and coloration, which make it difficult to see on the ground, are described by Roger Tory Peterson as a dead-leaf pattern. The under parts are rufous, while the upper parts are barred and mottled with rufous, black and gray.

Breeding grounds of the woodcock in the United States had been studied for sev-

Photographs by Allan D. Cruickshank, from Nat'l Audubon Society

The black-capped chickadee, upper left, and the slate-colored junco, are all-year residents at Moosehorn, and here, too, may be seen the brown-capped chickadee. In summer the eastern kingbird, lower left, and the ruby-throated hummingbird come to Moosehorn from their South American winter homes. All four of these birds range widely in the East and may be seen on a number of refuges.

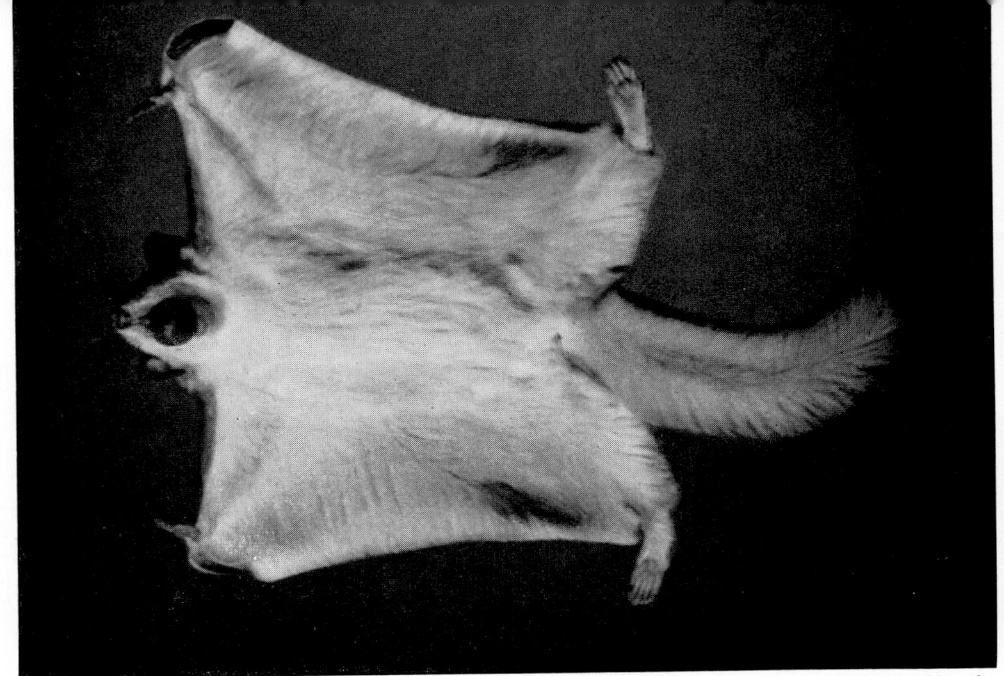

Photographs by Ernest P. Walker, courtesy Nature Magazine

With "wings" spread and flat tail serving as rudder, above, a flying squirrel glides with a nut in its mouth. Below, a flying squirrel goes to work on a nut. These appealing little creatures, with large eyes, are nocturnal and are seldom seen. Two species inhabit North America, the larger, the northern flying squirrel, living in the forests of Canada and parts of northern United States; while the eastern squirrel makes its home in forested areas of our eastern states.

If you invade his woodland territory, the amusing red squirrel will quickly let you know, with a tirade of enraged scolding, that he wants you to get out p. d. q.

V. B. Sheffer
Fish and Wildlife Service

eral years with a view to discovering a tract especially favored by these birds. Its breeding range extends from our southern states to Nova Scotia, west to southern Ontario, northeastern Minnesota and southern Manitoba. It winters southward from New Jersey, the Ohio Valley and southern Missouri to south Texas and Florida. Eastern Maine was known to be one of the best breeding areas. When Moosehorn, in the heart of this breeding area, became available by transfer from the Resettlement Administration it was selected for a refuge not only to give protection to the woodcock and its favored habitat, but also to enable the Maine Cooperative Wildlife Research Unit to study the habits

Allan D. Cruickshank, from Nat'l Audubon Society

The sweet song of the white-throated sparrow sounds through spring and summer meadows of Moosehorn. Not including subspecies, the sparrow clan is large, numbering over thirty kinds.

and requirements of the species under favorable conditions. The necessity of learning more about this bird stemmed from the fact that it was a persecuted species, being avidly sought by gunners, and its survival was by no means certain. Scientific management might help to save it.

Excellent as was the ecology of the refuge area for breeding woodcock, the biologists have improved it by clearing well-spaced areas of shrubs and trees to provide additional openings to be used by the birds as "singing grounds." The woodcock's use of its singing grounds is described by Frank M. Chapman, in his *Handbook of Birds of Eastern North America:* "The cloak of night always lends a certain mystery to the doings of nocturnal birds, and more often than not their habits justify our unusual interest in them. Few of the mating evolutions of our birds are more remarkable than the sky dance of the woodcock. He begins on the ground with a formal, periodic *peent, peent,* an incongruous preparation for the wild rush that follows. It is repeated several times before he springs from the ground, and on whistling wings sweeps out on the first loop of a spiral which may take him three hundred feet from the ground. Faster and faster he goes, louder and shriller sounds his wing song; then, after a moment's pause, with darting, headlong flight, he pitches and zig-zags to the earth, uttering as he falls, a clear twittering whistle. He generally returns to near the place from which he arose, and the *peent* is at once resumed as a preliminary to another round in the sky. In the gray of early morning, this strange performance is repeated." These fantastic evolutions occur here during the last part of April and the early days of May. At the refuge it is sometimes possible to see several males performing at the same time.

Headquarters is on the Moosehorn Unit. The address is Box 285, Calais, Maine. It is reached six miles west of Calais on U. S. Highway 1 toward Houlton. The Edmunds Unit is on the same highway, thirty-six miles south of Calais. The Edmunds Unit contains an excellent picnic area and a campground for trailers and tents.

NATIONAL BISON RANGE, south of Flathead Lake, in northwestern Montana, is an area of high grassy hills, with occasional patches of ponderosa pine and Douglas fir and groves of trembling aspen. The Jocko River, bordering the refuge on the south, is grown with willow, alder and birch, as is also Mission Creek inside the northern boundary. Both of these streams flow into the Flathead River, just west of the refuge. The area is twenty-nine square miles in extent, and was established in 1908 to help save the bison from pending extinction. Here, too, are elk, whitetail deer, bighorn sheep, pronghorn antelope and Franklin's and blue grouse.

Bison once roamed from western Pennsylvania, Kentucky and Georgia, to eastern California, south to Texas and north to Great Slave Lake in northwestern Canada. The Great Plains were its favored habitat, however, for it was here that early explorers found the herds stretching from horizon to horizon. The bison filled many important needs of the plains Indians—its hide, meat, sinews, and in fact, every part of the body was used.

Although the Indians killed, at the same time they preserved the bison population. It was with the advent of the white man that the carnage began. Men bragged about killing hundreds of the great animals. Some killed for the hide, some for the meat, often only the tongue, and left the carcass to rot. The slaughter went on unchecked, partly because it was realized that bison destruction meant wiping out the plains Indian, who was a threat to advancing civilization. The plains were white with bleaching bison bones; later even these were harvested commercially for fertilizer, and train-loads of them were shipped to eastern cities. When the Union Pacific Railroad first spanned the continent,

The giant of our western grasslands finds sanctuary on the Bison Range.

The author

and other roads were moving west, they brought gunners into the bison country quickly and easily, and to entice business, some railroads advertised killing from the moving trains.

Just before the turn of the century, the monarch of the plains had nearly vanished. It was not until 1893 that President Grover Cleveland signed a bill making it illegal to kill bison in Yellowstone National Park—the first national legislation offering any protection to the species. In 1905, President Theodore Roosevelt established the Wichita Game Preserve, now the Wichita Mountains National Wildlife Refuge, Oklahoma, which was stocked with fifteen head from the Bronx Zoo. That same year, a group of men deeply concerned over the bison's threatened extinction, banded together to form the American Bison Society. The first accomplishment of the organization was to establish the National Bison Range and purchase animals with which to stock it. At this time, efforts also were carried on by the Dominion Government to save and restore the bison in Canada.

The Bison Range now supports between three hundred and four hundred head. To explore the area, and to search for the bison—they are by no means always conveniently located on the nearest slope for the visitor to see—and to come suddenly on a hundred or more tranquilly grazing in that wild, primitive setting, is to experience one of the greatest thrills the refuge system has to offer.

Dr. William T. Hornaday, for a number of years president of the American Bison Society, wrote in a report to the Society, March, 1910: "The American people have thus

Three hundred bison roam free and wild over the hills of the refuge.

The author

The author

Supper time on the Bison Range.

become owners in perpetuity of what we believe to be the richest and the most beautiful grazing grounds ever trodden by bison hoofs. We have seen the best portions of the American great buffalo plains all the way from Texas panhandle to the sweet grass hills of northern Montana, and for abundance of rich grass, pure water, winter shelter, picturesque interior and picturesque surroundings, the Montana National Range is absolutely beyond compare."

On the day of our visit to the refuge in August, clouds wreathed the grassy heights, and rain fell intermittently, as we wound up along the truck trail in search of bison, antelope, elk and deer, and hopefully, bighorns. A number of sleek blacktail deer were resting along the lower slopes when we came into view, and in graceful bounds made off over the nearest ridge. Once, high up along the skyline, the mist made silhouettes of a dozen elk; and down again in the low country, three antelope appeared in the landscape of gray-green sage. Unlike the deer, these tawny animals did not bound, but, holding their backs level, ran swiftly away, white rump patches flashing. Rounding the end of a long ridge that descended from the heights, a vast cirque-like slope came into view, and far away on its grassy incline that ascended steeply to the highest points along the range of hills, we saw a hundred bison. Their coats, almost black in the rain, showed distinctly against the pale color of the grass. There was no sound except the rush of gentle wind through the grass around us, but as we approached, the roarings and gruntings of the huge bulls became increasingly audible, for this was the mating season, and there was much restlessness. Two bulls engaged in combat, and one slightly wounded moved swiftly away, limping on three legs.

Here, indeed, was a glimpse back into primeval times. In a setting as wild and undisturbed as it had been for countless centuries, the bison unmolested, were carrying on their natural happy lives. Well could we imagine that beyond these hills and the distant mountains that added their beauty all around, were more bison, and beyond them still others, and that the hundreds of thousands, yes, millions, that once roamed the grasslands of the western plains were still living there—the thundering herds that pioneers and the railroad builders knew.

Fine as the National Bison Range is, one cannot help but look upon some of the adjoining hills beyond present refuge boundaries a bit covetously; for if the range could be extended to include a sizeable part of them, many more bison could be supported. The hills extend eastward, grassy summit after grassy summit, with areas of green conifer forests, all equally good bison habitat. Perhaps someday this area can be added to the refuge. But equally impressive, perhaps, would be the establishment of a large area of wild grassland as a national monument or a wildlife preserve in the Great Plains—a vast region of gently rolling short grass prairie—where several thousand head of bison, elk and antelope might range.

Headquarters is in the refuge, and the address is Moiese, Montana. The area is reached south from Kalispell, Montana, over U. S. Highway 93, eighty-seven miles to Ravalli, to the junction with U. S. Highway 10A, seven miles right, to a right hand road to Moiese. North from Missoula, it is reached forty-four miles to the same right hand road to Moiese. The refuge can be visited readily by tourists traveling between Yellowstone and Glacier national parks. Obviously, it would be dangerous to visitors and disturbing to the animals to permit visitors to roam at will in the area. Accordingly, an enclosure containing a number of bison has been constructed at headquarters, and this is encircled by a road from which to see the animals. There is a picnic area in the refuge.

Here one gains a glimpse back into primitive times when millions of bison covered the plains.

E. P. Haddon, Fish and Wildlife Service

Courtesy Nature Magazine

No creature is more majestic than the Rocky Mountain elk.

NATIONAL ELK REFUGE is located in Jackson Hole along the foot of the Gros Ventre Mountains, in northwestern Wyoming. It adjoins Grand Teton National Park on the northwest. Established in 1912, its thirty-seven square miles provide a wintering ground for the Jackson Hole herd of Rocky Mountain elk.

When the refuge biologist told us to return to a certain place at sunset time, we had no idea of the sight that was in store for us. We had been told a few elk were summering on the refuge, and we thought we might see two dozen. Earlier, with binoculars, we had seen twenty animals grazing slowly through the screen of cotton-woods that fringed the far side of the grassy expanse. Now, as we came up over a ridge a hundred feet or so above the plain, we beheld the spectacle of 200 elk scattered over a square mile of rich grass. Their brown coats and the green grass and cotton-woods were bathed in the warm light of the setting sun, and the whole entrancing scene was backed by the jagged blue wall of the glacier-streaked Teton Mountains.

The need for the refuge points up a fact that has been apparent for a long time, namely, that Yellowstone, like many other national parks, while providing summer range for wildlife, does not contain adequate winter range. Because of the limited size of the elk refuge, it only partly makes up for the serious lack of winter habitat. The cause of the difficulty is that man has taken over for his own use the land that once belonged to the elk. In primeval times, these animals wandered over a wide region. They went into the higher altitudes in summer—to the lower slopes of the northern Tetons, the luxuriant, flower-filled meadows of southern Yellowstone and the forested slopes of the Teton National Forest. Then in winter they migrated to the lowlands where temperatures were milder and snow not so deep as in the mountains. Ranches and urban communities have now usurped much of this winter range and made extensive winter wandering almost impossible.

This land limitation creates another problem: Because man has not adjusted his economy to live with mountain lions, wolves and bobcats, he has systematically hunted these fine animals down and killed them, or worse, has strewn poisoned meat across the land to lure them to their deaths. In primitive times, these animals, because they are meat-eaters, kept the populations of elk and deer from becoming too large. Without this natural check on the herds, the elk are increasing beyond the capacity of the available limited land to support them. Some plants, especially certain shrubs and aspen trees, which the elk like to eat, are being so heavily browsed that they are disappearing. Whereas we are trying to help most species to increase, with the elk we must find a way to keep its numbers within the carrying capacity of the range.

It is especially important to control the populations of deer and elk on wildlife refuges and national forests, and in national parks and national nature monuments. Public shooting helps outside the park and monument areas, but policy permits no public shooting in the parks and monuments. Here Park Service employees have congressional authority to control the herds. To reintroduce the mountain lion and the wolf would be one answer to the problem, but the livestock ranchers would not hear of this. It becomes increasingly clear that we cannot continue to have the wonderful wild creatures for our enjoyment unless we are willing to give them sufficient land; for they, like ourselves, have definite requirements of food and shelter, without which they cannot survive. If we are to

This elk calf, in refuge habitat, stands knee-deep in grass as rich as it must have been during pre-Columbian centuries.

The author

A. P. Nelson, Fish and Wildlife Service

The Elk Refuge is full of activity in winter, for it is then that the animals have migrated from their high summer ranges to these lower altitude grasslands; but there is not enough natural feed here for the hundreds of elk, and the Fish and Wildlife Service must provide hay.

keep on taking land away from the wild birds and mammals—land in those few favored places where they still exist—or if we are unwilling to give back to them a little of that which we have foolishly encroached upon, then we shall have to forego the pleasure of seeing and having them around.

The Rocky Mountain elk is a magnificent creature. It once ranged from New York and southeastern Ontario south to Georgia, west to northern New Mexico, eastern Utah, Idaho, north through eastern British Columbia and Alberta and southern Manitoba. (Scientists have classified the animals of Manitoba and eastern Saskatchewan as a separate species.) During recent years, many successful efforts have been made to restock suitable parts of our country with the Rocky Mountain elk. The species should not be introduced to parts of our country where it did not occur naturally.

To see the elk in large numbers moving across the slopes and through the valleys of the highly scenic refuge is to take a look back into primeval times, to gain some small sense of the continent as it was before the arrival of the white man. Autumn is a time to enjoy the refuge and the nearby national parks and national forest. Snow may already whiten the peaks, and the lowlands along rivers and streams are aglow with yellow aspens. The elk are moving down from the uplands, seeking the best feed, and hills and valleys echo with the bugling of bulls—the voice of the autumnal wilderness—for this is the time of the mating of elk. Everywhere there is rivalry between the big antlered males engaged in rounding up harems. Attempted seductions by younger bulls often result in duels.

In winter, the refuge reaches its height of activity, for it is then that thousands of elk are here. While there remains sufficient natural feed for them, the animals forage for

As they wander over lowlands and hills, the elk offer one of the grandest wildlife shows in the refuge system. In primitive times elk ranged as far east as New York and Georgia, but the guns of the white man have killed them, and his spreading civilization has taken over almost all of the land that once was theirs. He who feels keenly the wonder and beauty in all nature, does not seek amusement through needless destruction of nature, for he knows such a pastime brings only remorse. The pressing need of our time is for a better understanding of wildlife and an attitude of sympathy toward it—an awakening to the rich reward that comes through appreciation of natural beauty. It is ignorance and prejudice that lead one to regard the wild birds and mammals as enemies or pests or mere objects for "sport." A world of fascination awaits him who would know nature intimately and as a friend.

E. P. Haddon, Fish and Wildlife Service

themselves, pawing through the snow to reach the grass; but when the supply is gone, it becomes the task of the Fish and Wildlife Service to provide hay for them. Such artificial feeding is far from desirable; but as long as there is not enough land for the elk to winter on and to find the food they need, there is no other way to prevent the herd from dying of starvation. Many people visit the refuge during the winter to see this great concentration of animals.

Other mammals of the Elk Refuge are moose, mule deer, coyotes, badgers, beavers, muskrats, and occasionally bighorn sheep which come down to the area in winter from the crests of the Gros Ventre Mountains. The avian population includes the rare trumpeter

swan, which has been brought here from Red Rock Lakes National Wildlife Refuge, Montana, to establish a breeding colony. This has been one of the few successful efforts to establish a new breeding colony of this rare bird. Here also are sage hens, long-billed curlews, willets, phalaropes, sandhill cranes, Clark's nutcrackers and waterfowl.

Headquarters is in the refuge, and the address is Jackson, Wyoming. The area is reached over U. S. Highway 89 south from nearby Yellowstone and Grand Teton national parks, and north from Salt Lake City, 273 miles mostly over U. S. Highway 89. Hotels and motor courts are available at Jackson, and there are many excellent guest ranches in the vicinity.

OKEFENOKEE NATIONAL WILDLIFE REFUGE in southeastern Georgia, protects a scenically unique cypress swamp, the outstanding area of its kind in North America. The refuge is 517 square miles in extent, but the total area of the swamp is more than 600 square miles, part of it being in private ownership and part in the privately maintained Okefenokee Swamp Park. Established in 1937 to give protection to the wilderness and its wildlife, it forms the headwaters of the Suwanee River, which flows across the Georgia line into Florida and on to the Gulf of Mexico. It is also the source of the Saint Mary's River flowing to the Atlantic. The foremost objective of the Fish and Wildlife Service in this area is to maintain primitive conditions.

The almost unblemished primeval beauty of the swamp is enhanced by a wide variety of plants and trees. A few of these are maidencane, which resembles a small bamboo, floating hearts, the blue-flowered pickerel weed, bladderwort, with yellow and lavender blossoms, tall pitcher plant, spatterdock, royal, cinnamon and chain ferns, and numerous kinds of moss add their colors and decorative outlines to the scene; while dahoon holly or cassina, buttonbush and fetterbush make dense borders around island forests of white bay, water, live and scrub oaks, persimmon, sassafras, willow, birch, the large-flowered magnolia, with its big, glossy evergreen leaves and white blossoms, red maple, longleaf

It is comforting to know that the bobcat lives in peace, as it has through countless centuries, in the wild beauty of Okefenokee Refuge

The author

Robert C. Hermes, from Nat'l Audubon Society

The facial expression of this bobkitten might lead one to suppose it knows all about man's traps, guns and poisons.

and slash pines, sweet and black gums and many other species native to the South.

It was a cold, clear day in January when we began our winding journey into the north side of the vast swamp. Our little boat in the hands of an able guide followed the water trail for seven miles. The dark water reflected the sky's brilliant blue. Cypress trees heavily draped in gray robes of Spanish moss, but without their delicate green leaves at this season, were mirrored in the still water. The forest extended on all sides, until we came into an opening called Sapling Prairie, a broad expanse of yellow grass; but this is not a grassland of the usual kind. In places you can walk on it, but if you stand still you will

Okefenokee is a haven of safety to the mink, for as long as it stays inside refuge boundaries, it will never know the torture of the steel trap.

Maslowski and Goodpaster, from Nat'l Audubon Society

The author

East of Dinner Pond stands a forest of giant cypress trees.

The great horned owl flies silently througth the moss-draped forest, and its deep-toned calls drift far across the still water of the swamp.

Photographs by the author

Barred owls are numerous in Okefenokee, and when they call in the quiet of evening, they sometimes seem to be conversing.

The author

Narrow, lily pad waterways wind among tall gray trunks.

sink, for these grassy areas are floating islands. Narrow channels no wider than our boat wound through it. Now the view widened. Towering walls of gray forest stood around, and past the nearer ones others could be seen, and still others beyond. Soon the water trail entered the trees again, larger ones than before and taller and more impressive. On the dark shining water in the twilight of the dim mysterious aisles, grew yellow pond lilies and water lilies and the handsome green leaves of golden club or never-wet, now in bloom. Passing through this strand, the boat emerged into a small lake hemmed in by forest. Mallards and pintails, wood ducks and black ducks sprang from the water ahead and winged rapidly over the tree tops. Occasionally an American egret arose through the trees and flashed its white plumage across the sky. The strands of cypress opened and then closed around us, and opened again, and to the left larger trees than any yet encountered appeared. Their massive buttressed bases supported huge trunks that towered skyward, and their crowns were flattened and spreading. These ancient trees belonged to the swamp's original forest primeval.

Billy's Lake on the west side of the swamp is different. Here the open water is a mirror three miles long and three or four hundred feet wide. It is bordered by cypress, slender myrtles, white bay and magnolia. A raccoon searched for food in the mud along the shore; and an otter came to fish, while an osprey soared overhead. Evening turned the lake into a highway of molten copper. A barred owl called, then another and another, until the forest echoed with their hooting.

At Camp Cornelia on the east, the swamp presents still another aspect. Here are wide horizons, and the forest is confined to islands, where pine and gum sometimes take the place of cypress. And this is the home of the alligator and the Florida sandhill crane.

After exploring the Okefenokee wilderness, it is difficult to realize that commercial interests once tried to drain the swamp and then logged part of it, for the area did not drain, and the cut-over parts are healing. Lately the oil industry has tried to get in to do some test drilling, but the Department of the Interior, aware of the value of this wonderland, has refused to allow such destruction.

In spring and summer, the swamp is hot and humid and green, and its abundant life much more in evidence. Delos E. Culver, writing in *National Parks Magazine* for January-March 1947, gives his impressions of a spring visit: "The swamp lay shimmering in the midday heat enveloped in a silence unbelievable in this day and age. Its appearance seemed to carry us back to the pre-dawn of man. Our tiny boat turned its prow from the deep waters of a canal into a fringe of maidencane as we obtained our first view. Before us spread the primeval. It was as God made it, today, yesterday and a million years beyond. Stretching off to the horizon lay mile upon mile of shallow open swamp—a vast plain of clear amber water, dotted by islands near and far, with an occasional cypress skeleton standing. Perhaps the magnificent beauty is due in part to the uniform uncrowded distribution of plant life over the surface of the water that reflects the towering moss-draped pine and cypress between lily pads and golden club. Rising from the water on erect stems are the lavender blossoms of bladderworts, while around the shallow borders of islets grow clumps of 'southern trumpet' in full bloom. The latter, a species of pitcher plant, attains a maximum height of thirty inches.

"As regularly as day follows night, storm followed storm. There were four thunderstorms daily, accompanied by torrential rain. One minute we would be dripping; the next enveloped in steam as our clothing dried in the scorching sun. While the last faint rumble of a passing storm would die away in the northeast, there would be heard the first rumble of another approaching from the southwest.

" 'Listen to that,' said one of the guides on a rainy night. 'You don't often hear them fellows in the swamp. I been here all my life and I ain't heered them but once or twice before.' A weird call had sounded close at hand—a voice unknown to us. Had we been able to identify its maker, I am sure our amazement would have been even greater. It was not until our return to the North that a herpetologist friend informed us that we had heard a spade-foot toad.

The author

On Okefenokee's east side, wide vistas stretch away between islands of dense growth.

The author

An alligator basks in silent immobility.

"Nights, and particularly the dim hours following dawn, were sonorous with amphibian thunder. Rolling across the miles of swamp land, it was interspersed occasionally with the growl of an old bull alligator exhibiting his vocal powers in mighty tones that echoed and re-echoed.

"Somewhere from out of the distant past, as one gazes upon this primitive grandeur, there comes an indescribable feeling. Somehow it seemed that the civilization we knew but yesterday had passed, and here before our eyes the world had resumed its steady march of evolution through time. When regulations are issued for flying over wilderness areas, the Okefenokee Swamp should be among the reservations to which the regulations will apply. During our days in the swamp, the noise of airplanes—five in all—constituted the only discordant note.

"Tonight, months later, as a wintery wind howls about the windows and a cheery fire crackles within, memory carries us back, and, in a vision we are again sitting motionless in the hushed heat of a noon-day sun staring in fascination at a great saurian, replica of a by-gone age, as it basks in silent immobility. A red-shouldered hawk screams overhead and from afar comes the guttural purr of a sandhill crane. Then all is still."

A long list of birds has been recorded in the swamp. Besides those already named, there are the big black and white pileated woodpecker, with its flaming red crest, and the smaller red-bellied woodpecker. Here, too, are numerous waders—the Louisiana, great blue, little blue, green, and yellow-crowned night herons, rarely black-crowned night herons, wood and white ibises, which may be seen in sizeable flocks, the white ibises travelling silently in long undulating lines that weave among and over the cypress strands, the wood ibises, America's only true storks, wheeling above the swamp in majestic grandeur. The anhinga is here also. It can swim submerged, with only its head and slender snake-like neck showing. The large red-shouldered hawk is the most abundant of its group in the swamp. Some of the smaller birds are great crested flycatcher, chuck-will's-widow, Florida pine-woods sparrow and Carolina wren. The prothonotary warbler with its brilliant yellow head and breast is the most conspicuous and abundant of the warblers that occur here, including parula, Swainson's, magnolia, myrtle, pine, and black and white, some of which nest in the swamp, while others are winter visitors or migrants. Robins and catbirds winter here in great numbers. This once was the habitat of the big ivory-billed woodpecker, now extinct. Various mammals—bats, bobcats, opossums, mink, otters, skunks, black bears and whitetail deer dwell in the refuge wilderness. A hot, almost tropical climate during most of the year makes the swamp ideal for many kinds of turtles, frogs, toads and snakes, including the cotton-mouthed moccasin and diamond-backed rattler. The cougar once lived in this watery wilderness, but it has not been reported here since 1903.

During a drought in the early 1950's, Okefenokee's water levels dropped, and fire swept sixty-five percent of the refuge. Areas of cypress and pine were destroyed, and in places the fires burned underground. Lightning set a few, but most damage came from man-caused fires started outside. The Service believes a recently built water-retention sill across the outlet, and a fire-break road, will help prevent future conflagrations.

Okefenokee headquarters is in the Post Office Building at Waycross, and the address is Box 117, Waycross, Georgia. People wishing to see what the swamp is like can do so by going to Okefenokee Swamp Park, eight miles southeast of Waycross, on U. S. Highway 1, to a paved branch road right, to the park. Here a half-hour boat trip takes visitors on a loop through a cypress forest on the edge of the refuge. Guides may be hired here also to take visitors—not more than two to a boat—into the refuge wilderness. To reach the west entrance, leave U. S. Highway 441 a half mile southeast of Fargo, Georgia, and go twenty miles northeasterly to Camp Stephen Foster at Billy's Lake, where meals, cabins, boats and guides are available. On the east side, the entrance is reached by leaving U. S. Highways 1 and 301 at Folkston and taking State Route 23 southwesterly seven miles, then west four miles on a graded road to Camp Cornelia on the Suwanee Canal, where boats and guides are available. The cooler months are best for seeing the refuge.

PELICAN ISLAND NATIONAL WILDLIFE REFUGE in the Indian River, on Florida's east coast, was the first of our federal refuges. It was set aside in 1903 to give protection to a favorite nesting place of the brown pelican. Covered with a solid stand of red mangrove, the island itself is only three acres in area. Well might we recall the adage that mighty oaks from little acorns grow, for the setting aside of this tiny refuge marked the beginning of the present vast system. The Fish and Wildlife Service is justly proud of Pelican Island Refuge, as is shown by the erection of a large sign here, which tells about the area's establishment through executive order, by President Theodore Roosevelt.

The brown pelican is represented by a subspecies along the California coast. The eastern species breeds south along our Atlantic coast from South Carolina to Florida, and along the gulf coast to southern Texas. It also inhabits the east coast of Central and South America to Brazil. Unlike the white pelican, which nests on inland lakes, the brown

The Fish and Wildlife Service is proud of little Pelican Island.

The author

The author

Like some weird prehistoric creature, a pelican flaps ponderously overhead.

The author

A colony of brown pelicans has nested at the refuge for years, but occasionally during a year or so, the island remains vacant.

is strictly a maritime species. It is often seen flying with characteristic lumbering wing-beats over coastal bays and inlets, or gliding in single file along the breakers on outer beaches. Seeing a fish below, it makes a shallow dive, quickly returning to the surface with the fish flapping in its bill or tossing about in its pouch.

The pelicans' breeding season begins about the first of November on Pelican Island, and the eggs, laid by December, hatch a month later; the young are able to fly at the age of ten weeks. From late October to the middle of March, the island is lively with the activities of brood-raising. Since refuge establishment, there have been years when the birds have deserted the island. Pelican colonies are unstable, the birds occasionally deserting a favored site for a year or more.

Other birds to be seen on or flying in the vicinity of Pelican Island are the frigate-bird, white ibis, anhinga, Louisiana, great blue, little blue and black-crowned night herons, and snowy and American egrets. The island is in a wide bay formed by the curving palm-fringed shore of one of the barrier islands that stretch along the coast. It is reached by boat from the small town of Sebastian, on U. S. Highway 1, twenty-one miles south of Melbourne and eighty-five miles north of West Palm Beach. To avoid disturbing the birds, visitors should not go ashore during the nesting season. There is no headquarters at the refuge. It is under the supervision of the Florida headquarters of the Fish and Wildlife Service at Delray Beach.

RED ROCK LAKES NATIONAL WILDLIFE REFUGE is located in southwestern Montana, fifty miles by road, west of the town of West Yellowstone. Established in 1935 primarily to provide sanctuary for the then rare and vanishing trumpeter swan, it comprises over fifty square miles of lakes, marsh and grassland at the foot of the Centennial Mountains along the continental divide. The south boundary of the refuge is, in fact, well up along the mountain sides, being over 9,000 feet in elevation in places. Most of the area is treeless, but clumps of Douglas fir dot the slopes, and there are several groves of Englemann spruce and numerous stands of trembling aspen along the south shore of Upper Red Rock Lake, while willow marshlands, the habitat of moose, extend east from the upper end of the lake.

At the time the refuge was established, it was believed there were fewer than fifty of the big white trumpeter swans still surviving in the United States. The fact is that today there are about 600 of these birds living within the Rocky Mountain environment, which includes the refuge, the lakes of nearby Yellowstone National Park, Grand Teton National Park and National Elk Refuge, in Wyoming. Continued protection is absolutely necessary, and it is all the more important now that a colony of about 500 birds in British Columbia has been endangered lately (1952) by commercial exploitation of the

A pair of trumpeter swans, five Barrow's goldeneyes and a muskrat make a lively scene at Red Rock Lakes.

Winston E. Banko, Fish and Wildlife Service

Winston E. Banko, Fish and Wildlife Service

Moose find sanctuary in the marshes and meadows above Upper Red Rock Lake.

wilderness of Tweedsmuir Provincial Park, which was part of the habitat of the Canadian swan colony. The Province of Alberta in Canada also has several flocks of these birds. As far as is known, the Canadian colonies are entirely isolated from those in the United States, there apparently being no migration between them.

In the days of waterfowl abundance, the trumpeters migrated long distances. Their range extended from the interior of Canada to the Mississippi Delta, and from north-

The blue lake stretches away beyond a screen of firs.

The author

Winston E. Banko, Fish and Wildlife Service

Trumpeters are even larger than whistling swans.

Ray C. Erickson, Fish and Wildlife Service

The pristine whiteness of the trumpeter matches the winter snow.

In summer, the marshes of Red Rock Lakes are the nesting grounds of the little sora rail, a species recognized by its gray breast, yellow bill and black patch on face and throat. Five other rails—black, Virginia, clapper, king and yellow—inhabit the marshes of the United States.

The author

western United States to the Texas coast and northern Mexico. Today they spend the entire year in the Red Rock Lakes-Yellowstone region. Their most important winter requirement is food to be secured in open water. This is available on the spring-fed ponds of the refuge, in Yellowstone National Park and along the north fork of the Snake River in Idaho.

Efforts to establish breeding birds in the National Elk Refuge have met with success; while attempts to establish colonies on Malheur National Wildlife Refuge in southern Oregon, Ruby Lake National Wildlife Refuge in northeastern Nevada, and Lacreek National Wildlife Refuge, South Dakota, have met with limited success.

The trumpeter swan is the largest of our North American waterfowl, exceeding even the big whistling swan in stature and strength. The whistler has a vastly wider range, however, migrating in spring and autumn in large numbers between its wintering grounds on our Atlantic and Pacific coasts and its breeding grounds on the bleak Arctic tundra. Like the whistler, the trumpeter is pure white with black legs and bill. It lacks the yellow spot on the bill commonly found on the whistler. It is said to be less wary than the whistler, although visitors to the refuge may have to be satisfied with seeing it far out on the lakes, as it does prefer a remote and isolated existence.

Trumpeters are believed to mate for life, pairing at the age of three, according to Fish and Wildlife Service biologists, and nesting at about five. In late February, a month before the period of mating, the birds begin to spend much of their time on the snowy ground near the open water of their feeding areas. It is during this period that they engage in vociferous trumpeting, their loud resonant calls sounding for long distances across the winter landscape. Nesting begins in May, muskrat houses often being used as nest sites. The eggs hatch about a month after incubation commences, and the cygnets leave the nest almost immediately to swim and, four months later, they are able to fly.

Besides moose, there are antelopes, beavers, muskrats, marmots, mink, otters, martens, badgers and ground squirrels inhabiting the refuge. Birds of the area include the handsome yellow-headed and red-winged blackbirds, marsh and rock wrens, Clark's nutcrackers, barn, violet-green and tree swallows, black terns, black-crowned night and

E. P. Haddon, Fish and Wildlife Service

The badger, an exceptionally plucky animal for its size, is gray with black and white markings on head. It lives on moles, gophers, rabbits and other rodents. The handsome Steller's jay, lower left, and the mountain chickadee find habitat among the Englemann spruces and Douglas firs of Red Rock Lakes.

Photographs by John L. Blackford, courtesy Nature Magazine

Olaus J. Murie

The neat little Bohemian waxwings range over western Canada and the northern part of our West, and may occasionally come to Red Rock Lakes. The smaller cedar waxwing has a much wider range, including our eastern states.

great blue herons, avocets, coots, water ouzels and, during migration, many species of ducks. Virgina and sora rails inhabit the rush-grown shores of the lakes.

Headquarters is in the refuge and the address is Monida, Montana. The area is reached by traveling west from West Yellowstone, Montana, over U. S. Highway 191, for twelve miles to Henry's Lake, then by gravel road thirty-eight miles to the refuge. From U. S. Highway 91 on the west, it is reached by turning east at Monida, on the Montana-Idaho state line, and traveling twenty-eight miles over a dirt road to headquarters. There is a picnic area with spring water on the refuge. The area may be used for overnight camping. The town of West Yellowstone provides overnight accommodations, and there is a country hotel at Monida. Summer is the time to visit the refuge.

Standley, courtesy Nature Magazine

[174]

Marmots live in the alpine meadows of the Centennial Mountains. In summer, tree swallows, lower left, dart and glide over the meadows and marshes of the refuge in search of flying insects; while the lark sparrow builds its nest in the grasses around the lakes.

Hal H. Harrison, courtesy Mass. Audubon Society

Courtesy Nature Magazine

REELFOOT NATIONAL WILDLIFE REFUGE in western Tennessee and adjacent Kentucky is two separate areas in the north end of Reelfoot Lake, the total being about sixteen square miles. The refuge was established in 1941 to provide a resting and feeding ground for migrating waterfowl along the Mississippi flyway. It is also a sanctuary for other species, some of them permanent residents. The Fish and Wildlife Service leases the area from the Tennessee Fish and Game Commission.

Much of the lake inside the refuge boundaries is open water, but a great deal of it is grown with a beautiful forest of cypress. As one drifts by boat in the dim light of this forest there is a sense of being in another world. The scene is so strange to unaccustomed eyes that one wants to exclaim over its fantastic effects. Here and there the water is paved with the big green leaves of yellow pond lily; and in spring and summer, the forest's beauty is heightened by the feathery leaves of the cypresses. Your boat drifts across open areas where the sun is bright and warm; it winds through cypress strands of mottled sun and shade, and travels the narrow lily pad lanes.

Amid such unique beauty, the visitor regrets to learn that large areas of the lake are not under protection. Some of the forest outside the refuge supports cypresses older and larger than any in the protected area. There has been some logging of these old trees, and great havoc has been wrought. It is to be hoped that the people of Tennessee will recognize the outstanding scenic quality of Reelfoot Lake before it is too late, and see that all the forested part is placed in the care of the Fish and Wildlife Service.

Reelfoot Lake was formed when the New Madrid earthquake of 1811 blocked the flow of the Mississippi River and depressed the land to form the present lake. Today, because of eroding soil from neighboring farm lands washing into it, the lake is well on the way to becoming dry land again. The soil on surrounding farms is fertile to a great depth, so that farmers are not threatened with immediate bankruptcy through erosion. It has been difficult, therefore, to induce them to employ sound soil conserving

The ruddy duck may be seen at Reelfoot only during migration. Smallest of our ducks, it is easy to recognize by its white cheeks.

C. J. Henry, Fish and Wildlife Service

Allan D. Cruickshank, from Nat'l Audubon Society

Great blue herons live in coastal and inland marshes and swamps, lakes and streams, and is a resident at Reelfoot, and practically every refuge with a suitable water area.

practices. The Fish and Wildlife Service is concerned over the rapidity with which the lake is silting. If it disappears, Tennessee will have lost not only one of its foremost beauty spots, but an important wildlife habitat.

Birds to be seen on the refuge and on adjoining lake areas include Canada geese and many ducks—blue-winged and green-winged teal, widgeons, blacks, pintails, shovelers, gadwalls, canvasbacks, ruddies, ring-necks, hooded mergansers and wood ducks, with mallards and lesser scaups the most abundant. Florida and purple gallinules, coots, least and American bitterns, pied-billed grebes, king rails, little blue, green, black-crowned night, yellow-crowned night and great blue herons also inhabit the area, and several species raise their young in a rookery known locally as Cranetown, high in the tops of tall cypresses outside but near the refuge. Cranetown is difficult to reach, but worth the effort; and the site should be included in the refuge. Birds to be seen here are American egrets, anhingas, double-crested cormorants and great blue and black-crowned night herons. Black and least terns can sometimes be seen flying over the open water of the lake; barred owls sound their calls from the depths of the forest; bald eagles nest in the area, and the big handsome flame-crested pileated woodpecker may sometimes be glimpsed swooping through the shadowy solitude of the forest. Peregrine falcons and red-shouldered hawks also come to the refuge; but only a few in the long list of song birds that are either permanent residents or migrants can be named: Black-billed and yellow-billed cuckoos, kingbirds, phoebes, wood pewees, rusty and red-winged blackbirds, white-eyed, yellow-throated and red-eyed vireos, scarlet and summer tanagers, blue grosbeaks, and orchard and Baltimore orioles are among the many.

During the spring migration, the refuge is sometimes alive with brightly colored warblers. These little birds at times swarm through the forests, their call notes coming

Warblers are less familiar to many people than some other birds. The hooded warbler, left, is bright yellow with a black hood, and the black-throated blue is blue above with black face and throat. Spring woodlands are melodious with their songs.

Photographs by Hal H. Harrison, courtesy Mass. Audubon Society

from all directions, as one attempts to identify them. To bird enthusiasts, a warbler swarm is one of the most thrilling events of the year. The prothonotary is a strikingly handsome warbler, with blazing cadmium orange on head and breast, fading to yellow below, jet black bill, blue-gray wings, greenish yellow back and gray tail. Most of the warblers are fine singers, and the prothonotary is no exception, its loud, clear notes ringing through the forest as it constantly moves about in the somber cypress shadows searching for insects. There are about seventy species of warblers and all of them are restricted to the western hemisphere. Of this number, more than fifty come to the United States to raise their young. Most of them spend the winter in Central and South America; while some travel as far as northern Canada and Alaska to breed. They usually migrate at night, and feed during the day. One cannot help but marvel at the long distances these feathered mites are able to go, over land and water, to reach their winter and summer homes.

Headquarters is near the refuge, at the town of Samburg, and the address is Samburg, Tennessee. The best way to see the area and the lake is by boat. Boats may be rented at a number of places on the lake shore. Overnight accommodations are available at several points and at nearby towns. The refuge may be visited at all times of the year, but winter is likely to be the least satisfactory. It is reached north from Memphis, Tennessee, over U. S. Highway 51, seventy-eight miles to Dyersburg, then over State Route 78, twenty-five miles to Tiptonville, and from there over state routes 21 and 22, about ten miles to Samburg. South from Paducah, Kentucky, it is reached over U. S. Highway 45, forty-nine miles to Fulton, Kentucky, and U. S. Highway 51, twenty-one miles to Troy, Tennessee, and from there over state routes 21 and 22, about fourteen miles to Samburg.

Kentucky Woodlands National Wildlife Refuge, described on another page, may be included on a trip to Reelfoot by people traveling southwest from Mammoth Cave National Park, Kentucky.

The ovenbird, a warbler, left, announces its arrival in spring with a loud song, and the chestnut-sided warbler, wearing a chestnut stripe on each side and a yellow crown, sings in shrubbery and trees of uplands.

Photographs by Allan D. Cruickshank, from Nat'l Audubon Society

Allan D. Cruickshank, from Nat'l Audubon Society

The anhinga or water-turkey nests at Reelfoot, where its fantastic form can be seen perching on the cypress trees or swimming in the lake.

The author

The cypress swamp at Reelfoot is one of America's beauty spots, but it will soon be filled with silt from eroding farms unless the State of Tennessee takes preventive action.

SAINT MARKS NATIONAL WILDLIFE REFUGE, one hundred square miles in area, is located on the coast of the Florida panhandle, thirty miles south of Tallahassee. It was established in 1931, primarily to protect the only Canada goose wintering ground in Florida at that time. The area includes a long stretch of shore line on Apalachee Bay, in the Gulf of Mexico, as well as marshes, sandy woodlands and five diked pools.

Archeologists have found evidence that Indians lived here a thousand or more years B. C. In 1513, Ponce de Leon, the first white man to arrive on the scene found the area inhabited by a large tribe of Apalachee Indians. In 1521, Ponce de Leon attempted to establish a Spanish settlement at the junction of the St. Marks and Wakulla rivers, a short distance downstream from the present town of St. Marks, which is just outside the refuge boundary. Hernando de Soto is believed to have spent the winter of 1539-40 in the vicinity of the refuge, shortly before he discovered the Mississippi River. The ruins of an old Spanish fort—Fort San Marcos de Apalachee—is still to be seen at the junction of the St. Marks and the Wakulla. Constructed in 1679, the fort was stormed and captured by 400 bucaneers in 1682. Stones were taken from the ruins in 1831 to build St. Marks Lighthouse, familiar to refuge visitors who drive to the end of State Route 59 to see shorebirds on the beach there.

Back of the beach is a wide area of salt and brackish water marsh, broken by meandering streams, ponds and mud flats occupied in November and December by a large concentration of Canada geese. Willets are common, as are ruddy turnstones, greater yellowlegs and Hudsonian curlews. King and clapper rails, marsh wrens and seaside sparrows, as well as ducks, come to these marshes, although the waterfowl more frequently visit the diked fresh water pools farther inland. The driveways along the tops of the dikes afford an excellent vantage point from which to observe the birds, alligators and an occasional mink or otter swimming in the pools. Here, too, are anhingas, handsome black birds that fly with snake-like necks stretched forward. Least and American bitterns, snowy and American egrets, little blue, great blue, black-crowned night and Louisiana herons add to the beauty of the pools as they stand reflected in the calm water. Among the ducks at St. Marks are gadwalls, greater and lesser scaups,

The ring-necked duck, winter resident at St. Marks, has a light band near tip of bill, and a dark back that distinguish it from the scaups with which it often associates.

Hugo H. Schroder, courtesy Nature Magazine

The author

Intelligent and readily befriended, the raccoon, inhabiting most of our country, is the victim not only of the steel trap, but of some of the cruelest acts conceived by the human mind.

green-winged and blue-winged teal, shovelers, mallards, pintails, canvasbacks, red-breasted and American mergansers, blacks, redheads and ring-necks; also coots, Florida and purple gallinules and double-crested cormorants. The gallinules with their wide-spreading feet are especially interesting to watch as they walk about on lily pads or along the grassy margins in search of food.

The dry, sandy, upland pine woods, mostly at the west end of the refuge, are the home of wild turkeys, bobwhites and whitetail deer. Loggerhead shrikes, flickers, Florida ground doves, cardinals, mockingbirds, meadowlarks, blue jays, brown-headed nut-hatches, Carolina wrens, pine and yellow-throated warblers, bluebirds, Florida pine-woods sparrows, towhees and gray kingbirds add song and color to these pinelands. Black and turkey vultures can be seen soaring high over the refuge or occasionally feeding on carrion.

Bordering the east dike of Stony Bayou pool, there is a picturesque woodland of pine and cabbage palm. Raccoons sometimes take a siesta among the concealing fronds of the palms; but if visitors linger too long on the dike, the 'coons clamber noisily down and retreat farther into the forest. This woodland area, if opened by trail, might become an attractive feature for exploration by visitors. It deserves fire protection to preserve its beauty.

The raccoon, with his black mask and ringtail, is found almost everywhere in our country except northern Maine. Its range extends from southern Canada to South

The double-crested cormorant is abundant on both coasts of Florida and northward in summer as far as Newfoundland and James Bay.

The author

The author

The lesser scaup, above, and the greater, sometimes occur in large numbers on their wintering grounds.

James Silver, Fish and Wildlife Service

The author

Cabbage palms form picturesque stands on St. Marks Refuge, and sometimes they are mixed with tall pines. These palm-pine forests deserve protection for the sake of their unique beauty.

America. Almost anything edible serves as its food, from fruit and berries to meat and insects. Its favored habitat is wooded country where hollow trees are used as den sites; but raccoons are adaptable and are as much at home in the Florida mangroves as in chaparrel of the West, where they sometimes use the burrows of other animals for shelter. The mating period is from December in the South to February in the North, and the young are born nine weeks later.

There are men who make sport of this appealing, intelligent animal in a number of cruel pastimes. Most such "amusements" involve the use of hounds. Although the raccoon is a plucky fighter for its size, and can sometimes resist two or three dogs, even though seriously bitten, it is no match for a pack of hounds, which sometimes tear it apart alive. That men can stoop to such cruel practices seems to indicate a defect in our national thinking, and in the education of our youngsters. Taught to enjoy wildlife for its own sake, and to feel sympathy and love toward it, instead of brutality

The author

The vultures are confined to no single refuge, but range widely over much of the United States. The turkey vulture, with a wing-spread of six feet, is larger than the black, and is distinguished from it by lighter color of flight feathers, longer tail and, in the adult, red skin on head and neck.

Allan D. Cruickshank
from Nat'l Audubon Society

The black vulture has a wing-spread of five feet, and bears a light patch on wing-tips, visible in flight. When the tail is spread, its edge forms a continuous line with the rear edges of the wings. Although the vultures may not meet our standard of beauty, they are superb flyers and fascinating to watch.

Photographs by
Allan D. Cruickshank
from Nat'l Audubon Society

A flash of blue darting amid the Florida scrub is likely to be the handsome Florida jay. Unlike the eastern blue jay and the Steller's jay of the West, this bird has no crest.

Allan D. Cruickshank
from Nat'l Audubon Society

and a desire to kill, young people not only make better citizens, but their attitude toward life and the world is bound to be more productive.

The western part of Apalachee Bay along the refuge shore is open to waterfowl shooting in season. There can be no question of the increased value of the refuge to waterfowl if all of the bay were closed. Certain points and islands that form the west shore of Apalachee Bay, inside the refuge, have been withheld from refuge management and protection, through local political pressure, and harm has been done here by real estate development. Interested people, particularly in Florida, should urge that all of these withheld areas be restored to the Fish and Wildlife Service and made available to wildlife.

Headquarters is in the refuge, and the address is St. Marks, Florida. It is reached south from Tallahassee over U. S. Highway 319, fifteen miles to Wakulla, then left four miles to Newport, and from there fourteen miles to headquarters. There are excellent hotels and motor courts in Tallahassee.

Arthur A. Allen, courtesy Nature Magazine

The blue jay is well-known throughout the East where its loud calls draw attention to its strikingly marked bright blue plumage. It is abundant in Florida and is found as far north as the Gulf of St. Lawrence. The white-eyed towhee inhabits the Florida scrub, and ranges north as far as North Carolina.

Allan D. Cruickshank, from Nat'l Audubon Society

SAVANNAH RIVER NATIONAL WILDLIFE REFUGE is located on both sides of the Savannah River in Georgia and South Carolina. Its twenty square miles include fresh water marshes, diked pools, cypress groves cloaked in dense veils of gray Spanish moss, and uplands of sweet gum and loblolly pine. The refuge was established in 1927 to provide a waterfowl wintering ground on the Atlantic flyway. It is about twenty miles above the mouth of the Savannah River. The main channel of the Savannah forms the west boundary of the refuge. Near the north boundary, the river branches into three meandering streams—the Back, the Middle and the Steamboat rivers—which flow into the main stream again, at or near the south end of the refuge. In early times the area was a rice plantation.

The refuge is reached from a by-pass road north of the Savannah River bridge on U. S. Highway 17. For those traveling between the Carolinas and Florida, this is but slightly longer. Headquarters is within sight of the by-pass, and near the buildings and for some distance along the north side of the highway, there is a diked pool, the resting and feeding place for great numbers of birds, especially in autumn and winter. South of the road, dikes form a number of large pools grown with aquatic food plants. Most visitors stop at headquarters to watch the birds in the exhibition pond; but it is possible also to drive along the dikes surrounding the larger pools. The rough, sandy driveways join a number of picturesque low islands shaded by spreading, moss-draped live oaks. The islands are ideal places for picnicking.

An exhibition pool at Savannah River is close to the highway, where tourists stop to watch the birds.

The author

Flournoy Photo, Virginia Game Commission

The bobwhite is a common resident on Savannah River Refuge, finding habitat along the dikes surrounding the pools.

The refuge seems to be well located to attract birds. It is excellent for spring bird-watching, when thousands of songbirds swarm through on their way north.

Marsh hawks glide low over the dikes in search of mice, and red-tailed hawks soar overhead. Some of the ducks that winter here are shovelers, mallards, blue-winged and green-winged teal, pintails, blacks, ruddies, gadwalls and wood ducks. Bobwhites find good living in the dense vegetation along the dikes. Snowy and American egrets, least bitterns, little blue herons, king rails, Florida and purple gallinules, anhingas, coots, woodcocks, Wilson's snipes and turkeys also occur on the refuge, as well as such permanent resident songsters as mockingbirds, cardinals, mourning doves, gold-

Jack Dermid, from Nat'l Audubon Society

Marsh rabbits live in coastal areas from Virginia to Florida and southern Alabama. Because of the character of the country in which they live, they are not as well known as the cottontail and jack rabbit.

finches and red-winged blackbirds. Otters and raccoons are among the area's mammals.

The otter ranges throughout our country, except for the deserts of the Southwest, and it inhabits Canada to the limit of forests. It is an expert swimmer, as indeed it must be to catch its meals of fish. The body is slender, with short legs and thick tail, and the fur is dark brown, lighter and grayer along the belly and throat. The most striking characteristic of this fellow is his eagerness for fun. On stream banks he builds a mud

Photographs by Charles W. Schwartz

Otters live in swamps and marshes and along streams and lake shores across most of North America. Fond of play, they fashion mud or snow slides on stream banks for the fun of coasting on their bellies. At night, quail sometimes sleep in close circles with heads facing out.

The author

The wood duck is America's most beautifully marked and brightly colored waterfowl.

slide, and down it he slithers on his belly. In snow he takes a running start on the frozen pond or declivity, then flops down and coasts along. Of course, at Savannah, he enjoys no winter sports, for it seldom snows here.

There is a plant for the manufacture of the hydrogen bomb up-stream on the Savannah River, but there has been no evidence to show that this is having any adverse effect on the refuge water. A paper mill on the Georgia side of the river, visible from the refuge, pours wastes into the river, and this pollution works up into the refuge through tidal action. In certain winds, the mill pollutes the air over the refuge with strong chemicals that rise in thick clouds from the stacks. The story of air and water pollution in our country is a discouraging one, for while some commercial enterprises have tried to abate this dangerous effect of their operations, others have shown little concern about the harm they are doing.

Headquarters is in the refuge, and the address is Route 1, Port Wentworth, Georgia. It is reached on U. S. Highway 17, just north of Savannah, on the South Carolina-Georgia state line.

Tourists traveling north or south on U. S. Highway 17 can readily visit a number of other national wildlife refuges. In Georgia, there is Okefenokee, and in South Carolina, Cape Romain. For directions to reach them, see the texts on these refuges. Santee National Wildlife Refuge on U. S. Highway 15, is just south of Summerton, and Carolina Sandhills National Wildlife Refuge on U. S. Highway 1, is a few miles south of Cheraw, both in South Carolina. They are easily accessible over good paved roads. Carolina Sandhills is unlike any other refuge in the system. It is part of a broad wilderness of rolling sand hills forested with slash and longleaf pines and several species of low-growing oaks. A number of picturesque lakes dot the area, and it provides sanctuary for bobcats, gray foxes, beavers, turkeys, bobwhites and a large population of mourning doves. Local gunners have sought to open this refuge to quail shooting. Headquarters is in the refuge, and the address is McBee, South Carolina.

SENEY NATIONAL WILDLIFE REFUGE, located on Michigan's Upper Peninsula, is 150 square miles in area. It was established in 1935, and has become invaluable to mammals, upland birds and waterfowl. The area consists of woodlands and diked marshes along the valley of the Driggs River, and its varied landscape ranges from sedgy marshes and river bottoms to forests of spruce, red pine and aspen.

The Fish and Wildlife Service is especially proud of Seney. The Upper Peninsula once contained a magnificent primeval forest of pine, hemlock and hardwoods, which was completely logged in the late 1800's in one of the biggest lumbering booms ever known. Fires followed in the wake of the logging, and these spread into the marshes themselves. Then, in 1912, came the real estate promoters with their attempts to drain the marshes and turn them into agricultural lands, further damaging the once excellent wildlife habitat. In 1933, the Michigan Game Commission suggested that the federal government take the area and make it a national wildlife refuge.

Sharp-tailed grouse live in the prairie grass and brushland from Michigan to Minnesota and Wisconsin. This is one of the important species for which Seney is managed.

Charles W. Schwartz

On December 10, 1935, the government acquired the land under provisions of the *Migratory Bird Conservation Act* of 1929. Water was restored to the dried out marshes by construction of a system of dikes and other water control structures; and food and cover plants were seeded along the margins of pools and waterways. In addition to supplying good habitat for ducks and geese of the Mississippi flyway, the refuge preserves a valuable remnant of northern mid-west forest country. "The interspersion of wet marshes and pools, with knolls, islands and extensive ridges in the impounded area, together with the management of forest and meadow lands to condition them best for wildlife habitat," writes the Fish and Wildlife Service, "has provided an environment ideal for all species of wildlife indigenous to the lake states."

A notable feature of Seney is the large breeding colony of the big, rare sandhill cranes. The birds seek the more remote parts of the refuge to raise their young, but in autumn, when the waterfowl are present in large numbers, the cranes feed along the open marshy lowlands.

The crane, as it walks about in grassy or burned over areas to feed, has a decidedly stately mien; yet, the air of dignity vanishes when it performs its courtship dance. This is an amazing and unforgetable performance, which has won it renown among ornithologists and bird enthusiasts. Frank M. Chapman, in his *Handbook of Birds of Eastern North America,* quotes an eye-witness description: "During courtship and the early breeding season their actions and antics at times are ludicrous in the extreme, bowing and leaping high in the air, hopping, skipping and circling about with drooping wings and croaking whoop, an almost indescribable dance and din, in which the females (an exception to the rule) join, all working themselves up into a fever of excitement only equalled by an Indian war dance, and, like the same, it stops only when the last one is exhausted."

The refuge has the distinction of providing habitat for four different species of grouse—ruffed, spruce, sharp-tailed and greater prairie chicken—the latter now becoming rare at Seney. Sharptails require brushy grasslands, scrub oak barrens and bogs. Sharptails came into the Seney country and the Upper Peninsula after the logging and burning of forest lands there during the first two decades of this century, for the cleared land proved to be ideal sharptail habitat. These open areas are being carefully

Parent Canada geese form a protective guard fore and aft of the young flotilla.

C. J. Henry, Fish and Wildlife Service

Ray C. Erickson, Fish and Wildlife Service

Some broods of the Canada goose number as many as ten, but four to six are more usual.

preserved in the refuge, for as soon as young forest trees cast shade across the dancing grounds, the sharptails will leave. Frederick and Frances Hamerstrom and Oswald E. Mattson in their pamphlet *Sharptails into the Shadows?* give an account of the habitat requirements of these grouse and the threat to the survival of the species as a result of forest plantings in Wisconsin. Their description of the courtship dance is fascinating: "Suddenly . . . within the twinkling of an eye . . . one cock spread his wings, blew up his lavender air sacs, and started to dance. His feathered legs buzzing like a mechanical toy and his feet beating a rapid tattoo, he danced and cooed. So still was the morning that the sound of his cooing resounded far over the open plain. As the sun rose, more cocks took up the dance; and so, in the open plain by the oak stump, a dance ground was born. . . . So far no hen had appeared; early mornings and evenings the cocks gathered and fought and danced and cooed until each had his own territory. There was a vehemence in their cooing, not like the gentle-sounding dove. They danced as though possessed, and feathers lay upon the ground—torn out in fights—but still no hen had come. It was on a morning in April that a new intensity came upon the dance ground. It was still so early that the tails of the dancing cocks gleamed like will-o-the-wisps—white in the half light. Demurely the first hen walked the dancing ground. If she were aware of the tumultuous dancing cocks around her, she concealed it admirably. She walked slowly, occasionally pausing to peck at a blade of grass or an herb leaf . . . perhaps the avian equivalent of a yawn. Mornings and sometimes in the evenings the cocks came to dance and as May approached more and more often hens sought the dancing ground, and with each visit the fervor of the dancing cocks increased. Gradually, one by one, an awareness seemed to come over the hens. They spread or flicked their wings in invitation as they walked amongst the dancing cocks."

But Seney is an area of many habitats, for here, too, one may see common loons, and hear their wild, loud, wavering calls in the dusk of evening or in the early hours of morning; may hear the clear, ringing notes of the pileated woodpecker, and see Wilson's snipes and yellow rails in the marshy areas. Here, too, are woodcocks, greater and lesser yellowlegs and kingfishers.

As a waterfowl area, Seney is one of the finest in the refuge system. Canada geese breed here, and a number of ducks that find the area suited to their needs are blue-winged teal, widgeons, mallards, blacks, ring-necks, wood ducks and hooded and American mergansers.

The little wood duck is North America's most colorful waterfowl species, and while it is more common in the South, it ranges over nearly all of our country north to southern Canada. Most ducks build their nests on marshy ground, but the wood duck hides its nest in hollow trees in swamps or in wooded areas along the borders of streams and ponds.

John James Audubon says of wood duck courtship: "Here they are, a whole flock of beautiful birds, the males chasing their rivals, the females coquetting with their

Open grasslands are the principal habitat of the large gray sandhill crane. Although these birds are still abundant in some parts of the West, over much of North America they are almost unknown. The crane's courtship dance is one of the most remarkable performances of the avian world.

Allan D. Cruickshank
courtesy Nature Magazine

The author

The sandhill crane is four feet tall.

Aubrey Shaw, Jr., courtesy Virginia Game Commission

Whitetail deer and its subspecies inhabit most of our country and southern Canada, and wherever it lives it adds beauty and interest. Very prolific, it sometimes becomes overabundant locally.

chosen beaux. Observe that fine drake! How gracefully he raises his head and curves his neck! As he bows before the object of his love, he raises for a moment his silken crest. His throat is swelled, and from it there issues a gutteral sound, which to his beloved is as sweet as the song of the wood thrush to its gentle mate. The female, as if not unwilling to manifest the desire to please which she really feels, swims close by his side, now and then caresses him by touching his feathers with her bill, and shows displeasure toward any other of her sex that may come near. Soon the happy pair separate from the rest, repeat every now and then their caresses, and at length, having sealed the conjugal compact, fly off to the woods to search for a large woodpecker's hole."

In the late 19th century and early part of this, the wood duck was seriously reduced in numbers by shooting and by cutting of the wild swamp forests that were its habitat. In 1918, under the *Migratory Bird Treaty Act,* it was given full protection from shooting in the United States and Canada. This restriction still is in effect in some states.

The larger mammals of Seney are whitetail deer, beavers, muskrats, mink, otters, foxes, coyotes, raccoons, weasels, skunks and bobcats. Sometimes black bears and very rarely moose and timber wolves are seen.

On summer evenings at six o'clock, auto caravan tours are conducted for the enjoyment of visitors. Special arrangements are made for organized groups.

Headquarters is within the refuge, and the address is Seney, Michigan. The area is reached over U. S. Highway 2, twenty-three miles northeast of Manistique to the junction with State Route 77 at Blaney Park, ten miles north to Germfask, north two miles, then left to the refuge. Overnight accommodations are available at Germfask three miles from the refuge; at Seney five miles away; at Newberry thirty miles; and at Manistique thirty-five miles. The best time to see waterfowl in large numbers is in late summer and early autumn, although spring is also a time of varied wildlife activity.

A dweller of northern conifer forests, the white-winged crossbill, with rose-pink body and head and black wings and tail, is distinguished from its relative, the red crossbill, by two white wing-bars.

Photographs by
Allan D. Cruickshank,
from Nat'l Audubon Society

The evening grosbeak is familiar throughout the western and northeastern states, and its yellow, black and white plumage brighten many a feed tray in winter. Other grosbeaks—pine, blue, rose-breasted and black-headed—also are brightly colored and are excellent singers.

SUSQUEHANNA NATIONAL WILDLIFE REFUGE, established in 1939 by Presidential proclamation, primarily to give protection to canvasbacks and other inland diving ducks and whistling swans, is located in Maryland in the shoal water near the mouth of the Susquehanna River at the head of Chesapeake Bay. It contains twenty-nine square miles, and is unique among other refuges in that it is almost entirely a water area. It is part of the natural feeding grounds of one of the continent's largest concentrations of migrating canvasbacks, scaups, redheads and other diving ducks. Thousands of canvasbacks can be seen here at one time. Dr. Ira N. Gabrielson, former director of the Fish and Wildlife Service, says that the area, with its redhead grass, wild celery and sago pondweed, produces more food to the acre than any area known to Service biologists. Waterfowl use the refuge from early fall until freezing weather occurs. Just before the opening of the gunning season, the Fish and Wildlife Service places markers in the water to indicate refuge boundaries to keep it closed to shooting. During the autumn migration, the ducks can be seen from shore, but the best way to observe them is by boat. As you approach the huge rafts of birds, they rise from the water in waves, circle around and alight again as the boat moves past. Hundreds of the white whistling swans, which breed in arctic Canada, concentrate in the bay on their way to warmer wintering areas.

Seeing the canvasbacks and other diving ducks at Susquehanna, and realizing

Plumage of the canvasback is quite like that of the redhead, but the sloping forehead and lighter back of the former are distinguishing characteristics.

The author

H. M. Worcester, Fish and Wildlife Service

Although prized by gunners, shooting regulations and refuges are helping to slow the decline of the canvasback.

that they spend but part of the year there, the visitor cannot help wondering a little about how and where they spend the remainder of the year. Most of these birds breed in the prairie provinces of Canada, and an account of their activities from spring to late summer there, is given in the book *The Canvasback on a Prairie Marsh*, by Dr. H. Albert Hochbaum, who made an intensive study of ducks at the Delta Duck Station, Manitoba, in the late 1930's. A highlight of the book is the description of courtship activities. During courtship on the northern breeding grounds, the river ducks indulge in spectacular flights. Dr. Hochbaum says, "The courtship pursuit flights of the mallard, gadwall, baldpate, shoveler and pintail are of unbelievable grace. I can recall no marsh scene more moving than a party of gadwalls or pintails high in the air in the evening twilight, each drake attempting to outmaneuver the other, and the hen outmaneuvering them all." Concerning the flight of the canvasback, he says, "This nuptial flight is a graceful breath-taking affair. Now in swift, straight flight, now twisting, diving, turning, towering, the two birds course over the marsh, the hen always leading, the drake shadowing her every move. Many times during the flight the hen may rise sharply out of a steep dive or break abruptly to one side, the male speeding on for many yards before checking to follow again. After such a finesse, the hen may fly slowly until her mate is once more in pursuit."

The canvasback is one of the ducks most prized by gunners. As a result, during the 1920's, when waterfowl populations reached a low ebb because of destruction of habitat, overshooting and drought, the canvasback became dangerously reduced. Had it not been for the efforts of a comparatively few men, working through the federal government and private organizations to establish waterfowl refuges, the canvasback, as well as the redhead, ruddy, lesser scaup and possibly others, might have become reduced beyond the point of recovery.

Susquehanna is under the administration of Blackwater Refuge. Visitors may see Susquehanna by renting boats at Havre de Grace, Maryland, reached over U. S. Highway 40, thirty-seven miles northeast of Baltimore, and forty southwest of Wilmington.

TULE LAKE, LOWER KLAMATH and SACRAMENTO NATIONAL WILDLIFE REFUGES are located in northern California. The first two are on or close to the Oregon line, while the third is 150 miles in a direct line south. All are on the Pacific waterfowl flyway and provide superb displays during the autumn migration. Tule Lake and Lower Klamath are on Bureau of Reclamation lands.

When the white man first came to the Tule Lake region, a vast marsh-fringed lake covered the present refuge areas, and spread for miles beyond them. It was a wildlife haven the like of which we can hardly imagine. Today almost all of the original lake has disappeared through stream diversion and drainage to make way for farming. Tule Lake is close to Lower Klamath, and is separated from it by the low grass-covered Sheep Ridge. Nearby are two other refuges, Clear Lake to the east, and Upper Klamath in Oregon just north of the state line. The Klamath basin is under the jurisdiction of the Bureau of Reclamation, which regulates water for irrigation of farm lands. The Bureau is charged also with regulating water levels in the Tule Lake and Lower Kalmath refuges to insure that adequate supplies are available for waterfowl.

Lower Klamath and Tule Lake are under the same management, and they provide refuge for essentially the same species. Lower Klamath, thirty-five square miles in area, was established in 1908 as the first federal waterfowl refuge. Tule Lake was established in 1928, and it is fifty-eight square miles. Both consist of diked pools and crop lands. Hills and mountains in the distance provide a scenic background.

The white-fronted goose, named for the patch on face at base of bill, is one of a half dozen kinds of geese that migrate through Tule Lake, Lower Klamath and Sacramento.

Frank Dufresne, Fish and Wildlife Service

The author

The cackling goose, a far western species, is similar in coloration to the Canada, but is much smaller and darker.

At the height of the autumn migration in late October and early November, Lower Klamath and Tule Lake display one of the largest concentrations of waterfowl on the continent, with three to four million birds. The refuges serve also as breeding grounds for waterfowl, so that many birds are present throughout the year, except during the coldest months. Because these refuges are located at a "bottle-neck" in the Pacific flyway, there is little wonder that such great numbers of birds concentrate here. Geese and ducks raised from Hudson Bay west to Bering Sea funnel through the area. Impressive as the sight may be, it becomes less so when one realizes the vastness of the breeding grounds from which these birds come. Probably a greater number of different kinds of geese can be seen on these two refuges than on any others—white-fronted, Canada, lesser Canada, cackling, Ross's and lesser snow. Even the emperor goose has been recorded here as an occasional straggler. Whistling swans and white pelicans add their gleaming beauty to the scene, as well as such ducks as the handsome cinnamon teal, shovelers, canvasbacks, redheads, American golden-eyes and very rarely Barrow's golden-eyes, buffleheads, ruddies, hooded mergansers and the more common species. Black-bellied and snowy plovers, willets, sanderlings, pectoral, least, red-backed, western and spotted sandpipers, Hudsonian and long-billed curlews, Wilson's snipes, greater and lesser yellowlegs, dowitchers, avocets, stilts, Wilson's and northern phalaropes and marbled godwits are a few of the shorebirds that inhabit the areas. The beautiful white American and snowy egrets were rare in the refuges ten years ago, but there are large colonies of American egrets at Tule Lake and

Upper Klamath, and a small but growing colony of snowy egrets at Tule Lake. Several species of owls also can be seen here, including the short-eared, which swoops and glides low over the marshes at sundown. California valley quail and the strikingly beautiful mountain quail haunt the dikes, and sierra and ruffed grouse and sage hens seek nearby brushy uplands. Among the waders are white-faced glossy ibises, great blue and green herons, and least and American bitterns.

Antelopes inhabit Tule Lake and Lower Klamath, while a breeding population lives at Clear Lake. Mule and blacktail deer, snowshoe hares, cottontail and jack rabbits and a long list of other mammals have been recorded here.

Both Tule Lake and Lower Klamath refuges were established with the provision that parts of them be open to autumn waterfowl shooting. About one third of each is used for this purpose. Such use of an area designated as a refuge defeats the purpose of wildlife protection, since the open areas provide no refuge at all to the birds during the shooting season.

For many years a controversy has raged over Tule Lake. Pressures on the side of the Bureau of Reclamation seek to have more of the refuge made available for homesteading and the raising of commercial crops, and pressures on the side of the Fish and Wildlife Service seek to have the area remain a refuge. The pros and cons are many, and the problem is extremely complex. What happens here may determine the future of the flyway. Refuge abolishment might seriously reduce or obliterate the flyway, which is a magnificent natural feature. How much ground there may be for compromise is not easy to say, but by giving away a little of the refuge now and a little more some other time is to tamper dangerously with nature. The refuge is already small, and the dry croplands within it, planted to barley, oats and rye, needed by the waterfowl, are being reduced. In late 1961, Senator Thomas H. Kuchel of California introduced a bill, S. 1988, which in effect would give recognition to the refuge status of Tule Lake and Lower Klamath. The proposed legislation was supported by the Secretary of the Interior.

During the southward migration, ducks sometimes literally cover the pools at Tule Lake as in this roadside scene at the refuge.

The author

The author

At Lower Klamath, the waterfowl can be seen as one drives along State Line Road on the refuge's north boundary.

In 1952 and 1953, when pressure was brought on the Department of the Interior to make certain parts of the area available to homesteaders, the Secretary of the Interior removed some of the requested area from the refuge. At the same time, certain lands adjoining Lower Klamath were placed under the protection of that refuge. However, the transaction resulted in a 6700-acre loss to waterfowl. And pressure for more land for homesteading continues. The question is this: Are we so poor a nation that we cannot afford to allow wildlife sufficient space for its needs? Already our government is paying huge subsidies for the overproduction of foods.

Headquarters for Lower Klamath and Tule Lake is within Tule Lake National Wildlife Refuge, and the address is Tulelake, California. Lower Klamath is reached from Klamath Falls, Oregon, fifteen miles south on U. S. Highway 97, to the junction with State Line Road, left to the refuge. Over the same highway, this junction can also be reached fifty-nine miles north from Weed, California. The pools of Lower Klamath border State Line Road on the south side for several miles. By continuing east a few miles, the visitor comes to the junction with Hill Road to the right, five miles to headquarters and Tule Lake Refuge. Both refuges can be reached on U. S. Highway 39 from Klamath Falls to Merrill, Oregon, then south on a gravel road to a junction with State Line Road. By following Hill Road south of headquarters, some of the pools of Tule Lake can be seen to the left, close to the road. Beyond here the road enters Lava Beds National Monument, which adjoins Tule Lake on the south. Overnight accommodations are available at the nearby town of Tulelake, California.

Sacramento National Wildlife Refuge, in the Sacramento Valley, was established in 1937. It comprises an area of diked pools and croplands, seventeen square miles in extent, and, being south of Lower Klamath and Tule Lake on the Pacific flyway, is the next stopping place for birds on their fall migration. The refuge is heavily used by pintails, well over a million of them being present during the autumn. Even more interesting is the fact that this refuge is the principal wintering ground of the rare little Ross's goose. The breeding ground of this species remained a mystery until the summer of 1940, when two officials of the Hudson's Bay Company found the geese nesting on islands in lakes on a tributary to Perry River near the northern coast of Northwest Territories. The species is a miniature of the lesser snow goose, which it resembles in every way but size. It is only as large as a mallard.

Sacramento has a level landscape broken here and there by an occasional clump of willows or cottonwoods, but like the foregoing refuges, it affords a grand waterfowl show in the fall. It is a popular stopping place for bird enthusiasts.

At this refuge there is another serious depredation problem. Agriculture has encroached on lands that once belonged to waterfowl, and the refuge is all that now remains for the birds. Farmers are aroused because the birds move out of the refuge onto adjacent crop lands to feed. If Sacramento were enlarged, this condition would be relieved.

Visitors should talk with members of a refuge staff whenever possible to learn interesting facts about the areas and their wildlife, and to become familiar with some of the administrative problems.

Sacramento headquarters is in the refuge, and the address is Willows, California. The area is reached south from Red Bluff fifty-nine miles over U. S. Highway 99W, which parallels the west boundary of the refuge. The entrance is on the left, just south of Willows. It is reached from U. S. Highway 40 at Davis, seventy-seven miles north on U. S. Highway 99W. The widest choice of overnight accommodations is at Chico, sixteen miles north from Willows to Orland and right twenty miles to Chico.

The gray California valley quail live in the chaparral and grasslands of Tule Lake and Lower Klamath.

H. H. Boswell, U. S. Forest Service

Peter J. Van Huizen, Fish and Wildlife Service

White-fronted geese feed on the croplands at Sacramento, above, and several species of geese, below, fill the air with flashing wings as they rise, and the din of their calls is heard afar.

The author

E. P. Haddon, Fish and Wildlife Service

The gray squirrel is familiar in eastern and central forests. At White River it shares the woods with the larger fox squirrel.

WHITE RIVER NATIONAL WILDLIFE REFUGE includes bottomlands of the White River, which is a tributary of the Mississippi, in eastern Arkansas. It is 182 square miles in area, thirty-five miles long north to south, and six miles at its widest. It was established in 1935 to protect waterfowl and other birds, as well as certain mammals.

The outstanding feature of this refuge is its southern bottomland hardwood forest. Although most of it is second growth, much of it today is of huge proportions, and there remain here and there towering giants. In places the effect is almost Amazonian, with vines clambering high among the trees. The White River winds in a tortuous course through the refuge, forming oxbows, and branching with a number of equally twisting tributaries. Throughout the forest are innumerable crescent-shaped lakes, remnants of former river channels, many of them rimmed with cypress trees.

Some of the important trees of the refuge are sweet and bitter pecan, water and honey locust, black and sweet gum, water tupelo, sugarberry, box elder, red birch, sycamore, persimmon, American and winged elms, green ash, cottonwood and seven species of oaks. Understory trees are buttonbush, swamp privet, water elm, red haw, rough-leaf dogwood, blue beech, deciduous holly and red mulberry.

The list of resident and migrating birds recorded in the area is impressively long. A few of the nesting species are black and turkey vultures, Mississippi kites, king rails, coots, barred owls, turkeys, bobwhites, pileated, red-bellied and red-headed woodpeckers, ruby-throated hummingbirds, yellow-billed cuckoos, purple martins, mockingbirds, bluebirds, short-billed marsh wrens, blue-gray gnatcatchers, bronzed grackles, meadowlarks, Baltimore and orchard orioles, and dickcissels. Some of the smaller migrants are Acadian flycatchers, Arkansas and eastern kingbirds, wood pewees, phoebes, brown creepers, winter and house wrens, yellow-throated vireos, purple finches and red-eyed towhees. The waders—the egrets and herons—are well represented on the refuge. The mallard is by far the most abundant duck at White River, more than half a million being on the refuge lakes in early January. Blue-winged and green-winged teal come to the refuge, along with pintails, widgeons and many others. Canada geese are abundant in winter, but blue and lesser snow geese and whistling swans are rare. The only waterfowl that nest on the refuge are the wood duck and less frequently the hooded merganser.

Black bears, whitetail deer, gray and fox squirrels, swamp rabbits, raccoons, mink and otters are a few of the area's mammals.

The ivory-billed woodpecker once inhabited the primeval forests of the Mississippi Valley, including the forest of White River Refuge. The ivory-bill was the largest woodpecker north of the Rio Grande, exceeding in size even the pileated. Like the latter, it had a flaming red crest, the remainder of the plumage being black and white, but with a great deal more white than the pileated. The bill was ivory white. Its range extended as far north as southern Illinois, and up the Ohio Valley to southern Indiana, and it lived in the forests of the east from North Carolina to southern Florida. As late as the 1940's two pairs were known to inhabit the Tensas Swamp in Louisiana, just a hundred miles south of White River Refuge, and similar to it in many ways. This was a privately-owned tract of primeval southern bottomland hardwood forest—the only kind of habitat in which the ivory-bill could live, because its food requirements were certain grubs occurring in the dead trees of such a forest. In the 1940's, efforts were made to save the Tensas Swamp from being logged, as a last hope of perpetuating the ivory-bill; but these attempts were at least forty years too late. Reliable reports of birds persisting in Florida and South Carolina were made as recently as 1961.

In 1942, the National Audubon Society sponsored a report on the ivory-bill entitled *The Ivory-billed Woodpecker,* by James T. Tanner, who made exhaustive on-the-ground studies. Intensely interesting, it is worth anyone's time to read.

Even without the ivory-bill, the preservation of the Tensas Swamp would have been a worth-while achievement. It was, and the cut-over area still may be, one of the last

With glossy green head and neck and chestnut breast, the mallard is the most abundant of North America's ducks.

The author

Courtesy Nature Magazine

Several kinds of woodpeckers inhabit White River. Although the pileated is the largest, the red-headed, left, is the most showy with brilliant head, white breast and large white patches on black wings. Woodpeckers sometimes are condemned by fruit farmers who believe these birds kill trees. A woodpecker seldom if ever attacks live bark, but seeks dead wood to feed on the grubs it contains. Sapsuckers drill rows of holes in the bark of live trees.

The red-bellied has a bright red patch from top of bill, over head to back of neck, and this together with the black and white striping on back and wings make it easy to identify. Both species are more abundant in the southern states, although the red-headed sometimes wanders as far north as southern New England west to southern Manitoba, while the other goes to Minnesota and Maryland.

The author

The author

Spring rain inundates White River's forests.

Fish and Wildlife Service

The red wolf no longer inhabits the White River area, but a remnant population has been known to live in the Tensas Swamp a hundred miles south, and a few still may exist there. It will vanish soon unless a sanctuary is established for it.

habitats of the Texas red wolf, although trapping may bring this species to early extinction. It is gratifying to realize that in the refuge we do have, after all, a large tract of southern bottomland forest in federal ownership. Even though management of the area for wildlife may require some cutting, the Fish and Wildlife Service plans to preserve most of the area undisturbed, and allow it to return to its natural condition. With the long growing season of the southland, this should not take many more years. As similar bottomland forests elsewhere are harvested, the preserved forest of White River Refuge, with its abundant wildlife, will become increasingly unique.

In spring, the river bottoms are inundated by heavy runoff from the uplands, and it is necessary then to travel the waterways by boat to explore the refuge. During the drier seasons, parts of the area may be reached by winding dirt roads or by trails. Beautiful cypress-rimmed White Lake, a mile or two south of headquarters is frequented by visitors; and camping is allowed there on weekends.

One of the important functions of the Fish and Wildlife Service is to provide a growth of aquatic food plants each year for the thousands of waterfowl that come to the refuge in spring and autumn. Acorns of Nutall's, water and willow oaks, also are important food of the ducks and geese. To make the aquatic plants and the acorns available,

Peter J. Van Huizen, Fish and Wildlife Service

Spotted fauns of the whitetail deer are appealing. All too often people finding them, believe them to be lost from their mothers and take them home. This is a mistake, for the does are usually feeding nearby.

requires that water levels in the White River fluctuate seasonally—that is, a low stage is needed during the summer months to produce the food, and there should be a progressive rise during the late fall and winter to make this food available. The Corps of Army Engineers has built two dams on the White River watershed above the refuge, and more dams are proposed. If the dams do what they are intended to do, they will take the crest off the winter floods, and increase the minimum stages during the summer months. The latter will cause much harm by preventing production of the aquatic foods.

Arthur A. Allen, from Nat'l Audubon Society

The ivory-billed woodpecker, largest of its kind north of Mexico, once ranged far up the Mississippi Valley and along the southern Atlantic states, but logging of primeval hardwood forests, the only habitat in which it could survive, has brought it to extinction.

Headquarters is on the west bank of the White River, close to the refuge, and the address is Saint Charles, Arkansas. It is reached south and east from U. S. Highway 79 at Stuttgart, Arkansas, twenty-seven miles over State Route 30 to De Witt, and sixteen miles over State Route 1, to Saint Charles and the refuge. There is a hotel at De Witt.

The least bittern, miniature by comparison with the American bittern, is colorful and adds beauty to marshlands throughout our country.

Hal H. Harrison, courtesy Mass. Audubon Society

WICHITA MOUNTAINS WILDLIFE REFUGE is one of the outstanding show places of the Fish and Wildlife Service. Located in southwestern Oklahoma, it was first established as a reserve for bison under the protection of the U. S. Forest Service. In 1935 it became a Fish and Wildlife Service refuge. Ninety-two square miles in extent, it consists of a rugged range of granite hills and ridges that rise from undulating valleys of grassland. The hills extend west for a few miles beyond the refuge boundary, where cultivated fields are carried to the very bases of the granite outcrops. In contrast, the wild beauty of the refuge country is much as it was in primeval times, with rich, thick grass covering the rolling valleys between the picturesque outcrops. Narrower valleys are sometimes densely forested, and the trees extend up the slopes in scattered stands and groves. Although many of the rocky slopes and sharp ridges and peaks are exposed, groves and small stands of woods are scattered over them. The granite is broken and eroded into house-size boulders that appear heaped up helter-skelter, and the vegetation on narrow benches and in the gorges produces an effect of decided charm. During the days of the Civilian Conservation Corps, a number of small dams were built to conserve water runoff, and more than twenty blue lakes of various sizes now dot the landscape.

Three old bison bulls laze in the picturesque landscape of Wichita Mountains.

The author

Allan D. Cruickshank, from Nat'l Audubon Society

The scissor-tailed flycatcher, with pink, gray, white and black plumage, has streaming tail feathers unlike any other songbird in the United States. This extraordinarily beautiful bird is a member of the avifauna of Wichita Mountains.

A thousand bison roam wild and free in small herds over its grasslands, adding immeasurably to the fascination of this beautiful refuge. Many elk, antelope, whitetail deer, and smaller mammals such as raccoons, striped and spotted skunks, badgers, gray foxes, coyotes, mink, bobcats, cottontail and jack rabbits and prairie dogs also live on the refuge. This is indeed one of the nation's finest mammal sanctuaries. The impression one gains is not unlike that produced by the fabulous wildlife reserves of Africa.

Among the refuge trees there are four species of hackberry, flowering and roughleaf dogwoods, black willow, bitternut, pecan, black walnut, redbud, cottonwood, red cedar and eight species of oaks, with post oak the most abundant. The refuge is a garden of wild flowers, and some of the species to be seen here are butterfly weed, bright blue prairie larkspur, day flower, spiderwort, white prickly poppy, Venus' looking-glass, downy paintedcup, showy and cut-leaved rayless gaillardia, small blazing star, false indigo, the red wine cup and three species of cactus—tufted and Bailey's hedgehog and prickly pear, which have large colorful blooms in spring.

Wichita Mountains has a bird population that equals the mammals in interest. Since the ranges of many eastern and western birds meet or overlap here, the area is of keen

The author

On spring nights the weird notes of the chuck-will's-widow sound from the wooded areas of Wichita Mountains. Prairie dogs have "towns" on the refuge, and here they are safe from persecution. Almost everywhere else throughout their formerly wide range in the West, they have been poisoned to make way for agriculture.

E. R. Kalmbach, Fish and Wildlife Service

Philip A. DuMont, Fish and Wildlife Service

A flock of Franklin's gulls, with gleaming white bodies and black heads, come to the blue lakes of Wichita Mountains.

interest to bird-watchers from both east and west. The list of feathered creatures is lengthy and only a few can be named: The fantastic pale gray scissor-tailed flycatcher, with its black and salmon-color markings and streaming forked tail—one of North America's most beautiful birds—is a summer resident on the refuge, as are lark sparrows, eastern bluebirds, painted buntings, eastern and western meadowlarks, summer tanagers, cardinals, yellow-billed cuckoos, roadrunners, western tanagers, blue jays, Carolina,

Maslowski and Goodpaster, courtesy Mass. Audubon Society

The red plumage of the cardinal draws attention to this handsome bird wherever it occurs.

canyon and rock wrens, mockingbirds, loggerhead shrikes, spotted towhees, nighthawks and the chuck-will's-widow which latter sounds its loud call at nightfall—a strange utterance that one might imagine coming from the heart of a tropical jungle. Wild turkeys are present, and a strutting gobbler is a memorable sight. During the winter you may see mountain bluebirds, Brewer's blackbirds, red-shafted flickers and spotted towhees. A strikingly colorful reptile, the large green and yellow "mountain boomer" or collared lizard, is quite abundant on the refuge.

During the afternoon we wandered afoot through the narrow, wooded confines of Hollis Canyon, where there is a very small stand of the extremely rare bigtooth maple, *Acer grandidentatum*, and continued on to a level grassy glade at the canyon's western end, where the post oaks grow large. Deer along the road to Grama Lake were particularly handsome in the sunset as they wandered through the tall yellow grass against a background of distant blue hills. Half a dozen bison bulls, old fellows who no longer sought companionship of the herd, lazed nearby. Then overhead, wheeling in wide circles against the brilliant blue, a flock of large and unfamiliar birds appeared. Long tails and sharp-pointed wings, predominantly gray, with white markings, these were Mississippi kites—magnificent rarities of the bird world. Since they now breed in only a few spots in the plains states, their range is much smaller than formerly.

Atop a ridge from which blue Grama Lake could be seen, a straggling flock of

Red-shafted flickers are permanent residents of Wichita Mountains.

Winton Weydemeyer, courtesy Nature Magazine

The author

From the summit of Mount Scott, visitors look west across the nearly primeval landscape of Wichita Mountains.

Franklin's gulls winged past to alight on the lake below. Graceful creatures, these, with gleaming white bodies and tails, and black heads.

As the sun's colorful afterglow filled the west, the white rump patches of three antelopes on a distant ridge reflected the last light of day. At our approach, a band of elk sped away, climbing a ridge to the west. There they stood in black silhouette, illuminated from behind by the fading glow of the western sky—a picture of incomparable primeval beauty.

The refuge protects a number of the famous Texas longhorn cattle, now known mostly in literature. These were brought here in 1927 to preserve the breed, for with the introduction of other kinds of cattle, the longhorn has vanished from our western ranges. In view of the part this lanky animal played in the early history of our West, it is fitting that a representative herd be saved for posterity. Some feel it might be more appropriate if the wild landscape of the refuge were to exhibit only native mammals.

Adjoining eastward is Fort Sill Military Reservation. The Army has coveted the refuge for artillery training, and, in 1955, it pressured Congress into approving a bill to authorize the use of 10,700 refuge acres for the purpose—a move vigorously protested by wildlife authorities; yet, hundreds of square miles of ranchland adjoining Fort Sill to the north and east might have served without injury to any existing values. In preparing for defense, we should destroy nothing that makes our country worth defending.

Headquarters is in the refuge, and the address is Cache, Oklahoma. The area is reached from the west over U. S. Highway 62, twenty miles east from Snyder, Oklahoma, to Cache, and from there, left six miles to the refuge. From Oklahoma City, it is reached southwest over U. S. Highway 62, 125 miles to Cache, and from there right to the refuge. Mount Scott, 2467 feet above sea level, highest point on the refuge, is at the extreme eastern end of the area. Its summit, reached by a paved road, offers visitors a view of the sanctuary spreading westward in a grand panorama of jagged hills, woodlands, grasslands and lakes. The northern half of the refuge is enclosed by a high fence, reserving this area exclusively for the large mammals. The southern half has been developed for visitors, and thousands use it for picnicking, swimming and camping. Here most of the lakes are located and there are several picnic and campgrounds in attractive settings. This area is traversed by good roads, most of them paved. Overnight accommodations are available at the nearby town of Lawton.

ALEUTIAN ISLANDS NATIONAL WILDLIFE REFUGE is the largest area under the protection of the Fish and Wildlife Service. Containing 4250 square miles, it begins on the east at Unimak Island off the tip of the Alaska Peninsula and extends west 1200 miles in the Aleutian chain, to Attu Island. It contains about fifty islands ranging in size from a mile to sixty miles in length, and dozens of smaller ones. Many rise from the ocean in sheer 2000-foot cliffs, over which waterfalls plunge into the sea. Some are volcanic, and have numerous extinct craters, cinder cones and lava flows, as well as glaciers. There are several active volcanoes, among which, steaming, snow-clad Shishaldin is the most symmetrical and highest, rising to 9387 feet above the blue sea at its base. The climate here is as stormy as any in the world, with fog and wind much of the year, but the winter temperature usually does not go below 15° Fahrenheit.

The islands are without trees, except for the dwarf willows a few inches high, but are covered with dense grass and thick, low-growing shrubs; and in spite of the harsh climate, the Aleutians are gardens of bright wild flowers in summer. Anemones sometimes form such dense patches on mountain sides that they look like snow. There are a purple and a white orchid, a brown and white lady's slipper, wild pea, pink Siberian spring beauty and bright yellow buttercups. The green inland valleys are grown with the white blossoms of parsnips, blue spikes of lupines and the brilliant blue monkshood. The Kamchatkan rhododendron, with its large brilliant red flowers, inhabits the banks of the fast-flowing mountain streams, and over the lichen and moss-covered slopes grow salmonberries, bunchberries and cranberries.

Sea otters nearly became extinct because man killed them for their fur. Protection is restoring them in the Aleutians and south to northern California.

Robert D. Jones, Jr., Fish and Wildlife Service

Robert D. Jones, Jr., Fish and Wildlife Service

Sea otters spend much time floating and feeding off shore.

Waterfowl that come to the Aleutians include the Pacific harlequin, Steller's eider, the handsomely marked old-squaw and the American scoter, and teal, mergansers, mallards and loons visit the island ponds. The emperor goose is a winter resident. Nearly twenty species of shorebirds come to the refuge including the Aleutian sandpiper and the black oystercatcher. Colonial sea birds occur in the islands in vast numbers on the ledges of the cliffs, and these concentrations, one of the wonders of nature, are a chief reason for establishing the Aleutians as a refuge. Puffins, murrelets, cormorants, various species of gulls and others constitute the principal inhabitants of these great bird cities.

A noted authority on the Aleutian Islands and its bird colonies is Dr. Ira N. Gabrielson, who, while he was director of the Fish and Wildlife Service, traveled as far west as Amchitka, about three fourths of the length of the island chain. In his article *America's Greatest Bird Concentrations,* in *Audubon Magazine* for January-February, 1941, he describes a flight of auklets on Kasatochi Island: "As the sun sank toward the horizon these birds began to leave their nests in increasing numbers and to fly out over the water in front of the great slides that harbored the colony. There were flocks of thousands, each a swiftly moving ribbon or patch against the sky, twisting and turning in their evolutions like sandpipers. The flocks played around and over each other until the air seemed awhirl with birds. Sometimes one long ribbon would cross another, both undulating as they went and alternately showing white and dark in the sun. As it became a little darker, one after another of these great flocks came sweeping with a roar like a waterfall over the rock where I was sitting. The flocks passed overhead, but

H. C. Kyllingstad
from Nat'l
Audubon Society

The rare bristle-thighed curlew breeds in western Alaska, and migrates through the Aleutian Islands on its way to the Hawaiian Islands where it winters.

The slaty blue-gray Aleutian sandpiper breeds in Alaska and winters south to the coasts of Oregon and Washington. It associates with black turnstones and surfbirds.

J. Malcolm Greany,
Fish and Wildlife Service

Sigurd T. Olson, Fish and Wildlife Service

The handsome gray emperor goose, with scaled pattern on body, white head and back of neck and white tail, is a winter resident in the Aleutian Islands. Its breeding grounds are on the marshy west coast of Alaska between the mouths of the Yukon and Kuskokwim rivers.

hundreds of individuals dropped like falling leaves to land all around me on the rocks. Some took off again to join one of the flocks but most of them stood quiet for some time, looked around, and finally disappeared into their burrows."

Mammals of the refuge are the brown bear, the wolverine, the Alaska Peninsula hare and certain small rodents, including the lemming. The blue fox was imported to several of the islands from the mainland, for commercial purposes several years ago. These foxes are the largest land mammals on the outer islands. Various sea mammals live in the bays and nearby waters of the Aleutians, most abundant of which is the northwestern harbor seal. Here, too, is the rare bearded seal. Killer whales travel through the expanses of the Bering Sea and come to the bays and channels of the island chain, together with porpoises. But of greatest interest is the sea otter, because not many years ago it nearly became extinct. One of the foremost objectives of the Fish and Wildlife Service, in administering this refuge, is to enforce protective laws governing the sea otter. When

Allan D. Cruickshank, from Nat'l Audubon Society

The black brant, very similar in size and markings to the Atlantic brant, migrates through the eastern Aleutian Islands on its way from its breeding grounds on the Arctic Ocean coast of Alaska, to the west coast of the United States where it winters. Large concentrations of the species appear at beautiful Cold Bay, below, and Izembek Bay, an area designated a refuge of the Bureau of Sport Fisheries and Wildlife in 1960.

Robert D. Jones, Jr., Fish and Wildlife Service

Alaska was owned by Russia, the animal was slaughtered ruthlessly for its fine fur; and the slaughter continued for many years after the territory became the property of the United States. Only because the few remaining animals were widely scattered, was the species saved from extinction. Today this furbearer is under complete protection, and its population is slowly gaining. It occurs in a number of locations, notably in the Delarof and Rat islands. According to Robert D. Jones, Jr., of the Fish and Wildlife Service, this region has come to be known as the sea otter belt. It extends from Tanage on the east to Kiska on the west and apparently includes all of the islands in between, a distance of 160 miles. Other otter population centers are at Amelia Island, Unimak Island and in the Sanak Islands.

The sea otter lives on sea urchins, mollusks, crabs and to a small extent on fish. Measuring from four to five feet from tip of tail to tip of nose, its rich fur is brown black, often grizzled, with head and ears much lighter. It spends a great deal of time lazing or feeding in the kelp beds off shore. When approached, it shows more curiosity than fear, a cause of its near extinction. The single young cannot swim at birth, but floats effortlessly. During the early months of life it is kept close to its mother resting on her chest while she floats on her back. In bad weather, the otters haul up on the beaches.

The teeth of the sea otter deteriorate with age, and although normally the animals

This airplane view shows one of the Aleutian Islands' several active volcanoes, Mount Shishaldin, on Unimak Island, rising from a sea of clouds.

Dean Freiday

Dean Freiday

The Aleutian Islands are highly scenic as shown in this view on Umnak Island, where the islands rise abruptly from the surf of the Pacific on the south and Bering Sea on the north.

crush the shells of sea urchins with their teeth, during later years they are unable to do this. Instead, they bring up a small rock from the bottom of the sea, which they place on the chest, and crack the urchin shell against it.

The range of the sea otter in North America extends as far south as the coasts of Oregon and northern California, where they can be seen playing or resting in the offshore kelp beds. They deserve the best protection we can give them.

Refuge headquarters is at Cold Bay, and the address is Cold Bay, Alaska.

KENAI NATIONAL MOOSE RANGE is only a little smaller in area than the big Desert Game Range in Nevada. It is ninety-two miles north-south, and fifty miles east-west, and it embraces 3214 square miles. The refuge was established, in 1941, to give protection to the big Kenai moose. It is situated on the west side of the Kenai Peninsula, on Alaska's south coast. Although a fourth of the refuge includes part of the Kenai Mountains, which form a scenic backdrop along the east side, the larger part of the area consists of bogs, lakes, river valleys and low ridges. It lies between Turnagain Arm on the north and Sheep Creek on the south, with Cook Inlet on the west and the Kenai Range and the Chugach National Forest on the east. The refuge is drained by four principal rivers—the Swanson, the Chickaloon, the Kenai and the Kasilof—the two last having their origin in the Harding Ice Field and its glaciers, whose waters flow north into Lake Skilak and west into Tustumena Lake.

Kenai is vast and rugged, and it provides a fine sample of the original Alaska wilder-

The largest moose in North America are those on the Kenai Moose Range.

Floyd McDowell, Montana Fish and Game Commission

J. Malcolm Greany, Fish and Wildlife Service

Antlers of the moose sometimes attain a spread of six feet, while the animal occasionally measures seven feet and more at the shoulder, and weighs a thousand pounds.

Charles W. Schwartz

The red fox is not abundant at Kenai, but for the sheer pleasure of seeing this handsome furbearer, it deserves strict protection on the refuge.

Adolph Murie, National Park Service

A high degree of intelligence is possessed by the red fox, but this too often is referred to as slyness or craftiness, and the animal condemned because of it.

ness. Unfortunately, part of it is being used for agriculture and settlement. The forests consist of small trees, mostly black spruce in the bogs, and aspen and the white-barked Kenai birch on lake shores, with dense growths of alder and willow covering the low ridges between the lakes.

The moose is North America's king of the deer tribe, and the Kenai moose is the largest of the species. Bulls weigh from 1400 to 1800 pounds, and stand as high as seven and a half feet at the shoulder. The palmate antlers, sometimes exceeding six feet in spread and weighing up to eighty-five pounds, are shed annually. The Fish and Wildlife Service finds that, in order to keep the moose population within the limits of the range to feed it, there must be an open season each year for public shooting of the animal. The wolf is a native species here, and if it were given protection, and a few were permitted to live on the refuge, the moose population problem might be partly taken care of by them. This would require less reduction by artificial means.

Other Kenai mammals are brown and black bears, mink, beaver, muskrat, lynx, otter, weasel, wolverine, coyote, the white mountain goat and the handsome white subspecies of the bighorn—the Dall sheep—which now numbers several hundred head in the refuge. Red foxes, as well as wolves, are now extremely rare.

A varied population of land birds includes ptarmigans, ravens, Alaska jays, white-winged crossbills, ruby-crowned kinglets, pine siskins, redpolls, robins and brown-capped chickadees. Mallards, green-winged teal, pintails, golden-eyes and harlequin ducks come to the refuge in summer to nest, and lesser Canada, emperor and white-fronted geese and brant migrate through. The bald eagle also occurs here. For many years, Alaska paid a bounty on the bald eagle, encouraging its killing throughout the territory; but this action was bitterly opposed by those who recognize not only the absurdity of rewarding our citizens for killing the bird that has been chosen as our national emblem, but also because the bald eagle is a magnificent creature that deserves utmost protection for the pleasure many people derive from seeing it. On July 1, 1952, the eagle bounty was repealed. This

U. S. Forest Service, courtesy Am. Forestry Ass'n

Alaska brown bears inhabit Kenai. The Kodiak Island brown bears are North America's largest, and cattlemen on the island have sought to have this magnificent creature exterminated.

was brought about when the Secretary of the Interior issued an order modifying the Alaska game law, ending the bounty payment and giving the eagle its long-needed protection. It is ironic that the same session of the Alaska Legislature which terminated the eagle bounty, placed a bounty on the wolverine, one of the rarest and most interesting of North America's furbearers.

Refuge headquarters is at the village of Kenai, in the refuge, and the address is Kenai, Alaska. The area can be reached by airplane from Seattle, Washington, to Seward, a flight of unimagined beauty over the spectacularly scenic mountainous coastal islands of British Columbia and southern Alaska. From Seward, the road runs north to the junction with the Sterling Highway, left across the refuge to the villages of Soldotna and Kenai; and it can be reached south from Anchorage to the same highway junction to the right. Cabins and meals are available at Soldotna, and rooms and meals at Kenai. There are two campgrounds on the shores of beautiful Skilak Lake.

There are more than a dozen national wildlife refuges in Alaska. Forrester Island and Hazy Islands refuges, on the southern coast, protect auklets, murres, cormorants, gulls and puffins. Tuxedni Refuge, across Cook Inlet from the Kenai Moose Range, contains kittiwakes, as well as most of the species at Forrester and Hazy islands. Kodiak National Wildlife Refuge, on mountainous Kodiak Island, is the habitat of the big brown Kodiak bear, the largest carnivore in the world. To save their cattle from molestation, the residents of the island have asked that the bears be exterminated. Kodiak sea cliffs

Kenai also contains black bears, a species having a range throughout most of North America.

E. P. Haddon, Fish and Wildlife Service

Photographs by Wm. E. Ackerknecht, Fish and Wildlife Service

A superb primitive wilderness of forests, lakes, mountains, glaciers, rivers, marshes and coast constitute the Kenai Moose Range. For this it should be preserved intact, as well as for the sake of its wildlife.

Adolph Murie, National Park Service

Both the handsome white Dall sheep, a species of bighorn, above, and the white mountain goat, find sanctuary at Kenai. On unprotected areas, these animals become targets merely to provide mountable heads. They deserve protection.

A. E. Hutchinson, courtesy Am. Forestry Ass'n

Charles J. Ott

Trapped, shot and poisoned wherever it lives, the lynx, typifying northern wilderness, has high esthetic value, and deserves better treatment.

swarm with colonies of tufted and horned puffins, glaucous-winged gulls, murres and cormorants. Semidi National Wildlife Refuge, consisting of eight islands southwest of Kodiak, is inhabited by Pacific fulmars, harlequin and eider ducks, horned and tufted puffins, kittiwakes, California murres, pelagic and white-crested cormorants, Aleutian rosy finches, Semidi wrens, savannah, song and fox sparrows and Pribilof snow buntings. From the Aleutians northward to Bering Strait, there are some of the largest colonies of

Joseph S. Dixon

sea-birds known. Bogoslof Island, which is one of the Aleutians, but which has been established as a separate refuge, contains large herds of sea lions, as well as colonies of glaucous-winged gulls, California and Pallas's murres and red-faced cormorants. The murre colonies here are far larger than those of the other birds, and are, in fact, the largest murre colonies to be seen anywhere.

The beautiful Izembek National Wildlife Range, located at Cold Bay and established in 1960, is protecting the Grant's caribou, a herd of which has been increasing here lately on the Alaska Peninsula. The area is also an important waterfowl habitat, particularly for cackling geese and brant. During migration, the emperor goose, which

The willow ptarmigan, upper left, and the white-tailed ptarmigan, inhabit a number of Alaska refuges. The wolverine, already extremely rare because of trapping, is a resident of the Kenai wilderness, yet the Alaska Legislature has put a bounty on it. A member of the weasel tribe averaging about forty inches in length, it is courageous even when confronted by an enemy many times its size.

R. W. Shufeldt,
courtesy Am. Forestry Assn.

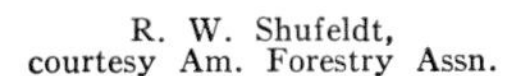

breeds on Alaska's west coast, in the vicinity of Nunivak Island, migrates to and through the Cold Bay country, wintering there and in the Aleutians, as well as along the southern coast. Occasionally a straggler will wander to the coast of northern California. However, it is not an abundant species, and because it belongs chiefly to coastal Alaska, it is not often seen by bird enthusiasts.

The three islands of the Pribilof Islands Reservation, in the Bering Sea, best known for its fabulous herds of fur seals, the surplus of which are taken each year for commercial use of the skins, is also the habitat of many bird colonies. Crested, paroquet and least auklets, red-legged and Pacific kittiwakes, red-faced cormorants, pigeon guillemots, Pribilof sandpipers, glaucous-winged gulls, Pallas's murres, long-tailed jaegers and tufted and horned puffins, as well as a few land birds including Pribilof snow buntings and Aleutian rosy finches are found on Saint George Island; almost all of these in addition to the Pacific godwit, inhabit Saint Paul and Walrus islands.

Nunivak National Wildlife Refuge, comprising the sixty-mile long Nunivak Island,

Fur seals spend their birthing and breeding period on the shores of the Pribilof Islands Reservation in Bering Sea.

V. B. Scheffer, Fish and Wildlife Service

V. B. Scheffer, Fish and Wildlife Service

Fur seal bulls are six feet long and weigh five hundred pounds.

off the west coast of Alaska, is the habitat of emperor and lesser Canada geese, and is now the home of a herd of the rare muskox. In 1930, the Fish and Wildlife Service brought thirty-four head from their native habitat in Greenland to Fairbanks, Alaska. Later, the herd was moved to this grass-covered island, where it is gaining in numbers. In 1957, there were about 150 head.

The original range of the muskox extended from northern Boothia Peninsula, in Northwest Territories, south to Chesterfield Inlet, on the west coast of Hudson Bay, west to Great Slave Lake and north to Coronation Gulf on the Canada mainland. It occurred also on a number of islands in the District of Franklin, including Prince of Wales, Melville, Bathhurst and Cornwallis. Over most of this region it has been greatly reduced, and in many places extirpated. It inhabits the northern and eastern coasts of Greenland as far south as Scoresby Sound.

This heavy-set creature with its thick horns and shaggy coat has a unique method of defense. When attacked, a group of them forms a circle, the animals standing closely

V. B. Scheffer, Fish and Wildlife Service

Steller's sea lions, shown here on Bogoslof Island Refuge, are larger and lack the fine coat of the fur seal. Bulls sometimes measure thirteen feet in length and weigh 2000 pounds.

side by side, with their heads facing out, each individual ready to meet the enemy. This served well when the attackers were wolves; but, in the words of Glover M. Allen, in his book *Extinct and Vanishing Mammals of the Western Hemisphere*, it "was often its undoing when attacked by men with modern guns, for the entire group might then be killed at close quarters." The depletion of this interesting member of our North American fauna has been the result of shooting by Eskimos, explorers and trappers for food for themselves and their dogs. A great deal of needless killing has been done.

Detailed information on how to reach Forrester and Hazy Islands, Tuxedni, Kodiak, Pribilof Island and Nunivak can be obtained from the Fish and Wildlife Service, Department of the Interior, Washington 25, D. C.

Although relatively few of us may be privileged to take a trip to Alaska, we can, nevertheless, derive satisfaction from the knowledge that there are reservations in that very large state that are being guarded by our federal government, and that the wonderful wildlife that inhabits these areas will continue to exist as long as the refuges are main-

Following the discovery of the Pribilof Islands by the Russians in 1786, the fur seals were nearly wiped out. Protective regulations and treaties restored the herd so that, by 1918, a regulated annual take became possible.

Karl W. Kenyon, Fish and Wildlife Service

Red-faced cormorants inhabit a number of the Alaska coastal refuges, where they breed on the cliffs and rocky islands. Here they mingle with other bird species of the rugged Alaska coast.

Photographs by
Karl W. Kenyon,
Fish and Wildlife Service

Least auklets nest in huge numbers on the sea cliffs of some of the Alaska refuge islands, and their flights during the breeding season are one of nature's most thrilling sights.

Frank Dufresne, Fish and Wildlife Service

The muskox, still thriving in parts of northern Greenland and a few spots in far northern Canada, has been shot needlessly and greatly reduced. A small herd was brought to Nunivak Island Refuge a number of years ago, and is doing well there.

tained and protected. Pictures of these refuges and of the wild birds and mammals that live on them, and writings by those who live on or travel to them, will always be a source of pleasure. For this reason and for the sake of the wilderness and the wildlife itself, we must constantly see that Congress appropriates sufficient money to adequately protect our Alaska refuges.

The granting of statehood to Alaska, in 1958, wisely provided for the continuation of the national wildlife refuges under federal protection. There are still many unprotected areas in the state that are extremely important to wildlife that deserve to be saved from the ruin of commercial exploitation and given refuge status.

The statement that man does not live by bread alone, though hackneyed, is true all

Stanley G. Jewett, Fish and Wildlife Service

California murres, above, like the auklets, form large nesting colonies on the sea cliffs in a number of the Alaska refuges. They breed as far south as the central coast of California, wintering as far as southern California. The strikingly marked Pacific loon breeds on the Arctic coast and in the interior valleys to the Seward Peninsula, but during migration it comes to the Aleutian Islands, Kenai Moose Range, Forrester Island and other refuges.

Allan D. Cruickshank, from Nat'l Audubon Society

Charles J. Ott

The long-tailed jaeger, above, is a summer resident on several Alaska refuges. Two other species are the pomarine and parasitic jaegers. The blue fox, a color phase of the white Arctic fox, is an introduced species at Nunivak Island.

Olaus J. Murie

Photographs by V. B. Scheffer, Fish and Wildlife Service

Pallas's murres, above, and kittiwake gulls, are abundant along the sea cliffs of the Alaska coast and off shore islands, and comprise a large part of the bird populations here.

Allan D. Cruickshank, from Nat'l Audubon Society

the same. Because of our increasingly mechanized and hectic life, more and more people are turning to nature for relaxation and refreshment; and because our population is rapidly growing, wilderness and wildlife are becoming ever more valuable. As the years go by and civilization moves steadily into our remaining wild lands, the wilderness so eagerly sought by an expanding population is increasingly less adequate to fill the growing need. To one who recognizes the effect of human encroachment on wild land, it becomes apparent that we are confronted with a most urgent responsibility to ourselves and future generations to retain the wilderness and wildlife habitats already protected in refuges, and to dedicate as many more areas to the permanent preservation of wilderness and wildlife as may be possible and feasible.

Surfbirds, above, nest in Mount McKinley National Park in south central Alaska, and migrate along the Pacific coast as far as the southern tip of South America. During migration they visit Forrester Island. The little snow bunting raises its young in the Arctic, but in migration it visits a number of the Alaska refuges, coming south for the winter as far as Oregon, Wyoming and Colorado. It is especially appealing when on the wing, for then it appears almost entirely white.

Arthur A. Allen
courtesy Mass. Audubon Society

HAWAIIAN ISLANDS NATIONAL WILDLIFE REFUGE is situated in the Pacific Ocean near the extreme western end of the Hawaiian Archipelago, extending about 1500 nautical miles northwest from Honolulu and contains a number of small lava islands and coral reefs, including Bird Island, Necker Island, French Frigate Shoals, Gardiner Island, Laysan Island, Lysianski or Peel Island, Pearl and Hermes Reef, and Cure Island. Laysan Island is the largest in this Leeward group. It is a coral atoll about two miles across, encircling a lagoon of a hundred acres. Three square miles in area, the refuge was established in 1909 to save from extinction several species of island birds, including the Laysan albatross, the Laysan teal and the Laysan rail. Prior to man's interference, the island was covered with grass and other plants, and contained a stand of sandalwood and fan-leaf palms.

Twenty-three bird species are known to Laysan; five were found nowhere else; three are gone. To Laysan from far across the rolling ocean come thousands of sea birds to lay their eggs and raise their young—such species as Laysan and black-footed albatrosses, frigate-birds, tropic birds, shearwaters, Bonin Island petrels, gray-backed, white and sooty terns. Besides these there were four species of land birds and one waterfowl that occurred nowhere else in the world—Laysan honey-eater, Laysan miller-bird, Laysan finch, the flightless Laysan rail and Laysan teal. The lagoon and waters of the outer reefs of the atoll are alive with countless forms of marine life.

The dance of the black-footed albatross.

Philip A. DuMont, Fish and Wildlife Service

V. B. Scheffer, Fish and Wildlife Servce

The albatrosses, with a wing-spread of seven feet, spend all their time over the open ocean, except for the breeding season.

Laysan was discovered in 1828, and the first authentic literature on it was Rothchild's *Avifauna of Laysan*. Another important contribution to the literature of this and other islands in the Leeward group is *Birds of Laysan and the Leeward Islands, Hawaiian Group*, by Walter K. Fisher.

The first great tragedy to strike little Laysan Island took place in 1909, when one Max Schlemmer, catering to the millinery trade, rounded up a group of Japanese workers and came to the island and slaughtered the birds by countless thousands for their wings. It was this act that spurred refuge establishment. Fortunately, Schlemmer was interrupted by officers of a U. S. revenue cutter in time to prevent total extermination of the bird colonies. Schlemmer, his Japs and the wings of more than 300,000 birds were taken to Honolulu for legal action. The feathers were burned later. Evidence showed that methods of extreme cruelty had been used in killing the birds.

In 1902, the bird population on Laysan Island had been estimated to be between seven and ten million. By 1911, through the appalling destruction of these birds for plumes, the population was reduced to an estimated 1,016,224. Of this total, the sooty tern comprised about one third of the number, while the Laysan and black-footed albatross had 180,000 and 85,000 individuals respectively.

Laysan's next fateful event was the freeing of rabbits there. Again the culprit was Schlemmer. Apparently he thought these animals would provide a source of food for ship-wrecked mariners. In a short time the rabbits had multiplied so that nearly all

The blue-faced booby, related to the gannet, is a large sea bird whose range extends from the Bahama Islands and the West Indies to the islands of the Pacific, including the Hawaiian Islands. The name "booby" may derive from the bird's habit of not flying from an enemy, but standing its ground and using its bill in self-defense.

Photographs by
Alexander Wetmore

Frigate-birds breed on the Hawaiian Islands Refuge, where their characteristically narrow, tapering wings and long forked tail make their identification easy when in flight. A different species breeds in the Bahama Islands and visits the Florida keys in the vicinity of the Great White Heron Refuge.

Karl H. Maslowski
from Nat'l Audubon Society

As graceful as all the terns, the sooty, black above and white beneath, breeds on oceanic and coastal islands in the tropics, including the Hawaiian Islands. Little is known about this species, and concerning its habits there are still several unsolved mysteries.

The friendly white or fairy tern of the Hawaiian Islands has an ethereal beauty accentuated by large black eyes and blue-black bill. Although a bare branch or crotch serves as nest, the single egg seldom falls, and the young clings firmly.

Alexander Wetmore

Alfred M. Bailey, from Nat'l Audubon Society

The Laysan teal is a native of Laysan Island in the Hawaiian Islands Refuge, and of nowhere else. With fewer than 500 individuals, it may be one of the rarest ducks in the world.

grass and other vegetation was eaten and killed off, sand dunes formed, and the atoll became a wasteland. In 1912, a group of four scientists spent three months on Laysan attempting to exterminate the rabbits. Since the animals used the burrows of birds for shelter, the effort resulted in only a temporary reduction. However, the finch and the rail were transported to Eastern and Sand islands of the Midways. A few individuals of the teal still remained at Laysan, but the honey-eater and the miller-bird became extinct. It was not until 1924 that another group of scientists succeeded in ridding the island of the rabbits. Latest reports state that vegetation is returning. However, in the meantime, rats, which came ashore from boats stopping at Eastern and Sand islands, wiped out the defenseless rail there, so that it can never be restored to Laysan.

The rail was somewhat of a clown. Six inches long, brown, with darker feathers on top of head and back, and with red eyes, this bird lost its ability to fly, probably because it had no natural enemies and because its food supply was abundant. Describing the habits of the bird, Professor Fisher says: "It is one of the most naive, unsophisticated and wholly unsuspicious birds in the whole avian catalogue. At times it is confiding and familiar in deportment, yet at others holds aloof with some show of reserve. It will occasionally hide behind a bunch of grass, as if afraid, then suddenly come forth with entire change of demeanor and examine the intruder. One can never tell how he will be received by the next rail. Often they scurry away, as if pursued by a *bête noir*, but an insect will stop them in their mad career, and, having partaken of the interruption, they seem to forget their former fright and walk about stretching their necks in a highly inquisitive manner. Their ideas seem to flash by in kaleidoscopic succession and within a minute they make as many false starts as a healthy monkey. One can scarcely imagine more amusing and foolish little birds than these." No one ever again will have the fun of watching this odd little fellow. Through the ignorance and carelessness of man, it has disappeared forever, as many interesting, beautiful creatures already have. Island birds and mammals are especially vulnerable to the destruction of habitat.

Professor Fisher's visit to the island was in 1902, and from his description, one gets the impression that Laysan was a Garden of Eden. He was there in May, when the atoll was brilliant with flowers of many kinds. The birds had no fear of him or the others of his party, coming close to inspect them, and even in some cases allowing themselves to be stroked. The dance of the Laysan albatross gave the party amusement. Professor Fisher's description of it is well worth recording: "Two albatrosses approach each other bowing profoundly. They circle around each other nodding solemnly all the time. Next they fence a little, crossing bills and whetting them together, pecking meanwhile, and dropping stiff little bows. Suddenly one lifts its closed wing and nibbles at the feathers underneath, or, rarely merely turns its head and tucks its bill under its wing. The other bird during this short performance assumes a statuesque pose and either looks mechanically from side to side or snaps its bill loudly. Then the first bird bows once and, pointing its head and beak straight upward, rises on its toes, puffs out its breast, and utters a prolonged nasal groan, the other bird snapping its bill loudly and rapidly at the

The Laysan albatross performs the same amazing dance as the black-footed, during which there is a great deal of bowing, groaning and snapping of bills.

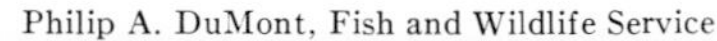
Philip A. DuMont, Fish and Wildlife Service

same time. Sometimes both birds raise their heads and either one or the other utters the indescribable bovine groan. When they have finished, they begin bowing at each other again, and presently repeat the performance . . . but many variations occur. Sometimes three engage in the play, one dividing its attention between two. They are always polite, never losing their temper. The whole affair partakes of the nature of a snappy drill, and is more or less mechanical. If one stands where albatrosses are reasonably abundant, he can see as many as twenty couples hard at work bowing and groaning on all sides. If I walked up to them, they would stop and gaze in a deprecating way, and walk off bowing still, with one eye in my direction. Having reached what they considered a respectful distance, they would fall to and resume their play. Should one enter a group of albatrosses engaged in this diversion and begin to bow very low, the birds would sometimes walk around in a puzzled sort of way, bowing in return."

While the sea-birds continue to come to the islands in somewhat lesser numbers, the tragic fact remains that three species that once lived here have now vanished from the earth forever. To prevent other species from vanishing, not only here but elsewhere in the world, is going to require more than the mere establishment of sanctuaries, the drafting of laws and the employment of wardens. It will require the widest dissemination of information throughout the whole world to win public sympathy for all the wild creatures and an understanding of their needs. The International Union for the Protection of Nature, with headquarters in Brussels, Belgium, is endeavoring to do this.

Paul H. Baldwin, writing about Laysan Island in *Audubon Magazine* for November-December, 1945, said, "Even if we are held from traveling by our life circumstances, the knowledge that Laysan is 'a place of wonders' is enriching and inspiring, whereas the knowledge that such a beauty spot has been despoiled and impoverished through the carelessness of men is disquieting. Though the rail is gone, remote Laysan with its remaining rich seabird life is still valuable to us. Let us take care of it."

An agreement between the Hawaii Board of Commissioners of Agriculture and Forestry and the Fish and Wildlife Service was approved on December 28, 1951, for the joint administration and supervision of this island group. Under the agreement, the Board has undertaken the posting of the lands, using the Fish and Wildlife Service boundary markers. Permits for entry are issued by the Board, while permits for the taking of specimens for scientific purposes continue to be issued by the Service. Conservation officers designated by the Board have been empowered as deputy game management agents. This additional protection for one of our most remote refuges has proved very successful.

The Hawaiian Islands Refuge is not easy to reach, and it is not the intention here to arouse interest in going there, but instead to show how precarious has become the position of rare and wonderful life forms in a world now largely dominated by human beings. Here, in this isolated spot, is a little remnant of the paradise that once was.

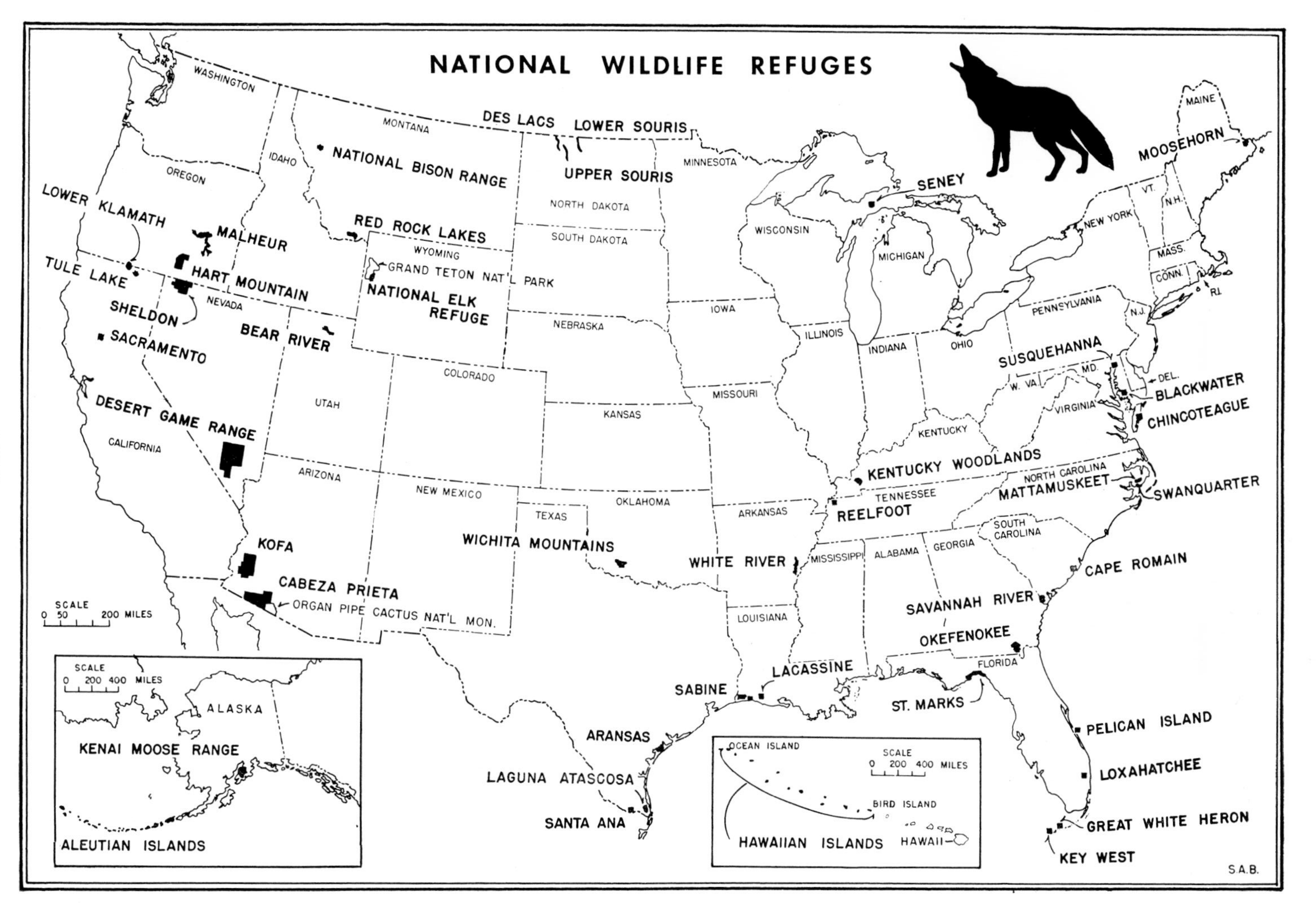

NATIONAL WILDLIFE REFUGES
WASHINGTON
MONTANA
DES LACS
LOWER SOURIS
NATIONAL BISON RANGE
UPPER SOURIS
MINNESOTA
SENEY
MOOSEHORN
MAINE
IDAHO
OREGON
NORTH DAKOTA
LOWER KLAMATH
MALHEUR
RED ROCK LAKES
WYOMING
SOUTH DAKOTA
WISCONSIN
MICHIGAN
NEW YORK
VT.
N.H.
MASS.
CONN.
R.I.
TULE LAKE
HART MOUNTAIN
GRAND TETON NAT'L PARK
NATIONAL ELK REFUGE
NEVADA
SHELDON
SACRAMENTO
BEAR RIVER
NEBRASKA
IOWA
ILLINOIS
INDIANA
OHIO
PENNSYLVANIA
N.J.
SUSQUEHANNA
MD.
DEL.
BLACKWATER
W. VA.
VIRGINIA
CHINCOTEAGUE
COLORADO
UTAH
MISSOURI
KANSAS
DESERT GAME RANGE
CALIFORNIA
KENTUCKY
KENTUCKY WOODLANDS
NORTH CAROLINA
MATTAMUSKEET
SWANQUARTER
ARIZONA
NEW MEXICO
OKLAHOMA
TENNESSEE
REELFOOT
TEXAS
ARKANSAS
SOUTH CAROLINA
WICHITA MOUNTAINS
KOFA
WHITE RIVER
MISSISSIPPI
ALABAMA
GEORGIA
CAPE ROMAIN
CABEZA PRIETA
ORGAN PIPE CACTUS NAT'L MON.
SCALE
0 50 200 MILES
LOUISIANA
SAVANNAH RIVER
OKEFENOKEE
FLORIDA
LACASSINE
SABINE
ST. MARKS
SCALE
0 200 400 MILES
ALASKA
KENAI MOOSE RANGE
ALEUTIAN ISLANDS
ARANSAS
LAGUNA ATASCOSA
SANTA ANA
OCEAN ISLAND
SCALE
0 200 400 MILES
BIRD ISLAND
HAWAIIAN ISLANDS
HAWAII
PELICAN ISLAND
LOXAHATCHEE
GREAT WHITE HERON
KEY WEST
S.A.B.

There can be no real civilization which does not take into account justice to dumb animals. How, so far, has the human race met its duty toward the great creation of dumb creatures committed to its care? It has met it without intelligence, without justice, and without mercy.—ROBERT INGERSOLL.

Sanctuaries and Other Refuges

National Parks

EVERGLADES NATIONAL PARK, established in 1947, is one of our country's foremost bird sanctuaries. Situated on the southern tip of the Florida peninsula, it contains 2342 square miles of marsh dotted in places by hammocks or islands covered with dense jungle growth, upland areas of pine and palm, and salt water fringes of mangroves. The park includes also the shoal waters of Florida Bay with its keys, and part of the Ten Thousand Islands along the west coast. Egrets, herons, ibises, terns, gulls and ducks of several species inhabit the area, in addition to brown pelicans and a wintering colony of white pelicans. Frigate-birds, anhingas, purple and Florida gallinules, chuck-will's-widows, roseate spoonbills, sora rails and a long list of other birds also may be seen in the park. Alligators and various mammals, such as whitetail deer, black bears, skunks, bobcats, raccoons, otters and the rare sea mammal, the manatee, are native to the park. Cougars are present but rare.

Besides its amazing wildlife population, Everglades National Park is a botanist's paradise. Several kinds of palms are native, including the royal, largest and most majestic of the group, the tall, slender-trunked paurotis palm, the silver palm and various palmettos. Here, too, are orchids and a large variety of other flowering plants.

Headquarters is at Homestead, Florida. The park is reached from Miami forty miles south on U. S. Highway 1 to Florida City and west on State Route 205 to the park. The park can be seen by driving along the road to Coot Bay, where there is a restaurant,

The manatee, a water mammal twelve feet long weighing 500 pounds or more, lives in the coastal fringes of Everglades National Park. A photograph of it in a natural setting would be nearly impossible to take, but this museum habitat group shows it admirably.

Chicago Natural History Museum

and where boats are available for going into the various waterways on the west side. It can be enjoyed by joining the tours conducted by the National Audubon Society. The Society takes visitors by station wagon and by boat to see some of the bird concentrations and other important park features. Arrangements may be made by contacting the National Audubon Society, 311 East Flagler Street, Miami 32, Florida. The park is open all year.

GLACIER NATIONAL PARK, in western Montana, on the international border, embraces 1583 square miles of the most spectacular part of the Rocky Mountains, great U-shaped valleys carved by ancient glaciers, innumerable lakes and a magnificent forest of conifers, especially on the west side of the continental divide, which runs through the park. Glacier, important as a wildlife sanctuary, is the home of elk, whitetail, blacktail and mule deer, moose, bighorns, mountain goats, black and grizzly bears, bobcats, mountain lions, coyotes and a long list of smaller mammals and many birds.

The park is one of the last strongholds of both the grizzly bear and the mountain

The mountain lion, magnificent American cat, is the embodiment of wilderness.

Plummer, courtesy Texas Game and Fish Commission

lion. Where the lion occurs in national parks—Big Bend, Sequoia, Kings Canyon and Zion—it is given strict protection. Elsewhere, it is still being hunted down and killed. It also survives in some of the wilderness areas of the national forests of the West, but is not protected there. The animal's original range extended throughout much of North America from southern Canada to Florida and Mexico, south to southern Argentina in South America. A person fortunate enough to see a mountain lion in the wild may well count it a red-letter day. It is wary of man, as well it might be, under his constant persecution. From the time the white man came to the western hemisphere, he was determined not to get along with this handsome cat, and he set at once to the task of killing it wherever it lived. There have been but few reports of the mountain lion attacking and killing man, but livestock interests have been so vociferous about mountain lion depredations, real or supposed, on sheep and cattle, that men have been employed to hunt it with hounds.

The man who takes a mountain lion by setting a pack of hounds after it has performed no feat of courage or shown unusual intelligence. Indeed, to shoot a mountain lion treed by hounds hardly seems worthy of praise. Yet mountain lion hunters proudly pose with their kill and have their pictures published for all to see. To take the life of any wild creature, whether out of necessity or for amusement, is remorseful, and not an action to brag about.

The mountain lion is invaluable as a control to deer and elk populations. Where it has been extirpated, deer and elk always have caused serious problems as, for instance, in the case of the elk herds of Yellowstone National Park and the deer of the Kaibab National Forest, where few lions remain. As a handsome and extremely interesting member of our North American fauna, it deserves consideration and a more sympathetic attitude toward it on the part of man. The wilderness whose trails no longer bear the footprints of the mountain lion has lost much.

Glacier National Park headquarters is at West Glacier, Montana. The park is reached by the trains of the Great Northern Railway, which make two stops at the park—one at East Glacier Station and the other at West Glacier Station. Visitors may take Glacier Park Transport Company buses from either station and make the trip by the scenic Going-to-the-Sun Highway over Logan Pass, returning to the railroad again at the other station. The park is reached by road from the east over U. S. Highway 89 from Great Falls, Montana, and from the west over U. S. Highway 2 from Kalispell, Montana. Motorists can drive north along the park's east side over the Blackfeet Highway to the Canadian border and visit the adjoining Waterton Lakes National Park, in Alberta.

MOUNT MCKINLEY NATIONAL PARK, in south central Alaska, is an area of rolling tundra hills and glacier-fed rivers, with the majestic Alaska Range rising along the park's south side. Mount McKinley, the highest mountain in North America, is 20,300 feet above sea level. It forms a snowy backdrop for most of the park landscapes. The area is 3030 square miles in extent, and provides sanctuary for many mammals. Among these are the barren-ground caribou and the wolf. Other park mammals are the Dall sheep, moose, Toklat grizzly bear, the rare wolverine, red fox, marmot, parka squirrel, cony, porcupine, lynx, mink, marten, beaver and coyote. The bird population includes a number of waterfowl, golden and bald eagles, little brown cranes, Pacific golden plovers, wandering tattlers, long-tailed jaegers, snowy owls, Arctic terns, Bohemian waxwings and Arctic three-toed woodpeckers.

The barren-ground caribou, which once roamed over much of Alaska in herds of untold thousands, living mostly on ground-growing lichens, has been greatly reduced by shooting. Descriptions of the caribou herds in migration, by eye-witnesses, are nearly unbelievable.

Dr. Olaus J. Murie made a study of the caribou for the U. S. Biological Survey (now the U. S. Fish and Wildlife Service), and in his report, *Alaska-Yukon Caribou,* 1935, he says that he never saw one of the vast herds often mentioned by other observers, but

Adolph Murie

he tells about witnessing "an extensive movement on the hills at the divide between Twelve-mile Creek and McManus Creek in the region between Fairbanks and Circle. Long single files of animals were winding through a little valley, up to a hill top, across a saddle, and onward to another hill, which was so speckled with caribou as to present the appearance of a snowy slope covered with a scattered stand of stunted black spruce.

The gray wolf, above, exists today only in a few large wilderness regions, principally in Canada and Alaska, including Mount McKinley National Park, where it is protected. A creature of highest intelligence, it provides an unforgettable thrill for one fortunate enough to see it. Let us make certain it never wanders down the fading trail to oblivion. The handsome animal shown was raised in captivity. At left is the cony, smaller than a cottontail rabbit. It lives in the mountain talus slopes of Mount McKinley, Glacier and Yellowstone national parks.

Fred M. Packard

The animals counted numbered 2500, and it was estimated that there were in all about 3000, for others were coming from behind the mountains." Dr. Murie says, "It is common to hear of 'whole hillsides moving with caribou,' or of a herd 'passing for hours.'" He says that the Yukon-Tanana herd was by far the largest included in his study, and he states that the animals in Alaska and Yukon Territory together might number anywhere from one to two millions.

Such accounts remind one of the descriptions of the millions of bison that once swarmed across our western plains. Is the caribou facing a fate similar to that of the bison? Formerly, caribou occupied most of Alaska, but today their main concentration is in the east central section of the state. Already the country along the Bering Sea coast knows them no more, for herds of reindeer imported from Asia for commercial purposes have taken over this region. Says Dr. Murie: "The caribou's greatest menace is not the wolf, nor the hunter, but man's economic developments." And he adds, "Caribou require much territory. A serious decrease in numbers should be guarded against as Alaska becomes more thickly settled and many of its frontier conditions pass."

Although the caribou migrates through parts of Mount McKinley National Park, the herds sometimes seen here wander beyond the safety of park boundaries. There is a

A caribou calf.

Jim D. Rearden, courtesy The Alaska Sportsman

Olaus J. Murie

Millions of caribou once thrived in the Alaska wilds, but the reindeer introduced from Asia for economic reasons, has already taken over much caribou habitat.

very real need for wider protection being given this large interesting member of the deer tribe before it is too late.

In some respects, the wolf as a species is in a worse plight than the caribou. Mount McKinley is almost the only National Park Service area in which the wolf survives today. The history of the wolf on our continent is a story of continuous effort to exterminate it with poison, trap and gun. So successful has this effort been, that the gray wolf probably exists today in no more than two places south of the Canadian border, one of them the roadless area of the Superior National Forest, Minnesota. Occasionally an animal may stray into Glacier National Park from the wilderness of the Canadian Rockies. Protection of the wolf in Mount McKinley is in accord with the excellent national policy that all native wildlife shall be given strict protection in the national parks and monuments. Those who enjoy all wild creatures for their own sakes, have regarded Mount McKinley National Park as most important in preserving this species. In spite of national park policy, gunning interests have sought to have the Park Service shoot every wolf in the area. The esthetic value of this animal—which so thoroughly typifies the wilderness—is inestimable. Park visitors who have been fortunate enough to see this intelligent creature running free and wild have derived a thrill that almost no

Caribou travel in herds of hundreds in search of the lichens on which they feed, and rivers are no obstacle to them, as shown by the scene below.

Courtesy Nature Magazine

other animal can give. Tales to the contrary, there is no authentic record of the wolf attacking a human being in North America.

Dr. Adolph Murie, former biologist, Fish and Wildlife Service, made a study of the wolves in the park, and afterwards wrote *The Wolves of Mount McKinley*. A condensed version of this book, omitting its more scientific phases, was published in *The Living Wilderness*, The Wilderness Society, Washington, D. C. Dr. Murie discovered a wolf den, and he spent days and nights on a slope across the valley opposite to it, watching the home life of the animals. As with people, each wolf, he found, had its own characteristic habits. Fur coloration differed with individuals, so that Dr. Murie was able to distinguish one wolf from another wherever he saw them. He watched the pups at play; saw the adults coming from and leaving for the hunt; watched them chasing caribou and singling out an animal for food; and he observed them in their relationships to the other animals of the park, such as the Dall sheep, fox and grizzly bear.

Describing an instance of activity preliminary to going on a hunt, Dr. Murie says, "Considerable ceremony often precedes the departure. Usually there is a general get-together and much tail wagging. On May 31, I left the lookout at 8:30 P. M., since the wolves seemed, after some indications of departure, to have settled down again. But as I looked back from the river bar on my way to camp, I saw the two blacks and the two gray males assembled on the skyline, wagging their tails and frisking together. There they all howled, and while they howled, the gray female galloped up from the den a hundred yards and joined them. She was greeted with energetic tail wagging and general good feeling. Then the vigorous actions came to an end, and five muzzles pointed skyward. Their howling floated softly across the tundra. Then abruptly the assemblage broke up. The mother returned to the den to assume her vigilance, and four wolves trotted eastward into the dusk."

As a member of the fauna of North America, having one of the noblest places in the literature and traditions of our country, the wolf deserves all the protection we can give it in Mount McKinley National Park and wherever else it exists.

Headquarters is in the park, and the address is McKinley Park, Alaska. The park is reached by the Alaska Railroad, 348 miles from Seward on the south coast, and from Fairbanks, 123 miles. By road it is reached from Paxson, on the Richardson Highway, west 156 miles over the Denali Highway to Cantwell and north twenty-seven miles to the park. Campgrounds and a hotel are open from June 1 to September 15.

OLYMPIC NATIONAL PARK, in the far northwest corner of the United States, on Washington's Olympic Peninsula, contains a range of mountains rising 7923 feet above sea level, with an unblemished forest of conifers covering the lower slopes. The highest peaks are streaked with glaciers and gleaming snowfields all year; but the most important feature of the park—one that distinguishes it from all other national parks—is the dense evergreen rain forest on the west side of the Olympic Mountains. Grown in deep moss and dripping with rain most of the year, the trees of this forest reach heights of 200 feet and over, with the Sitka spruces usually the largest, and the western hemlocks attaining almost equally impressive size. Part of the area became a national monument in 1909, but in 1938, with boundaries extended, it was designated a national park. It is an almost roadless wilderness of 1321 square miles.

Mammals of Olympic include blacktail and whitetail deer, black bears, bobcats, snowshoe rabbits and beavers. The high moist meadows are the home of the mountain beaver, a small, dark brown rodent that looks more like a gopher than a beaver. Probably it was given this name because it sometimes cuts down trees. The trees it cuts, however, are usually small saplings. For a den, it digs a burrow and a system of tunnels.

Mountain lions exist in the park, but are rare. There are also a few of the white mountain goats in the high alpine country; but the largest mammal of Olympic is the Roosevelt elk. Darker and even larger than the more abundant Rocky Mountain elk, this

The author

A herd of the Roosevelt elk lives in Olympic National Park, and smaller herds are being preserved in a few other areas.

species originally ranged through the rainy coastal belt from Vancouver Island, in British Columbia, to northern California. It spends the summer in the grassy meadows at or above tree line, and in autumn it comes down along forest trails to the low valleys, returning to the high country again in spring. In primitive times, mountain lions, as well as wolves, served to keep the elk population from becoming too abundant. Today, with no wolves and but few mountain lions to do this important job, the elk are showing indications of becoming too numerous here, and when they migrate beyond park boundaries they are shot by gunners during an annual open season. The Walt Disney film *The Olympic Elk*, one of the *True Life Adventure Series*, has made these animals famous.

Several smaller herds of the Roosevelt elk can be seen, notably at California's Prairie Creek State Park, near Orick.

Olympic headquarters is in the park, and the address is Port Angeles, Washington. The area is reached over U. S. Highway 101, which encircles the park. The park is open all year.

YELLOWSTONE NATIONAL PARK is one of our country's foremost mammal sanctuaries. Situated at a high elevation in the Rocky Mountains of northwestern Wyoming, with parts of its borders extending into Montana and Idaho, the park is 3472 square miles in area. It is the home of black and grizzly bears, bison, antelopes, bighorn sheep, elk, coyotes, mule deer, moose, martens, fishers, otters and many smaller mammals. Famous for its geysers and brilliantly colored thermal pools and the magnificently scenic Canyon of the Yellowstone River, with the Upper and Lower falls, this park is a true remnant of the once primeval continent. Much of the area shows the result of titanic volcanic forces active centuries ago. Its plateaus and mountains are covered with forests of conifers interspersed with wide areas of grassland and the beautiful fragrant gray-green sage. Lakes of the park are the habitat of the rare trumpeter swans, which are also found in the Red Rock Lakes National Wildlife Refuge just a few miles west, in Montana. (See Red Rock Lakes Migratory Waterfowl Refuge.) In summer, an island in Yellowstone Lake is the habitat of a breeding colony of white pelicans.

The grizzly bear once lived in certain mountains of the Southwest, in the Sierra Nevada of California, the Cascade Mountains of Oregon and Washington and in the Rocky Mountains from Montana south to southern Colorado and northern New Mexico. In our country it now survives only in a few spots in the Rocky Mountains. These are principally Glacier, Yellowstone and rarely Grand Teton national parks, and in parts of the national forest wilderness areas of Idaho and western Montana. A few grizzlies are surviving in the Rio Grande Grizzly Bear Management Area, situated partly in the Upper Rio Grande Wild Area of the Rio Grande National Forest and partly in the San Juan Wilderness Area of the San Juan National Forest, in southwestern Colorado. This area is closed to the killing of bears under a regulation adopted in May, 1954,

The pine marten, an attractive furbearer, is trapped throughout its range in northern conifer forests and the high mountains of the West, but is protected in Yellowstone and other western national parks.

Bob Casebeer, Montana Fish and Game Commission

National Park Service

Over almost all of its original range in the rugged mountainous regions of the West, the grizzly bear has been extirpated, so that today it can be seen only in Yellowstone, Grand Teton and Glacier national parks, and in two or three national forests.

by the Colorado Game and Fish Commission. It is enforced by rangers of the U. S. Forest Service and by wardens of the Game and Fish Commission. The area is in the heart of a wilderness, and is accessible by trail only.

Its shoulder hump, much larger size and the grizzled coloring of its coat help to distinguish the grizzly from the much more abundant black bear. While the black bear is an agile tree climber, the big grizzly almost never climbs. Its great size and strength make it king of the wilderness, for it has no creature to fear but man. Visitors to the national parks in which this fine animal lives, would do well to avoid making any attempts toward friendliness, the best policy being to keep a safe distance and mind one's own business. If provoked or startled, the grizzly may attack.

To permit the grizzly bear to vanish from the few wilderness spots of our country where it still may be seen, would be unnecessary and tragic. One of the truly magnificent creatures of North America, it has immeasurable esthetic value. This value was expressed by Sigurd F. Olson, President of the National Parks Association, in a talk before the 1954 National Convention of the Izaak Walton League of America: "We were riding through a dense stand of spruce in the bottom of a canyon. I got off my horse to lead it around a windfall, and there in the center of the trail I saw the track of a grizzly. We never did see the bear, although we found where it had scratched great marks in the bark of a spruce as high as it could reach. From that moment on the country changed. It was the land of mountain men of another century, the country of Lewis and Clark, part of the old West. Those grizzly signs belonged to the intangibles."

Yellowstone headquarters is in the park, and the address is Yellowstone Park, Wyoming. The park is reached south from Livingston, Montana, over U. S. Highway 89, and north from Jackson, Wyoming, over the same highway by way of Grand Teton National Park; from Cody on the east, it is reached over U. S. Highway 20, and from Idaho Falls, Idaho, on the west over U. S. Highway 191. The park is open from May 15 to October 15.

The beautiful tassel-eared Abert squirrel is protected in several national parks and monuments from northern Colorado to New Mexico and west to northern Arizona. It is large and conspicuous in the open ponderosa pine forests where it lives.

Much more rare than the Abert is the Kaibab squirrel, also a tassel-eared species. It is confined to the Kaibab Plateau bordering the north rim of Grand Canyon. Dark of body, the most noticeable feature of this squirrel is its snowy white tail.

Photographs by
Joseph S. Dixon

THE FIRST of our national parks was Yellowstone. It was established by Act of Congress, in 1872, after the Washburn Expedition, sent to explore the area, in 1870, had made a report to Congress recommending the entire area be set aside as a national park.

That Congress followed this advice was one of the most constructive moves that our federal legislators ever made, as far as the protection of wildlife in our country is concerned. It set a precedent and a pattern for the preservation of wildlife and wilderness areas that was to spread all across our country and our territories. Had Congress failed to do this, many mammals and birds that today are making their last stand principally in the national parks, might long ago have vanished from our land.

As wildlife sanctuaries, the national parks—twenty-six of them—are of utmost importance. They preserve some of the most superb primeval wildlife habitat on the continent. In regard to wildlife, National Park Service policy allows nature to take its course. It might be termed a policy of "hands off." Only in rare instances does the Service interfere, such as when a species may require help to survive, or when one species becomes overabundant to the detriment of itself and other species.

Besides the national parks, there are thirty-six national nature monuments, also in the care of the National Park Service, which are under inviolate protection and serve as wildlife sanctuaries. Such areas as the beautiful Chiricahua, Saguaro and Organ Pipe Cactus monuments in southern Arizona, and Joshua Tree, Death Valley, Pinnacles and Muir Woods in California, protect many kinds of native birds and mammals. Most of the monuments are highly scenic and contain superb botanical exhibits. Dinosaur National Monument, in Utah and Colorado, is one of the largest and finest of our monument areas. In 1955, the Bureau of Reclamation attempted to have Congress authorize construction of the Echo Park and Split Mountain dams in this area. The dams were only two of approximately thirty units proposed for construction in the Upper Colorado Water Storage project. If such engineering works should be permitted here, they would not only ruin the primitive landscapes and habitats for the protection of which the monument was established, but would constitute a threat to the entire national park and monument system. Similar threats have occurred to various parks before, but the Dinosaur dam proposal resulted in the bitterest struggle between park defenders and the commercial forces of destruction that has occurred in the whole history of the nature protection movement in the United States. The integrity of our national parks and monuments must never be violated, for as soon as this happens there will begin the deterioration of the system to the common level of other commercially used lands, and their value to wildlife will be reduced or lost.

State Parks and State Refuges

Almost every state has a system of parks, and many of these are large enough and wild enough to contribute importantly to the protection of birds and mammals. California stands in the lead in the state park field, for not only are many of her parks large in area, but they are numerous and contain a great variety of country. The Anza Desert State Park, located west of Salton Sea, is a vast desert region; while contrasting with it are the cool, moist redwood parks in the northern part of the state. Prairie Creek State Park, one of these, is noted not only for its giant redwood trees, but also for its herd of Roosevelt elk. The animals often can be seen in the open meadows by motorists driving over U. S. Highway 101, north of Orick and south of Klamath. Here the highway runs across the park's rich meadowland hemmed in by the towering walls of the forest.

Minnesota's Itasca State Park is a large wooded area with lakes and streams—the headwaters of the Mississippi River. Custer State Park in South Dakota is notable for its herds of bison, elk and antelope. New York has establshed a number of excellent areas, foremost being the Adirondack and Catskill parks. These are mountainous and heavily forested, and provide habitat for deer and most of the smaller mammals, upland birds and songbirds native to this part of the country. The New England States, particularly Maine, New Hampshire, Vermont and Massachusetts, have good state park systems, as have the Carolinas, Maryland, Virginia, Florida and Texas.

In addition to their parks, most of the states have extensive systems of wildlife refuges, totalling many hundreds of areas. As early as 1870, California established Lake Merritt at Alameda as a refuge. Indiana probably came next in establishing a refuge, 1903, the same year in which the national refuge system was begun. By far the greater number of state refuges exist for the purpose of maintaining a supply of birds and mammals for the pleasure of the gunner. Even so, the habitats thus protected and managed are helping to preserve not only the hunted species, both migrant and permanent residents, but also songbirds and others. Perhaps the most peculiar feature of the state refuge systems is that almost all of them are financed with funds derived from the sale of hunting and fishing licenses. This means that if the wildlife is to be protected, it must be subjected to killing.

A few of the hundreds of state refuges are Pennsylvania's Pymatuning Lake, Indiana's restored Kankakee Marsh, Iowa's Rice Lake and Round Lake and Illinois' Horseshoe Lake, for waterfowl, and New York's North Pharsalia and Idaho's Payette, for deer and other mammals.

In National Forests

CONDOR REFUGE, also known as the Sespe Wildlife Preserve, is a rugged mountain area of fifty-four and a half square miles situated in the Los Padres National Forest, in southern California. Densely covered with various chaparral species of shrubs and trees, including canyon live oak and ponderosa pine in the canyons, it was established in 1947 through an order of the chief forester, U. S. Forest Service, to protect the foremost nesting and roosting habitat of the rare California condor. In 1951, oil and gas operations in the area were restricted through a public land order of the Secretary of the Interior.

The condor, which is a vulture, has a wingspread measuring up to nine and a half feet, the largest of all the birds of North America. The adult condor is recognizable in flight by its black plumage and white patches on the under sides of the wings. The patches are widest near the body, tapering toward the tips of the wings. As with other vultures, the head and neck are without feathers, the skin of the condor's head being orange or yellow, grading to gray on the neck, with patches of red and purple. Immature birds have less white under the wings, and the head and neck are gray.

The thrill of seeing one of these birds can hardly be overestimated, and every nature enthusiast harbors the hope that during his lifetime he may be afforded at least one glimpse of a wild condor in flight. Flocks of them have been seen, and one observer reported seeing forty-three at once on the Tejon Ranch, in 1947.

The California condor, a vulture with wingspread up to nine and a half feet, is the largest bird of North America. White markings on the under sides of the wings identify it. In primitive times these magnificent creatures ranged over a wider area than they do today, for then there were many more of them, and nesting grounds were more numerous. The estimated four or five dozen surviving individuals are strictly protected now on their only breeding ground.

Allan D. Cruickshank,
courtesy Nature Magazine

Carl B. Koford, from Nat'l Audubon Society

What bird enthusiast has not dreamed of someday seeing a California condor soaring over its native wilderness?

Some soaring species, such as the bald eagle and the white pelican, ascend to the limit of human vision. It is interesting to speculate on the heights to which a condor will soar. Carl B. Koford, who made a three-year study of the life and habits of the condor at the refuge, and afterwards wrote *The California Condor,* Research Report No. 4, of the National Audubon Society, 1953, believes the condor does not go higher than 10,000 feet above sea level; but high altitudes probably are reached only while soaring above mountains. Mr. Koford makes a number of comments concerning the flight of the condor. He says that he believes the birds can soar for more than an hour without flapping, and says he has seen them glide in a straight line for eight minutes, alternating the long straight glides with periods of circling to gain altitude. The soaring of the condor, he says, produces a steady hissing whistle, probably caused by the emarginated primary wing feathers. The sound is sometimes audible from as far away as a hundred yards. He states that many of the contour feathers are constantly fluttering while the bird soars.

The dominance of one bird over another is shown in a number of ways, one of which is by chasing. Koford has observed pursuit flights taking place throughout the year at the roosting sites, and most frequently on days of high wind. He says, "The usual behavior in a chase is for one condor to overtake another by fast flex-gliding (with wings arched and flexed). The pursued bird dives downward, twisting from side to side, flapping at the end of the swoop as if to gain every possible inch of altitude. Then the birds soar peaceably, or the attack is repeated. In only three or four of more than a hundred observations did the pursuer appear to touch the pursued bird. Often the chase continued for eight or nine minutes and extended over a distance of more than one mile." Koford adds that on occasions the glide toward the pursued bird may begin from as far as half a mile away. An attacking bird, he says, sometimes turns on its side at the start of a dive. The dive he describes as producing a distinctive roar like the sound of escaping steam. Koford has estimated the average flight speed at about thirty miles an hour. Of course, this would vary greatly depending on the direction of flight in relation to the direction and velocity of the wind. Another interesting observation by Koford is that condors can fly in fog. He says, "Many times I have seen them soaring through the edges of broken fog or circling and rising up out of sight into the base of a cloud."

Condors live on the flesh of dead animals, and there is no record of one making an attack on a live animal. Concerning the condor-golden eagle relationship, he says that repeatedly one or two eagles will defend their right to feed on a carcass, swiftly chasing off a condor that dared to approach too close.

About the food supply of the condor, Koford expresses the opinion that in primeval times the birds fed on the carcasses of wild animals, including sea mammals and fish that washed up along the ocean shore. In the early 1800's, with the rise of the California missions, vast herds of cattle were introduced and were allowed to graze over wide areas. This produced food for the condors. An era of large ranches followed the decline of the missions, and there continued to be an abundance of food on the range. After 1870, sheep began to take the place of cattle in some areas, and these also provided the condor with plenty of food. In recent years, however, the cultivation of land for crops, and scientific methods of livestock raising have reduced livestock mortality on the range. Koford believes that this, together with shooting, egg collecting and molestation, may have been an important factor in bringing about the present restricted distribution and scarcity of the birds.

Koford found that condors probably do not breed until they are five years old, and that they raise only one chick about every other year. So low a breeding potential is another factor against condor survival as a species, and it only serves to emphasize the necessity of giving the bird the greatest possible care and consideration. In the vicinity of their nesting and roosting areas, the birds are extremely sensitive to disturb-

Carl B. Koford

The Condor Refuge is a rugged mountain area in Los Padres National Forest. It is difficult of access and should remain so for the sake of the birds.

ance by man. Blasting or the noise of road-building machinery a mile away will disturb them. Koford states that one man can keep parent birds away from their nest all night or prevent the feeding of the chick for an entire day merely by allowing himself to be seen within 500 yards of the nest for only a few minutes once or twice a day. To avoid such disturbance, nests should not be approached closer than half a mile.

Because of the serious plight of the species, probably no one should be permitted to enter the nesting and roosting areas of the refuge, even to photograph the birds. There are already excellent photographs of condors in black and white and in color, as well as in moving pictures, and under present circumstances there should be no necessity for taking more.

Today the California condor is in serious danger of becoming extinct. One of the rarest birds in our country, its population consists of not over sixty individuals. Its breeding range in primeval times may have covered a wider area than it did when first recorded in the early part of the 19th century, for condor bones have been discovered as far east as Brewster County, Texas, and in New Mexico, Arizona and Nevada. Although in the early 1800's, nesting condors were seen as far north as Monterey Bay, the present range centers in Ventura and Santa Barbara counties. How many more years the condor will survive cannot be told, but no effort should seem too great to preserve it and to help it increase in numbers. Alden H. Miller, Professor of Zoology and Director of the Museum of Vertebrate Zoology, University of California, in the preface to *The California Condor*, says, "Man will certainly fail to save the California condor unless he tries to save it, and the trying is eminently worth while as anyone with even the most rudimentary appreciation of nature will agree who has actually watched wild condors living in their native mountains."

The refuge, which is under the protection and administration of the U. S. Forest Service, eventually should provide maximum benefit to the condors. Under the public land order of the Secretary of the Interior, January 16, 1951, a sixteen square mile area was withdrawn from surface entry. The withdrawal recognizes all valid existing rights by issuing permits for the use and occupancy of the land to holders of valid oil and gas leases acquired prior to January 16, 1951. Outside the sixteen square mile withdrawal, but inside the exterior boundaries of the refuge, regulations are even more lax. Here, permits for use and occupancy are issued to holders of oil and gas leases, applicants or assignments, and their authorized employees and agents, upon submission of reasonable evidence of their holdings or employment by those with holdings, and to geologists, oil prospectors, engineers or surveyors engaged in actual survey or exploratory work. All permits, except those relating to leases issued prior to January 16, 1951, contain the restriction that there shall be no use or entry within a half mile of a condor nesting site active within three years. Permits are issued also to authorized water and flood control employees for official work, and to holders of valid mining claims, and cattle grazing is being continued by former permittees. Fishing is allowed along certain streams in the area, but gunning and trapping are not allowed, except on the private inholdings, where the order does not apply. No permits are issued for camping, riding and hiking.

One need not enter the refuge in order to see the condors. The birds often range up to fifty miles and more in a single day, and they can be seen from vantage points along various mountain ranges and in a number of valleys that are easily accessible. One should not expect, perhaps, to see a condor every day, but a careful observer at a favorable location should not have to wait too long to be rewarded.

The Forest Service has suggested that the refuge be studied to determine whether there are suitable locations along its borders where visitor observation points might be established. Such observation spots, if limited and carefully placed, might be desirable. A location or two, where the public could observe condors coming from and returning to their refuge might provide one of the most thrilling wildlife exhibits in our country. The Forest Service is directing visitors to Thorn Point Lookout reached by road and trail northeast of Ojai, and to Whitaker Peak Lookout reached over a low-standard road west from U. S. Highway 99, about ten miles north of Castiac.

There are other locations outside the refuge, from which condors may be seen. One is the summit of Pine Mountain, reached north from Ojai thirty-four miles on U. S. Highway 399. Another spot is Bear Mountain, reached south from Bakersfield on U. S. Highway 99 ten miles to a road left. Follow this road beyond Arvin to a location near the mountain. The birds may sometimes be seen flying in this vicinity. Olin S. Pettingill, Jr., in his *A Guide to Bird Finding West of the Mississippi* says that condors may occasionally be seen flying across U. S. Highway 99 between Lebec and Gorman. Mount Pinus, west of Lebec, is also a likely location.

A refuge advisory committee composed of three members—the president of the National Audubon Society, the director of the Museum of Vertebrate Zoology, at the University of California, and the assistant regional forester, U. S. Forest Service, in charge of wildlife management, advises the supervisor of Los Padres National Forest, Santa Barbara, on policy matters pertaining to the management of the refuge. The Forest Service and the National Audubon Society are financing a patrolman for a period of eight months every year. The most interesting and informative material on the condor is the above-named report, *The California Condor*. Priced at $3, it is obtained from the National Audubon Society, 1130 Fifth Avenue, New York 28, N. Y. Information about the refuge is available from the Supervisor, Los Padres National Forest, U. S. Forest Service, Santa Barbara, California.

Private Sanctuaries

HAWK MOUNTAIN SANCTUARY is located in eastern Pennsylvania, on a spur of the Kittatiny Ridge, just north of Reading and west of Allentown. The sanctuary was established in 1934 to give protection to migrating hawks and eagles. It is a little over two square miles in extent, and is administered by the Board of Directors of Hawk Mountain Sanctuary Association, a Pennsylvania corporation, with an office in New York City.

The Lookout is the sanctuary's focal point. This is a high promontory on the ridge, 1540 feet above sea level, and a thousand feet above the cultivated valleys on each side. It affords sweeping views to the west, north and east. Directly below the Lookout, the ridge drops abruptly to form a saddle, beyond which it rises again in a picturesque mountain profile. The ridge is densely forested with hardwoods, stunted along the crest, and gay in spring with the blooms of laurel, azalea, dogwood and rhododendron.

Hawks and eagles on autumn migration fly above the slopes and summits of mountains and ridges, to be buoyed aloft by warm air currents that drift up the slopes and rise into the sky. The Appalachian ridges serve the hawks ideally, and they follow these ridges for hundreds of miles in their southward journey. The hawk flights are a wonder

A female marsh hawk soars above the Lookout on its autumn journey.

Enoch Reindall,
courtesy Nature Magazine

Maurice Broun

From the Lookout there are wide views across the forests and farms of Pennsylvania.

of nature. As expressed by Mrs. C. N. Edge, founder of the sanctuary, "They are to the eye as music to the ear." The fame of the hawk flights has now spread so widely, that thousands of people come to Hawk Mountain every year to enjoy them. The rocky outcrop at the Lookout on any bright autumn day is like a grandstand loaded with enthusiastic spectators, who bring with them binoculars and cameras.

But it has not always been like this at Hawk Mountain. Among farmers and "sportsmen" hawks are regarded all too often as "vermin." Until 1934, the Lookout, in autumn, was the *rendezvous* of men armed with pump guns, automatics and double-barreled shotguns. For years they knew about the hawk flights. Richard H. Pough and Henry H. Collins, energetic workers in the nature protection field, were the first ones to learn about the "hawk-shoots" on the Kittatiny Ridge, and they came to Hawk Mountain, then known as Blue Mountain, to investigate. Soon afterwards, writing in *Bird Lore* (now *Audubon Magazine*), Pough said, "On top of Blue Mountain above Drehersville, Schuylkill County, an appalling slaughter is going on. . . . First the broadwings in September, and out of this flight I would say sixty were shot. Then came the sharp-shins and Cooper's hawks—thousands of these were killed. The enclosed photographs show 218 birds picked up in about an hour last Sunday morning at one stand. Among others I have found five ospreys, a protected bird, of course, but one that will be shot every time, along with eagles, sparrow hawks, flickers, blue jays, so long as hawk-shooting of this sort is

Allan D. Cruickshank, from Nat'l Audubon Society

An osprey glides past in the parade of hawks.

permitted . . . The birds are seldom retrieved, and I have found many wounded birds, some alive after several days."

It was not until the summer of 1934 that progress toward sanctuary establishment began. Mrs. Edge, Chairman of the militant Emergency Conservation Committee, had become aroused, leased the property on Blue Mountain, and later purchased it. She then engaged Maurice Broun to serve as warden, but without a salary at first, for there were no funds available at that time. Mr. Broun and his enthusiastic wife, Irma, took over; and the story of their experiences during the early years at the sanctuary are told by Mr. Broun in his thrilling book, *Hawks Aloft*.

Regarding the first few years of the sanctuary's history, Mrs. Edge, writing in the July-September 1950 issue of *National Parks Magazine*, said: "Our first contacts on the mountain had been with contentious and ignorant people—men, women too, arriving with guns, sullen because of the end put to their cruel 'sport.' It was, therefore, a pleasant surprise when friendly guests enthusiastically adopted Hawk Mountain for their own. They would sit (and through the years they continue to sit) enthralled with the spectacle of the birds. They confirmed our assertion that golden eagles, previously supposed to be birds of our West only, migrated past Hawk Mountain. They saw for the first time in their lives some rare hawk, the goshawk, perhaps, or, the more fortunate observers, the gyrfalcon. They studied, they compared notes.

"The whole aspect of Hawk Mountain had changed. The talk was of binoculars and cameras, not of guns; pride was in the identification of species, not in destruction. Many of the gunners sat among these, and numbers of them found the new visitors more interesting than the old group, and made friends among them. No preaching is done at Hawk Mountain. It is, 'judge for yourself.' Thus, many a man has learned that he gets a far greater thrill in watching the swift, smooth course of the eagle, or the dramatic dive of the falcon, than he ever had in the sighting of a mere flying target, ending in a mess of bloody feathers."

A tense moment at the Lookout, when all eyes are on a soaring hawk.

Charles E. Mohr

Hugh M. Halliday
from Nat'l
Audubon Society

For the beginner in bird study, hawks are difficult to identify, but the freedom and superb flight of these large birds are inspiring to watch. The goshawk is one of the accipiters, a group having rapid flight, swift wing-beats and long tails.

The red-tailed hawk, here eating a mouse, is one of the buteos, the large soaring hawks with broad wings and broad rounded tails. The rust red of this hawk's fan-like tail makes its identity certain.

Don Woodbridge
from Nat'l
Audubon Society

S. A. Grimes
from Nat'l
Audubon Society

Hawk Mountain protects not only migrating hawks, but gives sanctuary to all wildlife within its borders, including the pileated woodpecker, which is as large as a crow, and a year-round resident.

Among the songbirds that come to the sanctuary in spring is the scarlet tanager, with dazzling red body and black wings and tail. Other tanagers that migrate to our country from tropic lands are the Cooper's, summer, hepatic and western.

Allan D. Cruickshank
from Nat'l
Audubon Society

Charles W. Schwartz

No one in tune with nature could count it beneficial to destroy a red-tailed hawk.

The thousands of people who visit Hawk Mountain are slowly having an effect on the attitude of the Pennsylvania Game Commission, which, like almost every state division of wildlife, is sympathetic principally to the whims of the gunning fraternity. Much remains to be done for the protection of hawks by the commission, concerning which, Mrs. Edge says: "We regret to say that the laws protecting Pennsylvania's hawks, while decorating handsomely the statute books, have done little to save the hawks. Lawless shooting continues on other ridges, and we have yet to hear of an arrest for shooting a protected species. But within the commission are fine technicians who know the harm that is being done, and who are using their influence for good. The head of the Game Commission promised us that 'the entire hawk problem is going to be discussed carefully . . . with the hope of reaching some decision that will be the right thing to do.'"

The hostility of gunners and farmers toward hawks, as well as toward owls and certain mammals such as skunks and foxes, is largely the result of ignorance and prejudice handed down from generation to generation. Scientific study carried on for many years has shown conclusively that these species eat rodents and insects to an extent that far outweighs any harm they do in taking an occasional chicken. Mice, rats and grasshoppers are enemies of the farmer, and hawks and owls work night and day to rid farms and barnyards of these pests; yet at sight of a handsome hawk or owl, the farmer's first thought is to run for his gun.

"Sportsmen" are awakening to the realization that hawks weed out the weak and unhealthy individuals from among the so-called "game" birds, thus maintaining the vigor of the species.

Hawk Mountain Sanctuary can be enjoyed at all times of the year. The author

On summer evenings the voice of the whip-poor-will sounds from the sanctuary's woodlands.

Charles W. Schwartz, courtesy Nature Magazine

Robert L. Coffin, courtesy Mass. Audubon Society

The peregrine and other falcons have long, pointed wings, are swift, and soar only for short periods. They are smaller than the buteos.

has seen the hawks and eagles flying past under a brilliant autumn sky, and he has visited the area in late spring, when the songbirds are present. Hummingbirds come to feeders hung from the porch roof at the back of the headquarters building, pileated woodpeckers are frequently seen, and at dusk on June evenings, the gentle calls of whip-poor-wills sound from all parts of the wooded slopes, sometimes within a few feet of headquarters, where they can be seen with the aid of a flash light. At the Lookout, both golden and bald eagles are often observed, besides sharp-shinned, Cooper's, red-tailed, red-shouldered, rough-legged, broad-winged, marsh, goshawk, osprey, and pigeon hawks, kestrels and peregrine falcon and gyrfalcon, the latter a northern species coming this far south only rarely, having been recorded at the Lookout a number of times. Chimney swifts sometimes appear by thousands in a day, and at times nighthawks, related to the swifts and hummingbirds, fly past the Lookout in hundreds, usually in the late afternoon. Surprisingly, ducks, geese and swans have added the beauty of their flight formations to the sanctuary sky.

Hawk Mountain Sanctuary is truly an amazing place, one that every birdlover should visit. And *Hawks Aloft,* the story of the sanctuary, ought to be read by everyone with an interest in the outdoors. It is not only a success story of keen human interest, but it carries a message that deserves recognition everywhere.

Headquarters is at the sanctuary, and the address is Route 2, Kempton, Pennsylvania.

It is reached north from Reading on U. S. Highway 122, seventeen miles to Hamburg, and right on U. S. Highway 22, five miles to Lenhartsville, left six miles to Kempton. From Allentown, it is reached twenty-three miles west on U. S. Highway 22 to Lenhartsville, and right to Kempton. From Harrisburg, it is reached over U. S. Highway 22, fifty-six miles to Lenhartsville. Camping is allowed at the sanctuary for those who bring their own equipment, and overnight accommodations are available at Hamburg, Allentown and Reading. The sanctuary is open all year.

The kestrel, or sparrow hawk, smallest of our hawks, also is a falcon. Graceful in flight, it sometimes hovers over one spot while hunting field mice.

Karl H. Maslowski, courtesy Mass. Audubon Society

ARCADIA WILDLIFE SANCTUARY, 300 acres of meadow, marsh and woods, is located in central western Massachusetts, just west of the Connecticut River. The area is owned and protected by the Massachusetts Audubon Society. From 1932 to the time the area was presented to the Society, it was a private estate and was maintained as a sanctuary. Arcadia Marsh, which forms a wide crescent around Pynchon Meadows, once was an oxbow of the Connecticut. Nearby, but outside the refuge, there is an oxbow lake.

Close to 200 species of birds have been recorded in the area. Wood and black ducks breed here, and they are present throughout most of the year. Other waterfowl species to be seen during spring and fall migrations are pintails, widgeons, ring-necks, scaups, blue-winged and green-winged teal and American mergansers. Great blue, little blue, green, and black-crowned night herons and American egrets are summer visitors; while sora and Virginia rails, kingfishers, ospreys and marsh hawks are present also in summer. The list of resident and migrant songbirds is long and includes swallows of several species, bluebirds, towhees, vireos, scarlet tanagers, goldfinches, purple finches and several species of warblers. The mammalian population includes musk-rats, woodchucks, cottontail rabbits, raccoons, skunks, red foxes, otters, mink, chipmunks, moles, shrews, bats, and red, flying and gray squirrels, and meadow and white-footed mice. Arcadia is a sanctuary for numerous species of wild flowers, ferns, club mosses, shrubs and trees. Many plants that provide cover and food for wildlife have been introduced. Much of the sanctuary's woodlands will never be cut, and they are returning

Best known bird, perhaps, is the robin, whose arrival in our northern states in early spring is as cheering a sight as one could see.

William Z. Harmon

Karl H. Maslowski, courtesy Mass. Audubon Society

Let no farmer doubt the value of owls, for here is positive proof—a barn owl with a rat.

Frank M. Blake, Fish and Wildlife Service

Four young opossums take a ride on their mother's back. The opossum is the only North American mammal that carries its new-born young in a pouch.

to the condition of a primeval forest. To the south of the sanctuary the Mount Tom Range forms a scenic backdrop. Many people watch hawk migration flights from the summit of the range.

As with several of the other sanctuaries of the Massachusetts Audubon Society, Arcadia serves local communities as a recreational and cultural center. It is an outdoor laboratory for natural history research and education, and is used by classes from neighboring colleges. Campers come in summer, not only to study nature, but to spend several days in the sanctuary and on the trails of nearby Mount Tom and Mount Holyoke. The work of the Society serves as an example of what such an organization can do in furthering wildlife preservation, and in helping people to understand and enjoy nature.

Arcadia headquarters is in the sanctuary, and the address is Easthampton R. F. D. The area is reached north from Springfield on U. S. Highway 5 sixteen miles to Mount Tom Station, and left a short distance to the sanctuary road on the right. It is reached south from Greenfield, Massachusetts, on U. S. Highway 5 twenty miles to Northampton, then two and six tenths miles south of town, east on Lovefield Street six tenths of a mile to the sanctuary road.

IPSWICH RIVER WILDLIFE SANCTUARY, in northeastern Massachusetts, was established in 1951. It totals about three square miles in area, and extends for a distance of seven miles along the banks of the winding Ipswich River. It is owned and protected by the Massachusetts Audubon Society. The river is bordered by the Wenham Marsh with its wooded islands, and by the Great Meadows and uplands. Situated on the Atlantic flyway, the marsh serves waterfowl during migration, and it is the breeding ground for wood and black ducks. Most of the many songbirds that migrate northward into Maine and the maritime provinces of Canada have been recorded here, as well as the several resident species usually found in this part of the country. Mammals of the area include opossums, muskrats, otters, red foxes, and whitetail deer.

The sanctuary is contributing immeasurably to encourage hundreds of youngsters every year to appreciate nature, for a visit to the area is included in the Audubon School Course in Conservation and Natural Science, which is part of the curriculum of sixty elementary school classes in Essex County. In addition, more than a hundred youngsters attend the three sessions of day camp conducted at the sanctuary by skilled nature leaders during the summer months. A farm building on the property has been converted to serve as a center for the activities of the day camp, and a trailside museum will be added. Bird enthusiasts, nature groups, garden clubs and scout troops use the sanctuary's varied facilities for outings.

Headquarters is in the sanctuary, and the address is Topsfield. The sanctuary is reached about a mile north of Topsfield, on U. S. Highway 1 (Newburyport Turnpike), east three miles on State Route 97 and Perkins Row to the sanctuary.

Other sanctuaries of the Massachusetts Audubon Society are: Cook's Canyon, thirty-five acres of rocky gorge and pond in Barre, where the Society conducts a natural history program and maintains a children's nature camp; Drumlin Farm, 175 acres of woodland, ponds and farm at South Lincoln, site of the Louise Ayer Hathaway School of Conservation Education, Audubon Center, and Society headquarters; Marblehead Neck, fifteen acres of woodlands and swamp near Marblehead, an oasis for migrating birds; Moose

There is ideal stream-bank nesting habitat for the Louisiana water-thrush at Pleasant Valley Sanctuary.

Allan D. Cruickshank, courtesy Mass. Audubon Society

Robert C. Hermes, from Nat'l Audubon Society

The saw-whet owl occurs in a number of sanctuaries of the Massachusetts Audubon Society.

Hill, 250 acres of woodlands and pond twenty-five miles south of Boston—one of the country's oldest sanctuaries; Nahant Thicket, a four-acre swamp on the Nahant Peninsula, out from Lynn; Pleasant Valley, near Lenox, a square mile of wooded valley, site of a beaver colony; Sampson's Island, sixteen acres of sand and beach grass near Cotuit, on Cape Cod; Tern Island, supporting a colony of nesting terns best viewed from route 28, near Chatham Bars Inn; Wachusett Meadows, Princeton, a square mile of woods, swamp, and pasture; and Wellfleet Bay, 315 acres of Cape Cod pine forest, moor, and marsh, and site of Henry Boston's "Outermost House."

For further information, write the Massachusetts Audubon Society, South Great Road, South Lincoln, or Audubon House, 174A Newbury Street, Boston 16.

RAINEY WILDLIFE SANCTUARY, established in 1924, is located in Louisiana, and extends for eight miles along the gulf coast in Vermilion Parish. It comprises forty-one square miles of marsh owned and protected by the National Audubon Society. Serving primarily as a wintering ground for tens of thousands of blue geese and for smaller numbers of lesser snow geese, it also provides an inviolate sanctuary for the other species of waterfowl that winter in our southern states, including the mottled duck, which breeds in the area. Shorebirds are abundant, particularly during migrations, and numerous species of water birds can be seen here, in season, such as purple gallinules, least bitterns, king rails, white-faced glossy ibises, snowy and American egrets, and occasionally a few roseate spoonbills. Many kinds of songbirds breed in the sanctuary, including orchard orioles, loggerhead shrikes, red-winged blackbirds, yellow-throats, marsh wrens, boat-tailed grackles and kingbirds. Among the mammals there are muskrats, otters, marsh rabbits, whitetail deer and the nutria, which is a large rat-like rodent native to South America, released in southern Louisiana by mistake. At one time this animal almost obliterated the native muskrat, but fortunately hurricanes seem to hold it in check. Alligators also inhabit the sanctuary.

Headquarters is in the sanctuary, and the address is Abbeville, Louisiana.

Rainey, which is one of the largest and most important privately owned sanctuaries in our country, is open to visitors. It is reached over State Route 25 twenty-seven miles west from New Iberia to Abbeville, and south from Abbeville to Intracoastal City on the Intracoastal Waterway, where the Society's boat takes visitors to headquarters. Anyone wishing to visit the area must write to the National Audubon Society for a permit, instructions and information about accommodations. The Society's address is 1130 Fifth Avenue, New York 28, New York.

VINGT'UN ISLANDS WILDLIFE SANCTUARY is a group of four small islands in Galveston Bay, Texas. It comprises about four acres, and was established by law as a Texas state sanctuary in 1937. Sanctuary status was given the islands through the efforts of the Garden Club of Houston. The Houston Outdoor Nature Club has made supplemental plantings of shrubs on the islands to assist nesting birds. The National Audubon Society has protected the islands since 1931, and when the area was made a state sanctuary, the Texas Fish and Game Commission delegated to the Society full authority to continue to provide its protective service.

Vingt'un Islands Sanctuary contains the largest nesting colony of roseate spoonbills in the United States. Other species that inhabit the islands are white and white-faced glossy ibises, American and snowy egrets, Louisiana and Ward's herons.

Most people who have seen the spoonbill agree that it is one of the most beautiful birds of North America. Its bright pink wings flashing across the blue sky is truly an amazing and unforgettable sight. Its peculiar bill, shaped much like a spoon, as the name implies, suggests that the bird may have belonged to some far distant era of the past; the spoonbill, in fact, has survived through the almost countless centuries, from Pleistocene times.

In the book *Fading Trails, the Story of Endangered American Wildlife,* we find this statement: "The trail leading to the edge of the wide, shallow pond was well

Olin S. Pettingill, Jr., from Nat'l Audubon Society

Some regard the roseate spoonbill as America's most beautiful bird. Although this may be a matter of personal opinion, nothing could be more startlingly beautiful than these large waders fanning their bright pink wings against a brilliant blue sky.

marked. It was traveled by a large number of animals, and many of these animals were far bigger creatures than any that exist on the North American continent today. . . . Spread out across the flat, quiet waters of the pond were vast flocks of feeding birds—egrets, herons, ibises, ducks, geese, shorebirds—some that have their counterparts today, others that disappeared with the passing of the Ice Age. In the midst of this assemblage of birds flocks was a brilliant and startling and almost unbelievable sight. Surely the forces of creation had given way to an impulse, and indulged in a creative splurge, had felt a sudden and overwhelming desire for something closer to beauty than giant ground sloths. For here was a bird with plumage of a more delicate pink than the most fragile shell or the loveliest sunset. And splashed across its shoulders was a final dash of crimson which for sheer inspiration anticipated all of the great masters and outdid them."

But when the white man came to North America, the spoonbill was doomed to persecution. Its beauty was its own greatest enemy. On our southern shores, where the spoonbill and other handsomely feathered birds lived in the mangroves and swamplands, plume hunters made a lucrative business of slaughtering the birds and shipping their feathers to the cities, where they were used to make fans and screens and to ornament women's hats. The spoonbill formerly nested all along the coast of the Gulf of Mexico—Texas, Louisiana, Mississippi, Alabama and Florida—and it occurred in such great numbers that its post-breeding flight took it as far north as the Carolinas on the east, and far up the Mississippi Valley. But by 1890, the plume hunters had done such a thorough job that there were no nesting colonies left even in Texas, and by 1902 there remained only a few individuals on the mangrove keys and coastal fringes of the tip of Florida. The spoonbill had almost vanished from North America. Just in time, the National Association of Audubon Societies, now the National Audubon Society, became aroused and started a vigorous campaign to enlighten the public, and urged enactment of laws to protect the birds permanently. Furthermore, the Society undertook the establishment and protection of sanctuaries in Florida, a difficult task, for the few remaining birds were widely scattered. Opposition and ill-will toward the Society's wardens was keen among the plume hunters, and one warden, Guy Bradley, was murdered by the hunters near Cape Sable. A stone in Everglades National Park marks his grave.

Fortunately, the spoonbill still survived in large numbers on the coasts of Cuba, Mexico and South America. Annual post-breeding migrations from Cuba and north along the Mexican coast helped to restore the North American colonies. It is an interesting fact that spoonbill nesting colonies are usually located on islands.

Although the spoonbill population has been brought back to some extent, we should not take a complacent attitude toward its security. There are still many dangers facing this beautiful bird, one of which is oil operations on the gulf coast. This activity poses a constant threat to the spoonbill's feeding grounds, for pollution can wipe out the marine life on which the birds feed. The struggle to preserve our wildlife seems never to be completely won. It requires constant vigilance on the part of informed Americans everywhere, joined together in organizations like the National Audubon Society, to see that the last remaining habitats of the spoonbill and other birds and mammals are not disturbed. By this means alone can we and future generations continue to have the thrilling experience of seeing these creatures.

Vingt'un Islands Sanctuary headquarters is located at Smith Point, Texas. The Sanctuary is reached over State Route 124 south from Beaumont thirty-six miles to Whites Ranch, and from there southwest to Smith Point, where the boat of the National Audubon Society is available. For instruction on how to obtain a permit to visit the islands, see Rainey Wildlife Sanctuary.

The National Audubon Society patrols a number of other sanctuaries. In Texas, besides Vingt'un Islands, there are The Second-Chain-of-Islands, Lydia Ann Island, South Bird Island, Green Island and Bird Island. The Second-Chain-of-Islands consists of eight islands lying off Blackjack Peninsula and Aransas National Wildlife Refuge. The area is leased to the Society by the State Land Board, and it protects reddish, American and snowy egrets, roseate spoonbills, white ibises, oystercatchers, gull-billed, Caspian and least terns, black skimmers and brown pelicans. This is the northermost sizeable rookery of the reddish egret.

Lydia Ann Island, leased from the State Land Board, is located near Port Aransas, and it protects reddish, American and snowy egrets, Louisiana and Ward's herons, laughing gulls, willets, non-nesting roseate spoonbills and large, spectacular colonies of Cabot's and royal terns.

South Bird Island is in the northern part of Laguna Madre. Here the Society operates on a long-term lease under an act of the state legislature. The area protects laughing gulls, reddish and snowy egrets, Louisiana and Ward's herons and one of

Allan D. Cruickshank, from Nat'l Audubon Society

The reddish egret once was believed to be extinct, but under protection of the National Audubon Society's Texas sanctuaries and Everglades National Park, Florida, its population has been restored.

the two southern nesting colonies of the white pelican.

Green Island, in the south Laguna Madre, about thirty acres in area, is patrolled and leased similarly to South Bird Island. Unlike the other Texas sanctuaries, which are only slightly higher than the level of the water, this one rises several feet above sea level and is covered with a dense growth of small trees, which provide nest sites for the birds. It contains the largest rookery of reddish egrets in the United States. Other species are white and white-faced glossy ibises, American and snowy egrets, great blue and black-crowned night herons, least terns, and black skimmers, as well as non-nesting spoonbills and white pelicans.

Bird Island, in San Luis Pass just west of Galveston Island, provides protection for a nesting colony of brown pelicans. The Society does not maintain a warden here, but has posted the island.

In Florida, the Society guards the Alafia Banks, Green Key, Whiskey Stump and Big Bird Key in Tampa Bay; the southern Kissimmee Prairie and the western shore of Lake Okeechobee; Duck Rock off the southwestern coast of the Everglades, recently added to Everglades National Park; Cotton Key and that part of Cowpens south of the Intracoastal Channel in Florida Bay; Fishermen's and Hunter's islands, and other islands between these in Lake Worth; and the Society maintains station wagon and boat trips for visitors to Everglades National Park.

The Tampa Bay sanctuaries protect white ibises, brown pelicans, herons, egrets and cormorants. Of special interest is a large rookery of white ibises at Alafia Banks.

The vast Kissimmee Prairie is patrolled by a Society warden with the cooperation

Wray H. Nicholson, courtesy Nature Magazine

Those who join the Kissimmee Prairie tours of the National Audubon Society have the rare experience of seeing the Audubon's caracara, a crested vulture-like bird.

With long legs and thick bill, the rather comical caracara is confined to Florida's prairies, Aransas Refuge and parts of the Texas-Mexico border. It is eagerly sought by bird-watchers.

Allan D. Cruickshank from Nat'l Audubon Society

of the local people. Glossy, white and wood ibises, limpkins, the rare Everglade kites, Florida cranes, burrowing owls, Audubon's caracaras, bald eagles and egrets, as well as shorebirds, waterfowl and numerous migratory species are given protection here.

Duck Rock, a mangrove key of about an acre, is used by thousands of birds as a night roosting area. In late June and July, as many as 150,000 birds of many species including 200 or more spoonbills and several hundred frigate-birds come to the key every evening.

The National Audubon Society's Corkscrew Swamp Sanctuary of almost 6000 acres, located thirty-five miles southeast of Fort Myers, contains the last great virgin stand of cypress in Florida. Among the abundant wildlife to be seen there is the largest wood ibis and American egret rookery in the United States, as well as turkeys, otters, panthers and black bears. The area is scenically very beautiful, with its wide grassy lagoon encircled by the primeval cypress forest.

In addition to its protective work at the various wildlife sanctuaries, the National Audubon Society maintains four centers for educational purposes. These are the Audubon Center of Greenwich, Connecticut; the Audubon Center of Sharon, Connecticut; the Aullwood Audubon Center at Dayton, Ohio; and the Audubon Center of Southern California at El Monte. Further information about the Society's sanctuaries and how to visit them may be obtained by writing to the National Audubon Society, 1130 Fifth Avenue, New York 28, N. Y.

The Atlantic puffin breeds on islands from Greenland to Machias Seal Island off Maine's northern coast. With gray cheeks and broad bills tipped with red, these odd little birds are among the species that every bird enthusiast hopes someday to see.

Robert C. Hermes, from Nat'l Audubon Society

What monstrous folly, think you, ever led nature to create her one great enemy—man!—JOHN C. VANDYKE.

The Vanished and the Vanishing

It is intended here to discuss only a few of the rare and extinct birds and mammals of North America not already treated in foregoing texts, to show by these examples the dire importance not only of maintaining our present refuges and sanctuaries, but of establishing others. There is urgent need for more sanctuaries to protect kites and hawks, and for special sanctuaries to protect pinnated grouse, and such mammals as the key deer, the woodland caribou and the tule elk. Canada has established a number of far north wildlife reserves. The time may be approaching when the breeding grounds of geese, swans, polar bears and other species will require increased protection within these reserves. Exploitation of resources is moving northward and invading the vast silences of the northern wilderness. With every advance go traps and guns. The airplane has made it easy to reach almost any spot that a few years ago would have required great cost and effort. While there is still time, permanent inviolate sanctuaries should be established wherever species are endangered.

That the great auk no longer exists, and that you and I will never see one living in its former habitat, has no effect on our daily lives; but just as the world would be poorer were the music of Chopin obliterated and no one again could hear it, so the world is poorer because no one ever again will see the huge auk colonies that once thrived on little Funk Island.

Birds

Funk Island was never coveted by real estate developers. Petroleum companies never drilled for oil there, neither was the island grown with a mighty forest reduced to a mass of rotting stumps by the lumbermen. Nevertheless, it was the scene of a tragedy. Lying fifty miles off the east coast of Newfoundland, pounded by the raging

The Labrador duck became extinct by 1875, and there may be no photograph showing the bird in its natural habitat. These are museum specimens.

American Museum of Natural History

In 1904, the last flock of Carolina paroquets was seen in Florida. An attractive small parrot with bright green body and wings and yellow head, its loss is one of the most regretable of all. This is from the famous painting by John James Audubon.

Photographs from
Nat'l Audubon Society

Once numbering in flocks of millions that darkened the sun, the passenger pigeon became extinct when the last, a captive female, died in the Cincinnati Zoo in 1914. The species constituted one of nature's most impressive spectacles. Mounted birds are shown here.

Atlantic surf, this little rock-bound island contained one of the principal colonies of the **great auk.** Resembling a penguin, the auk was an excellent swimmer, but was flightless, yet it ranged south as far as the coast of New England and east to Iceland. The great auk became extinct shortly after 1850. As long ago as the 15th century, fishermen discovered that the auks could be kept alive aboard their boats and used for food as the need arose. Their eggs, too, were eaten. Huge numbers of the birds were driven or herded like sheep from their colonies onto fishing and whaling boats, which stopped at Funk Island for this purpose. The birds were slaughtered also for their oil, which was used in lamps, and for their feathers, used in quilts. The great auk was one of the first North American birds to become extinct as a result of human ruthlessness.

Little is known about the strikingly handsome **Labrador duck.** Its range extended along the coast of our northeastern states and the maritime provinces. Its feathers were sought for quilts, and it became extinct probably by 1875. Its disappearance was so sudden that it was gone before ornithologists were aware of it.

Many may feel that, among the several North American birds that have become extinct, the loss of the **Carolina paroquet** is to be more keenly regretted than most others. This little member of the parrot group, once the most widely distributed of its kind in our country, was brightly colored. Its body, wings and tail were green and its head yellow. It was sought as a cage bird; and because it liked fruit, it was considered a menace by fruit growers, and was shot by hundreds. Unfortunately, when one bird in a flock was wounded or killed, others would hover around the dead or wounded individual, thus making it easy to kill many more. The paroquet inhabited our southern states, coming as far north as Virginia, Kentucky and Illinois. The last little flock of paroquets was reported to have been seen in the vicinity of Lake Okeechobee, Florida, in 1904. It is the disappearance of a bird of this kind that should serve to awaken us to the urgency of protecting from extinction all birds and mammals. Our southern states today are truly poorer without the little paroquets to brighten and enliven its woodlands and gardens. We dare not, we must not again, permit so great a tragedy to occur. Yet, as these words are being written, the parrots that dwell in the jungles of the tropical lands south of us are being rapidly reduced in population. The **Puerto Rican parrot** has been pursued for years for the same reasons as the Carolina paroquet. This handsome green and blue parrot, in greatly reduced numbers, still inhabits the dense forest around the mountain of El Yunque de Luquillo. This area has been established as the Caribbean National Forest, and is administered by the U. S. Forest Service.

In referring to a book entitled *Extinct Birds*, by Walter Rothschild, the authors of *Fading Trails* make this comment: "Turn to the back of Rothschild's book. There, page after page of color plates portray parrots, macaws and paroquets which are now gone from the face of the earth. Most of them were gorgeous birds that will never be seen alive again. . . . Since Rothschild wrote his book, other parrots have slipped into oblivion."

Next to disappear from North America was the **passenger pigeon,** a bird that, during the days of market hunting in the last decades of the 19th century, existed in such uncountable millions that many people believed it never could become extinct. It was shot and it was enticed into baited nets. Forest trees containing hundreds of nests were chopped down to obtain the squabs, and night raids were made on roosts in which men clubbed the birds from the branches of the trees. During these raids farmers fattened their hogs on the carcasses that fell to the ground unretrieved. The birds were

George W. Field, courtesy Nature Magazine

The heath hen, eastern pinnated grouse, became extinct in 1932.

barreled and shipped by train loads to the city markets. The last survivor of the pigeon hordes, a female at the Cincinnatti Zoo, died in 1914. A typical pigeon flight, suggested by *The Passenger Pigeon,* by W. B. Mershon, is described in the chapter, *The Primitive Land.*

The **heath hen,** the most eastern of the four pinnated grouse, is now extinct. It once ranged on the sandy Atlantic coastal plain from perhaps as far north as eastern Massachusetts or southern Maine to Virginia. Martha's Vineyard Island was its last place of survival. About 200 birds were known to be there in 1890. Strenuous efforts were made to increase the number, and by 1905, the population had risen to around 2000 birds. This was a remarkable achievement, and it showed what can be done sometimes, before it is too late. In this case, birds should have been shipped out to repopulate other spots where suitable habitat remained; but this was not done. Devastating fires swept the Martha's Vineyard grassland, and birds and nests were destroyed to the point where the population was nearly wiped out. Predators, disease and perhaps some shooting reduced the remaining numbers, and by 1932, the last heath hen had vanished.

The **Eskimo curlew,** a member of the shorebird group, also probably has gone to oblivion, although very rarely somebody reports one as having been seen. Its breeding range is in the barren grounds of northern Canada and Alaska. After the young have taken wing in the latter part of summer, the birds migrate south to the maritime provinces and head out over the open ocean to the West Indies and South America to spend the winter in Chile, Argentina and Patagonia. The northward flight in spring takes them over the jungles of the Amazon country, and from there probably along the east coast of Central America and Mexico to Texas and on up the Mississippi Valley to their northern breeding grounds again.

The curlews fell victim to the market hunters. Moving in large flocks, they were taken in great numbers and shipped to the cities. The shooting of shorebirds has been outlawed, and most species have shown an increase. But as the gunners reduce other species, there is growing pressure to legalize the shooting of more abundant ones. There must never again be an open season on shorebirds, for even without being shot, they are having difficulty to survive because of ever shrinking habitats. Gulls and terns, too, must be kept on the protected list.

The **nene** or Hawaiian goose formerly inhabited the dry, grassy lava slopes of the mountains of Maui and Hawaii, at elevations of 1000 to 8000 feet above sea level. Before the coming of the white man, these handsome birds may have existed in flocks numbering several thousands; but when the white man arrived, he brought with him, among other creatures, three species of rats, and to get rid of these the mongoose was introduced. The rodents undoubtedly ate the eggs of the geese and perhaps attacked the geese themselves, particularly the young. In addition, the birds were shot for sport. Wild pigs and wild dogs are also said to menace the nene. The result is that today the nene is very close to extinction. A few birds are occasionally seen in Hawaii Volcanoes National Park. Efforts have been made to raise the nene on farms, not without some success, and, in 1960, and again in 1961, twenty marked birds were released—forty in all. These were seen later with the wild flocks, but nothing is known yet as to whether this has resulted in an increase of young.

Among the most graceful and beautiful birds of North America are the **kites.** There are four species, the swallow-tailed, the white-tailed, the Everglade and the Mississippi. All four have suffered severe reductions in population during the years our country has come under civilization. Because of their relationship to the hawks, gunners shoot them on sight, for to the gunners, the only good hawk is a dead one. The kites not only are not harmful to human interests, but, if anything, are beneficial. The author has had the pleasure of seeing three of the four species. Perhaps most unforgettable was the pair of white-tailed kites seen at Point Lobos Reserve State Park in California, in the summer of 1947. The birds, fluttering momentarily, were seen almost overhead through an opening in the dark green canopy of the ancient cypress trees, their plumage gleaming white like gulls, illuminated by the light of the westering sun, silhouetted against the rich blue of the sky. The original range of this bird is recorded as having been in three separate areas: the coastal belt of California, south into Lower California, the Texas coast northward into central Oklahoma, and Florida northward in southeastern Georgia and the southern part of the coast of South Carolina. The bird probably no longer exists in the eastern part of its range. In the other two areas it has become extremely rare; and latest reports are that the birds that formerly nested at Point Lobos have not been seen there in recent years.

Of the four kites, the Everglade is now the rarest. This bird is discussed in the text on Loxahatchee National Wildlife Refuge.

As quoted in *Fading Trails*, the naturalist Arthur Cleveland Bent has described the flight of the swallow-tailed kite as "beautiful in the extreme, unsurpassed in grace and elegance." And in the same book, Coues is quoted, "Marked among its kind by no ordinary beauty of form and brilliance of color, the kite courses through the air with a grace and buoyancy it would be vain to rival. By a stroke of the thin-bladed wings and a lashing of the cleft tail, its flight is swayed to this or that side in a moment, or

Alfred M. Bailey, from Nat'l Audubon Society

The nene of the Hawaiian Islands has reached dangerously low numbers, but efforts are being continued to increase the birds in Hawaii Volcanoes National Park, by raising them in captivity.

instantly arrested. Now it swoops with incredible swiftness . . . now it mounts in airy circles till it is a speck in the blue . . . All its actions display the dash of the athletic bird."

The former range of the swallow-tailed kite in North America was from northern Minnesota, southern Wisconsin, southern Indiana, North and South Carolina to Florida, Alabama and eastern Mexico. It winters in South America. Today, in our country, its range is limited chiefly to Florida, although there have been several recent records in Minnesota. Gunning is chiefly responsible for its decimation. The authors of *Fading Trails* say, "A beautiful and conspicuous target like a swallow-tailed kite seems to be more than the average gunner can resist."

The **Attwater's prairie chicken,** another of the pinnated grouse, once ranged over the coastal tall-grass prairie country of southwestern Louisiana, south in Texas to Cameron county, near Port Isabel, but it is now confined to a few isolated spots in Texas.

Overshooting and destruction of natural habitat by man are the causes of the prairie chicken's depletion. In reading of the ruthless shooting of this handsome bird, one wonders why it is not already extinct. Valgene W. Lehmann made a study of the species, and reported his findings in his monograph, *Attwater's Prairie Chicken, Its Life History and Management.* His discussion of shooting gives some idea of the former abundance of the bird. Cattlemen told him that "in early days the prairie chickens were relied upon to furnish fresh meat for the cattle camps. The task of killing forty or fifty prairie chickens was menial, the cook of the outfit usually attending to it . . . Ten or more piles of prairie chickens, each containing upward of a hundred birds, usually were left at the camp site to rot . . . Near Wharton, in the fall of 1894 or 1895, LeTulle found 340 (birds) piled where hunters had camped."

The prairie chickens' courting procedure is one of its notable characteristics. Says Mr. Lehmann, "Old-timers report that the deep booming courtship calls of the males once reverberated from the prairies with such force and monotony as actually to pain

Prairie chickens, particularly the Attwater's, have been so drastically reduced by shooting and habitat destruction that their future survival is precarious.

Charles W. Schwartz

sensitive eardrums." Courting takes place on booming grounds, where each male occupies a courtship station, which is visited by the female. "To attract the females," says Mr. Lehmann, "the cocks put on elaborate exhibitions, and their courtship antics are unbelievably weird. As a preliminary to uttering the call he stretches his neck forward. The erected ear tufts point forward; the spread tail is held vertically. The wings are extended downward and held firmly against the body and legs, the primaries almost touching the ground. The whole body appears strained. A short run forward is followed by stamping with the feet. Inflation of the air sacks is synchronized with the stamping. The first syllable of the booming is given before stamping ends, the male quickly jerking his head downward as he begins the call, and keeping it there until the air sack is deflated." Dueling between males is frequent, but seldom ends in death. According to Mr. Lehmann, opponents approach each other with necks extended, uttering whining notes, ear tufts erected, tails spread, wings drooped and air sacks deflated. Then, in unison, both birds leap off the ground, wings beating, and clash in mid-air.

Attwater's prairie chicken may vanish forever unless more and larger areas of its grassland habitat are restored and preserved.

Mammals

The **woodland caribou** once inhabited the northern forests from Newfoundland, Nova Scotia, New Brunswick, Maine, northern New Hampshire and Vermont and southern Quebec west to British Columbia; but now this handsome member of the deer tribe is threatened with extinction. The only place where it may be seen in the United States today is in the Superior Roadless Area of the Superior National Forest, in northern Minnesota. Small herds still survive in parts of Ontario, western Alberta, British Columbia and Quebec, where it is constantly subject to being shot for sport. The protection of the woodland caribou presents a special problem. To preserve it within an unfenced sanctuary is nearly impossible because although it may be in the sanctuary today, a few days from now it may have wandered far from protective boundaries. Island sanctuaries may offer the best solution.

Down along the western end of the Florida Keys, particularly on Big Pine Key and neighboring islands, there lives the smallest of the several species of North American deer. This little animal, which stands only twenty-six to twenty-nine inches tall at the shoulder, is known as the **key deer.** With the rapid alteration of the keys by real estate developers, and with consequent increase in human population there, not only has the habitat become reduced, but the species has been molested, particularly by gunners, who sent packs of hounds into the island thickets to drive the deer out, and then as the deer attempted to swim to other keys for safety, shot them. Recurrent fire swept parts of Big Pine Key, and on numerous occasions, the animals crossed the highway that traverses the chain of keys to Key West, and were killed by speeding automobiles.

By 1950, the deer had reached a dangerously low ebb in population, and organizations concerned with wildlife protection became interested to save the deer from pending extinction. The Fish and Wildlife Service, which had a warden on the keys, received the first donation of funds from the Boone and Crockett Club to provide protection. By 1953, the deer showed a decided increase. In 1954, a refuge for the deer was established, later enlarged, on Big Pine Key and on several nearby smaller keys, so that the survival of the species is being viewed with greater assurance.

The **tule elk,** smallest elk on the continent, once ranged through the valleys of California west of the Sierra Nevada, particularly the lower San Joaquin and Sacramento

America's smallest deer, the Florida key deer, which lives on several of the lower keys, a few years ago reached the low ebb of an estimated forty individuals. Protection has helped to restore them, thanks to a good sanctuary.

L. Niel Bell
courtesy Everglades
Natural History
Ass'n

valleys. By the early 1920's, the total population of the species, having been reduced by shooting and agriculture, was confined to a herd of about 400 animals on a ranch near Tupman, Kern County, in the San Joaquin Valley. Because there always was the danger that disease or some other cause might wipe out the elk while confined to one small area, a group of Californians interested in preserving the species, had a few of the animals moved to a fenced area in Yosemite National Park. The high country here was not the natural range of the elk. By 1933, the policy of the National Park Service, with regard to wildlife, had crystallized, requiring that no animal shall be kept under fence in the national parks, and that no species not native to a park shall be introduced or retained there. The Yosemite animals were moved, therefore, from the park to Owens Valley in 1933. Today the tule elk population consists of about fifty fenced animals on the San Joaquin Valley ranch, which exist under almost domestic conditions, and the Owens Valley herd of about 200 animals that roam freely in a superbly scenic area of about forty miles north-south, hemmed in by the Sierra Nevada on the west and the Inyo Mountains on the east.

But the Owens Valley herd seems to be in an increasingly precarious position. Although the Tupman herd may serve as a curiosity, it is the Owens Valley herd that presents the aspects of wildness and beauty so gratifying to the lover of nature. Owens Valley is owned by the City of Los Angeles, and in recent years the city has leased the lands to cattlemen. Today these men complain about having to share their ranges with the elk. There have been three open seasons for shooting the elk. The state of California appears to accept a somewhat nebulous guardianship over this herd, although in 1961 it expressed opposition to the demands for killing. The tule elk deserves the greatest possible protection we can give it. The need is for establishment of a permanent, inviolate sanctuary in Owens Valley to the exclusion of all conflicting interests and activities. The Committee for the Preservation of the Tule Elk, 5502 Markland Drive, Los Angeles 22, California, is working valiantly toward this objective. The organization needs your support because the future of the tule elk depends on the membership of the Committee. Through it, you are kept informed and, at times of emergency, told when and to whom to write and express your opinions and wishes. A tule elk sanctuary here not only would become a tourist attraction that would benefit the local communities, but also would give security to the species.

The now extinct **Merriam elk** once inhabited certain mountain areas in New Mexico and Arizona. According to Olaus J. Murie, in his book *The Elk of North America*, "Available descriptions of a few specimens indicate that *merriami* was larger than *nelsoni* and *roosevelt* and more uniformly colored, perhaps paler, with less contrast in color pattern, and it had 'more massive' antlers than *nelsoni*." It must have been a truly handsome creature; but it disappeared as a result of shooting and competition with sheep and cattle for its feed. During the last two decades of the 19th century, this species was abundant over its narrow range, and the last record of it occurred about

Only two small herds of America's smallest elk, the tule elk, still exist.

National Park Service

The author

**Here a band of tule elk is on the move.
This is part of the Owens Valley herd.**

1906 in the Chiricahua Mountains of southeastern Arizona. No effort or expense should seem too great to save the tule elk from a similar fate.

The islands of Penobscot Bay, in Maine, comprised the habitat of a mink that is said to have been twice as large as the well-known species. This was the **sea mink.** Like its smaller cousin its fur was in demand. These animals were not trapped, but hunted with dogs trained for the purpose. Sometimes the mink sought refuge in caves in the rocks. According to an account by Manly Hardy, "shovels, pick-axes and crow-bars" were used to dislodge them. The sea mink became extinct sometime toward the end of the 19th century.

The **sea elephant,** the largest member of the seal group, and the walrus, have become exceedingly rare. These two huge sea mammals occupy widely different ranges. The sea elephant lives in the warm, sunny waters off the coast and islands of southern and Lower California, while the walrus inhabits the northern coasts of Alaska, spending much time resting on the frigid cakes of drift ice.

The sea elephant was slaughtered for its oil, and by 1892, it had been reduced to a mere dozen individuals, which had sought safety on the beaches of Guadalupe Island. Actually, it was only a decline in the demand for seal oil that prevented extermination at that time. Slowly the population grew, but once again man took up the pursuit of the sea elephant. This time a manufacturer conceived the idea of canning the meat and selling it for cat and dog food. He operated under a Mexican Government permit. When it was discovered that the sea elephant was again threatened with extinction, strong protests were made, and the permit was not renewed. The sea elephant is again becoming more abundant, and it may be seen occasionally on some of the beaches of the southern California coast.

The **walrus** has been killed for its ivory tusks. Nearly half of the Alaska walrus population was wiped out prior to the 1880's, and the animal still is being killed for this purpose. The walrus ranges from Bering Sea east to the coast of Labrador. Some scientists have classified the animals of the western part of the range as a separate species.

The **harbor seal** inhabits the Atlantic coast, coming as far south as the harbors, coves and islands of the coast of Maine. On the Pacific coast it ranges from the Pribilof Islands to Lower California. The harp and hooded seals, found only on the Atlantic coast, formerly came as far as Maine in winter, but they are being persistently killed for their oil, and are dangerously close to becoming extinct. A foremost enemy of seals is the fishing industry. Believing that these interesting animals are a menace to the fish supply, the industry wages constant war on them. In 114 Pacific harbor seal stomachs, says Victor H. Cahalane in his *Mammals of North America,* salmon, the fisherman's catch, was found in only four. Seals add interest to our shores, and deserve rigid protection.

One of the strangest and rarest of North American mammals is the **manatee** or sea cow. Once these large dark creatures ranged along our Atlantic coast as far north as the Carolinas. Today the species is confined almost entirely to the tip of the Florida peninsula as far north as the vicinity of Miami, and occasionally along the lower west coast of the peninsula. It also inhabits the West Indies and the Atlantic and Caribbean coasts of South America. In our country, shooting has been the principal cause of the manatee's reduction. Although protected by state law and a $500 fine for killing it, the manatee is undoubtedly shot by poachers, particularly where it occurs outside the boundaries of Everglades National Park. If its protection could be enforced adequately, it might become a leading attraction to Florida's winter visitors. Experience has shown that the manatee loses fear of man when not molested.

For centuries **whales** have been sought for their oil and baleen or whalebone. An aura of romance and adventure adheres to the industry, especially as practiced in the days of sailing ships; but with the advent of "factory ships" or, as expressed by A. B. C. Whipple in his thrilling book *Yankee Whalers in the South Seas,* "floating mechanical slaughterhouses," and the invention of the harpoon gun with its explosive "warhead,"

Some urged killing this white whale when it swam up Maine's Penobscot River, but those with keener appreciation objected, and the whale lived to return to the ocean.

Bangor Daily News

Allan D. Cruickshank, from Nat'l Audubon Society

Even in the far reaches of the oceans the mammals are not safe from pursuit by man, where factory ships are reducing whale populations. The huge finback is a species showing a serious decline.

it has lost much of its former colorful picturesqueness. At the same time, the highly efficient modern methods of taking and treating whales have tended seriously to reduce the populations of these huge sea mammals.

By 1931, a decline, particularly of some species, such as the right whale, has become clearly apparent. In that year, an international agreement to ensure proper and effective conservation and development of whale stocks was signed in London. This agreement was replaced by a Convention signed in London in June, 1937, and the 1937 Convention was in turn amended by a series of protocols between 1938 and 1945. At Washington, D. C., in 1946, representatives of fifteen nations signed the International Convention for the Regulation of Whaling. This Convention entered into force on November 10, 1948. Its signatories recognized, among other things, that "the history of whaling has been overfishing of one area after another and of one species of whale after another to such a degree that it is essential to protect all species from further overfishing." The schedule to the Convention forbade the killing of gray and right whales, calves, suckling whales or female whales accompanied by calves; prohibited the killing of whales of certain species until they had reached specified minimum lengths; and closed specified areas of the Atlantic, Pacific and Indian oceans to the killing of certain species.

The 1946 Convention was a considerable step forward over the previous international agreements. An important feature was the establishment of an international commission to modify and amend the schedule to give added protection where needed, as research might dictate. Through the years, a number of modifications have been made; but protective efforts are hampered by a lack of knowledge of the life habits of whales. Ranging far and wide over the trackless wilderness of the open oceans, whales present an especially difficult problem to researchers. Today the right whale has become rare and the blue whale, which inhabits the Pacific and Atlantic oceans, particularly the southern hemisphere, is fast disappearing. These species formerly were among the most eagerly sought. With their decline, the finback of the Atlantic and Pacific, and others, are being taken more than they once were. Although the protection offered by the 1948 and preceding agreements has certainly prevented the disappearance of these valuable species, it is doubtful if the regulations now in effect will be sufficient to maintain the stocks of blue and finback whales at a level high enough to support a large-scale industry for many years.

The **American crocodile,** though not a mammal, seems to deserve mention here, for it is one of the two largest reptiles native to North America. Many people mistakenly believe that the crocodile and the alligator are one and the same. The alligator lives in fresh water, and is present in a number of the southeastern wildlife refuges. The crocodile is extremely rare in our country, its range being limited to the southern tip of Florida, where it lives in the shoal salt water along the shores of Florida Bay. Its full range extends down the island chain of the West Indies and along the northern coasts of South and Central America and Mexico. The crocodile can be distinguished from the alligator by its lighter coloring, the protruding teeth of the lower jaw, and by its long, narrow, pointed snout. As a rare and interesting species, the crocodile deserves complete protection within its small United States range. Someday it may become an attraction to Everglades National Park visitors.

It is a strange thing in history how little has been done to befriend the animal life about us. Mere witless killing, which is called 'sport' today, would inevitably give place in a better educated world to a modification of the primeval instinct, and change it into an interest, not in the deaths, but in the lives of beasts, and lead to fresh, and perhaps beautiful attempts to befriend these pathetic kindred creatures we no longer fear as enemies.

—H. G. Wells.

THESE REFUGES, TOO, ARE IN THE CARE OF THE FISH AND WILDLIFE SERVICE

Alabama

Wheeler, established in 1938, is fifty-five miles in area near Decatur, on the Tennessee River. It protects geese, ducks, quail, doves, muskrats, mink and raccoons. A resident manager is in charge, and the address is Box 1643, Decatur.

Alaska

Arctic National Wildlife Range, established in late 1960, contains 14,062 square miles of arctic tundra wilderness in the northeastern corner of Alaska. It extends along the Arctic Ocean coast and southward to include part of the Brooks Range, where Mount Michelson and Mount Chamberlain reach altitudes of more than 9,000 feet. Numerous lakes, marshes and streams are the habitat of waterfowl, while a hundred bird species in all are native in the area. Here, too, are grizzly and polar bears, Dall sheep, wolverines, wolves and large herds of caribou. Sad to report, this magnificent area is as yet far from secure, and it has no sanctuary status. Prospecting, mining and public shooting are permitted, and the 87th Congress, in 1961, refused to appropriate money for its protection.

Bering Sea, established in 1909, is six square miles in area on an island in the Bering Sea about 175 miles due west of Nunivak Island. It protects eider ducks, kittiwakes, auklets, puffins, Pribilof snow buntings and Arctic foxes.

Chamisso, established in 1912, is one square mile in area at the head of Kotzebue Sound. It protects kittiwakes, murres and puffins.

Clarence Rhode National Wildlife Range, established in late 1960, contains 2,924 square miles of wet tundra on the Yukon-Kuskokwim River delta of western Alaska. It extends from the mouth of the Kinak River north to Hooper Bay and east to Dall Lake and the head of Baird Inlet. It is part of a vast marsh, lake and river area that constitutes the largest waterfowl breeding ground in North America. It is the home of red and arctic foxes, mink, otters and muskrats. In time, the refuge boundaries should be extended to secure much more of this valuable wildlife habitat. Natives are allowed to shoot and trap in the area, and it is open to mining and mineral leasing, as well as oil and gas exploration and development. The 87th Congress, in 1961, refused to appropriate money for its protection.

Hazen Bay, established in 1937, is ten square miles in area on an island off the Bering Sea coast northeast of Nunivak Island. It protects the emperor goose and Steller's eider duck.

Saint Lazaria, established in 1909, is sixty-five acres in area on an island west of Sitka. It protects murres, auklets and puffins.

Simeonof, established in 1958, is an island of sixteen square miles for the preservation and propagation of the sea otter. The refuge includes all of the Simeonof Island and the island's tidelands together with all adjacent water areas, extending one mile beyond mean low water. Simeonof, one of the Shumagin group off the southeasterly coast of the Alaska Peninsula, is approximately 250 miles southwest of Kodiak Island.

Arizona

Havasu Lake, established in 1941, is seventy-one square miles in area on the Colorado River in California and Arizona near Needles, California. It protects bighorn sheep, muskrats, white-winged doves, Gambel's quail, herons and waterfowl. A resident manager is in charge, and the address is Box 1717, Parker.

Imperial, established in 1941, is seventy-three square miles in area on the Colorado River in Arizona and California north of Yuma. It protects bighorn sheep, Gambel's quail, waterfowl, white pelicans, herons, rails, muskrats and beavers. A resident manager is in charge, and his address is Box 1032, Yuma, Arizona.

Arkansas

Big Lake, established in 1915, is fifteen square miles in area between the Mississippi and the Saint Francis rivers east of Walcott. It protects waterfowl, quail, muskrats, raccoons and mink. A resident manager is in charge, and the address is Box 65, Manila.

Holla Bend, established in 1957, is an island of six square miles in the Arkansas River, Pope County. It is an important link in the Mississippi waterfowl flyway. The manager's address is Box 682, Russellville

Wapanocca was established in 1961, and contains five square miles in northeast Arkansas approximately twenty-five miles north of Memphis, Tennessee. This area has been a favored wintering ground for ducks and geese. The manager's address is Turrell.

California

Colusa, established in 1945, is three square miles in area in the Sacramento Valley east of Williams. It protects waterfowl and is administered jointly with Sacramento National Wildlife Refuge.

Farallon, established in 1909, aggregates about ninety acres, and includes the Farallon Islands twenty-five miles west of Golden Gate. It protects murres, auklets, guillemots, puffins and shorebirds. These islands are used by the U. S. Coast Guard primarily for navigational control.

Kern, established in 1960, contains seventeen square miles in the San Joaquin Valley and is managed with the Pixley Refuge for geese, pintails, mallards, and widgeons. The manager resides in Delano.

Merced, established in 1951, is about four square miles in extent, located sixteen miles northeast of the town of Merced. The purpose of the refuge is to provide adequate food to keep waterfowl from raiding nearby agricultural crops, particularly rice. The area is notable as one of the favorite wintering grounds of the rare, little, white Ross's goose, fewer than 10,000 of which are believed to exist. The tule goose, a large variety of the white-fronted, also winters here, and it is even less abundant than the Ross's goose. Both species nest in the same locality north of the Arctic Circle in Canada. The manager's address is Box 854, Merced.

Modoc, established in 1960, contains ten square miles in northeastern California, directly east of the Klamath Basin refuges. This area provides seriously needed nesting habitat for the Great Basin Canada goose. The resident manager's address is Alturas.

Pixley, established in 1958, contains six and a half square miles. It is administered jointly with the Kern Refuge, adding a much needed refuge southward in the San Joaquin Valley. The manager resides in Delano.

Salton Sea, established in 1930, is sixty square miles in area on the south end of Salton Sea north of Brawley. It protects shorebirds and waterfowl, including fulvous tree-ducks. A resident manager is in charge, and the address is Box 52, Calipatria.

Sutter, established in 1945, is almost two square miles in area in the Sacramento Valley west of Marysville. It protects waterfowl and is administered jointly with Sacramento National Wildlife Refuge.

Colorado

Monte Vista, established in 1952, contains eighteen square miles in the San Luis Valley of the south central part of the state. It protects waterfowl, doves and migrating sandhill cranes, avocets, Wilson's phalaropes and others. Great horned owls, marsh hawks and magpies are resident through the year, while golden and bald eagles are present in winter. Muskrats, skunks, rabbits, coyotes, bobcats, badgers, and weasels live in the area. Headquarters is on the refuge and the address is Monte Vista.

Delaware

Bombay Hook, established in 1937, is twenty-one square miles in area on the shore of Delaware Bay northeast of Dover. It protects muskrats, quail, mourning doves, shorebirds and waterfowl, particularly greater snow geese. A resident manager is in charge, and his address is Smyrna.

Florida

Anclote, established in 1939, is 195 acres in area on an island west of Tampa. It protects egrets, frigate-birds, cormorants, gulls and terns.

Brevard, established in 1925, is twelve acres in area on the outer beach of the east coast near Cape Canaveral. It protects brown pelicans, Florida mottled ducks, cormorants, herons and shorebirds.

Cedar Keys, established in 1929, is a half square mile in area, and includes three keys off the west coast near the village of Cedar Key. It protects brown pelicans, white ibises and herons.

Chassahowitzka, established in 1943, is forty-four square miles in area on the west coast south of Homosassa. It protects ducks, limpkins, Florida cranes and herons. A resident manager is in charge, and the address is Homosassa Springs.

Key Deer, established in 1954 to save the rare key deer, is ten and a half square miles in area. It is located on the Florida keys, principally Big Pine Key thirty miles east of Key West and about 130 miles by road south of Miami. The manager's address is Tavernier. (See comments about the key deer in the chapter *The Vanished and the Vanishing.*

Passage Key, established in 1905, is thirty-six acres in area on an island south of the mouth of Tampa Bay. It protects brown pelicans, herons, shorebirds, gulls and terns.

Sanibel, established in 1945, is three and a half square miles in area on Sanibel Island off the village of Punta Rassa, from where there is ferry service to the island. It protects waterfowl, herons, terns and shorebirds. The island's beaches are famous among collectors of sea shells. A resident manager is in charge, and his address is Sanibel.

Georgia

Blackbeard, established in 1924, is eight square miles in area on Blackbeard Island off the coast north of Brunswick. It protects sea turtles, ducks, shorebirds, herons and whitetail deer. A resident manager is in charge, but the area is administered jointly with Savannah River Refuge.

Piedmont, established in 1939, is fifty square miles in area north of Macon. It serves as a quail, mourning dove and beaver demonstration project. A resident manager is in charge, and the address is Round Oak.

Tybee, established in 1938, is a hundred acres in area near the coast at the mouth of the Savannah River east of Savannah. It protects shorebirds.

Wolf Island, established in 1930, is almost a square mile in area on an island north of the mouth of the Altamaha River. It protects brown pelicans and shorebirds.

Hawaii

Johnston Island, established in 1926, is a hundred acres in area 400 miles south of the Leeward group and about the same distance west of Hawaii, the largest of the group of Hawaiian Islands. It protects petrels, shearwaters, boobies, tropic birds and terns.

Idaho

Camas, established in 1937, is sixteen square miles in area north of Idaho Falls. It protects sage hens, sharp-tailed grouse, long-billed curlews and all species of waterfowl. There is a resident manager in charge, whose address is Hamer.

Deer Flat, established in 1909, is sixteen and a half square miles in area, and is superimposed on a Bureau of Reclamation project west of Boise. It protects waterfowl, including large numbers of geese, white pelicans, shorebirds, gulls and terns. There is a resident manager in charge, and the address is Route 1, Nampa.

Minidoka, established in 1909, is forty square miles in area on Lake Walcott Reservoir, a Bureau of Reclamation project in the Snake River south of Minidoka. It protects waterfowl. A resident manager is in charge, and the address is Rupert.

Snake River, established in 1937, is a half square mile in area, and includes a number of islands in the Snake River used by nesting Canada geese. It is located southwest of Boise.

Illinois

Chautauqua, established in 1936, is seven square miles in area adjacent to the Illinois River southwest of Peoria. Concentrations of nearly a half million mallards have occurred here in the fall. There is a resident manager in charge, and the address is Havana.

Crab Orchard, established in 1947, contains sixty-seven square miles and is easily reached from Carbondale, Carterville, Herrin, and Marion. This area, formerly an ordnance plant, was transferred by an Act of Congress. The eastern half is administered for wildlife management. Crab Orchard Dam, completed in 1938 by the Soil Conservation Service, forms the main lake of 7000 acres with a shoreline of about 125 miles. Much of the lake is located in the western half, which provides extensive recreational opportunities including picnicking, boating, camping and swimming. Crab Orchard is an important wintering area for waterfowl. Agricultural developments provide feed for these birds, particularly many thousands of Canada geese. The refuge manager's address is Route 2, Carterville.

Mark Twain, established in 1947, a continuation of the Upper Mississippi River Wild Life and Fish Refuge, contains thirty-six square miles extending southward from Rock Island, Illinois, in the states of Illinois, Iowa and Missouri. The area was acquired by the Corps of Engineers for the improvement of navigation in the Upper Mississippi River to Minneapolis. These lands were turned over for refuge use under a cooperative agreement. The manager's address is Box 225, Quincy, Illinois.

Iowa

DeSoto, established in 1958, contains eleven square miles in Iowa and Nebraska. It is about fifteen miles north of Omaha and fills a long recognized need for a resting and feeding place for migratory waterfowl, particularly geese, along this part of the Missouri River. Designated areas are being developed for recreation. The manager resides in Blair, Nebraska.

Union Slough, established in 1938, is three square miles in area northeast of Algona. It provides food for important waterfowl and upland birds. A resident manager is in charge, and the address is Titonka.

Kansas

Kirwin, established in 1954, is an area of seventeen square miles of rolling prairie and bottomland. Superimposed on a Bureau of Reclamation reservoir, it protects waterfowl, sandhill cranes, Franklin's gulls, white pelicans, herons, egrets, and mammals such as cottontails, jack rabbits, prairie dogs, beavers, muskrats and mink. It is located twenty-five miles south of Stockton and fourteen miles south of Phillipsburg. The manager's address is Kirwin.

Quivira, established in 1955, is ten square miles in area located thirty miles west of Hutchinson and twenty-five miles southwest of Great Bend. It provides protection for migrating waterfowl and Franklin's gulls, as well as quail and numerous song birds. Some mammals of the area are coyotes, badgers, rabbits, muskrats, mink, raccoons and skunks. The manager's address is Stafford.

Louisiana

Breton, established in 1905, is an island of eleven square miles in area lying east of the Mississippi Delta in Louisiana. It protects waterfowl, brown pelicans, shorebirds, gulls, terns, frigate-birds and black skimmers. Administered jointly with nearby Petit Bois and Horn Island off the Mississippi coast, the manager's address is Biloxi, Mississippi.

Delta, established in 1935, is seventy-six square miles in area, and includes two islands on the east tip of the Mississippi Delta. It protects waterfowl, including blue and snow geese, raccoons, mink, otters, muskrats, alligators and mourning doves. A resident manager is in charge, and the address is Pilottown.

East Timbalier Island Reservation, established in 1907, is a half square mile in area south of New Orleans on the Mississippi Delta. It protects brown pelicans, gulls and terns.

Shell Keys, established in 1907, is seventy-eight acres in area on several islands in Cote Blanche Bay south of New Iberia. It protects brown pelicans and royal terns.

Maryland

Martin, established in 1954, contains six square miles on Smith Island in lower Chesapeake Bay. A considerable part of the refuge was a gift from the late Glenn L. Martin. It provides much needed protection for diving ducks. Managed with Blackwater Refuge.

Massachusetts

Monomoy, established in 1944, is four square miles in area on a peninsula south of Chatham on Cape Cod. It protects waterfowl, particularly eiders and scoters, and shorebirds.

The refuge is not part of the Cape Cod National Seashore. There is a resident manager in charge, and his address in Chatham.

Parker River, established in 1942, is ten square miles in area on the coast east of Newburyport. This is the only federal refuge on the New England coast for black ducks. Increasing recreational pressure is being exerted on this refuge. There is a resident manager in charge, and the address is Box 190, Newburyport.

Great Meadows, established in 1944, contains 210 acres near Parker River Refuge, and is administered jointly with the latter. It is for waterfowl.

Michigan

Huron, established in 1938, is 147 acres in area on the Lake Superior shore of the Upper Peninsula, south of Copper Harbor. It protects double-crested cormorants, herring gulls and terns.

Michigan Islands, established in 1947, contains about twelve acres in the four islands near the tip of Michigan's Lower Peninsula. It protects herons, gulls and terns.

Shiawassee, established in 1953, is seven square miles in area in north central Saginaw County. It protects ducks, geese and whistling swans. The manager's address is Saginaw.

Wyandotte, established by an act of Congress in 1961, includes Grassy and Mammy Juda Islands in the Detroit River, about ten miles south of Detroit. It is not uncommon for 50,000 to 100,000 diving ducks to concentrate in this area, feeding on the luxuriant stands of wild celery. It is under the manager for Shiawassee Refuge.

Minnesota

Mille Lacs is a one-acre rocky island in Mille Lacs declared a refuge in 1915 to protect purple martins, which here nest in holes in the rock.

Mud Lake, established in 1937, is ninety-six square miles on Mud Lake north of Red Lake Falls. It is an important waterfowl nesting and migration area, and ruffed and sharp-tailed grouse are also protected here. It is one of the few areas on which moose are found. A resident manager is in charge, and the address is Holt.

Rice Lake, established in 1935, is twenty-three square miles in area on Rice Lake, east of Aitkin. It protects ducks, ruffed grouse, muskrats and beavers. The address of the manager is McGregor.

Tamarac, established in 1938, is fifty-four square miles in area northeast of Detroit Lakes. It protects ducks, ruffed grouse, prairie chickens, muskrats and beavers. A resident manager is in charge, and the address is Rochert.

Upper Mississippi River Wild Life and Fish Refuge, established by a special Act of Congress in 1924, is more than 300 square miles extending along both sides of the Mississippi River from Rock Island, Illinois, north to Wabasha, Minnesota. It protects waterfowl, muskrats and raccoons. The office of the manager is in Winona, Minnesota. A number of rangers are resident along the refuge area.

Mississippi

Horn Island, established in 1958, is an island of four square miles in area lying off the coast eight miles out from Pascagoula. It protects several species of shorebirds and waterfowl. Administered jointly with Petit Bois, the manager's address is Biloxi.

Noxubee, established in 1940, seventy square miles in area east of Louisville, protects ducks, turkeys, quail, mourning doves and deer. A resident manager is in charge, and the address is Brooksville.

Petit Bois, established in 1913, is an island of about one square mile in area lying off the Mississippi coast, twelve miles from Pascagoula. It protects brown pelicans, gulls and shorebirds. Administered jointly with Horn Island, the address of the manager is Biloxi.

Yazoo was established in 1936. The present six square miles failed to provide a satisfactory administrative unit. Acquisition of an additional sixteen square miles is dependent on resolving water drainage questions. A manager is resident at Hollandale.

Missouri

Mingo, established in 1944, is thirty-three square miles in area north of Poplar Bluff. Restoration of the former Mingo Swamp, an unsuccessful drainage project, adds another important area for waterfowl. A resident manager is in charge, and the address is Puxico.

Squaw Creek, established in 1935, is ten square miles in area south of Mound City. Huge flocks of waterfowl, particularly blue and snow geese, use this area in migration. It protects also white pelicans and muskrats. A resident manager is in charge, and the address is Mound City.

Swan Lake, established in 1937, is sixteen square miles on the Grand River northeast of Carrollton. Large numbers of waterfowl stop here in migration. Prairie chickens are protected, and this is one of the few places where this species remains in Missouri. A resident manager is in charge, and the address is Sumner.

Montana

Benton Lake, established in 1929, is nineteen square miles in area north of Great Falls. It protects waterfowl and shorebirds. There is a manager, and the address is Great Falls.

Black Coulee, established in 1938, is two square miles in area. It protects ducks and sage hens. Turner is the nearest town.

Bowdoin, established in 1936, is twenty-two and a half square miles on the Milk River north of Malta. Woody Island, one of several islands in Lake Bowdoin is famous for its waterfowl and its nesting white pelicans. Sage hens and antelopes are also present on the refuge. The manager's address is Malta.

Creedman Coulee, established in 1941, is four square miles in area north of Havre close to the Canadian border. It protects ducks, shorebirds, prairie chickens, sage hens and muskrats.

Fort Peck, established in 1936, is 1486 square miles in area, and is superimposed on the Fort Peck Reservoir, a flood control project of the Corps of Army Engineers, on the Missouri River near Fort Peck. Of this 575,589 acres is a waterfowl refuge, while the remainder, 375,237 acres, is administered jointly with the Bureau of Land Management for sharp-tailed grouse, sage grouse, pronghorns, bighorns and deer. The manager's address is Lewistown.

Hailstone, established in 1942, is three and a half square miles in area about thirty miles from Columbus. It protects ducks and sage grouse.

Halfbreed Lake, established in 1942, is five square miles in area near Hailstone Refuge. It protects ducks and sage grouse.

Hewitt Lake, established in 1938, is two square miles in area north of Malta. It protects ducks and sage grouse.

Lake Mason, established in 1941, is twenty-nine square miles in area about fourteen miles northeast of Roundup. It protects ducks, sharp-tailed grouse and sage grouse.

Lake Thibadeau, established in 1937, is six square miles in area north of Havre. It protects ducks, sharp-tailed grouse and sage grouse.

Lamesteer, established in 1942, is a little more than one square mile in area located near Wibaux, east of Glendive. It protects waterfowl and sharp-tailed grouse.

Medicine Lake, established in 1935, is forty-nine square miles in area east of the town of Medicine Lake. It is used by both migrant and nesting waterfowl, sandhill cranes, sharp-tailed grouse, shorebirds, gulls, terns, muskrats and badgers. The manager's address is Medicine Lake.

Nine-Pipe, established in 1921, is three square miles in the Flathead Indian Reservation north of Moiese. It protects waterfowl, shorebirds and muskrats.

Pablo, established in 1921, is nearly four square miles in the Flathead Indian Reservation, just north of the previously named refuge. It protects waterfowl, shorebirds and muskrats. This refuge and Nine-Pipe are administered jointly with the National Bison Range.

Pishkun, established in 1912, is thirteen square miles in area east of Flathead Lake and west of Great Falls. It protects ducks, shorebirds and sharp-tailed grouse.

Wild Horse was established in 1958. The five square miles were originally acquired from Agriculture under the submarginal land program and were transferred, together with War

Horse Lake and Yellow Water Reservoir, for refuge purposes. All are administered by the manager of Fort Peck Game Range.

Willow Creek, established in 1909, is five square miles in area west of Great Falls. It protects waterfowl, shorebirds and sharp-tailed grouse. This and the foregoing are on Bureau of Reclamation Projects.

Nebraska

Crescent Lake, established in 1931, is seventy-two square miles in area located north of the North Platte River, southeast of Alliance. It was one of the first refuges acquired under the *Migratory Bird Conservation Act* to protect waterfowl, sandhill cranes, long-billed curlews and antelopes. The manager's address is Ellsworth.

Fort Niobrara, established in 1912, is twenty-nine square miles in area east of the town of Valentine on the Niobrara River. This is one of the Service's four refuges fenced for large mammals. It protects bison, elk, beavers, prairie chickens, sharp-tailed grouse and waterfowl. A remnant herd of the Texas longhorn cattle is being preserved here. The resident manager's address is Valentine.

North Platte, established in 1916, is eight square miles on the North Platte River at Scottsbluff, superimposed on a Bureau of Reclamation project. It protects sandhill cranes, ducks and quail. The Chinese ring-necked pheasant has been introduced here.

Valentine, established in 1935, is 112 square miles located south of the town of Valentine. It protects sharp-tailed grouse, shorebirds and muskrats. The resident manager's address is Valentine.

Nevada

Anaho Island, established in 1913, is a third of a square mile on an island in Pyramid Lake, north of Reno. It contains one of the largest white pelican nesting colonies in the country.

Fallon, established in 1931, is twenty-eight square miles in Carson Sink, north of the town of Fallon. It protects waterfowl and California quail.

Ruby Lake, established in 1938, is fifty-five square miles in area, and is north of Strawberry and Ely and south of Wells, at the foot of the Ruby Mountains. It protects waterfowl, sage grouse, sandhill cranes, blue grouse and shorebirds. The resident manager's address is Ruby Valley.

Sheldon National Antelope Refuge, established in 1931, contains 34,131 acres in Nevada, which were purchased. The Bureau of Sport Fisheries and Wildlife has complete control of these lands. The Charles Sheldon Antelope Range, established in 1936, has 520,525 acres in Nevada and 627 acres in Oregon. These lands are administered jointly with the Bureau of Land Management. In addition, there are 23,373 acres of the range which is for large mammals only. The two areas are now managed as a single unit with Hart Mountain Antelope Refuge. Headquarters is at Lakeview, Oregon, Box 111. Subheadquarters are still maintained at the stations. (See Hart Mountain, page 77.)

Stillwater, established in 1948, is thirty-eight square miles in area near Fallon. It protects whistling swans, geese, ducks, herons, shorebirds and muskrats. A resident manager is in charge, and the address is Fallon.

Winnemucca, established in 1936, is fifteen square miles on Lake Winnemucca, a Bureau of Reclamation project, east of Pyramid Lake. It protects waterfowl, white pelicans and gulls.

New Jersey

Brigantine, established in 1939, is twenty-one square miles in area on the coast north of Atlantic City. It protects Atlantic brant, snow geese, ducks, quail, shorebirds and terns. The resident manager's address is Oceanville. Part of this refuge has been open to shooting since 1953, although the original purpose of the refuge was to provide inviolate sanctuary for the birds.

Great Swamp, established in 1960, contains 860 acres south of Morristown. The area was donated to the Bureau of Sport Fisheries and Wildlife, U. S. Department of the Interior.

Killcohook was established in 1934. It is two and a half square miles, and is located on the shore of the Delaware River near Pennsville, with one and a half square miles on the New Jersey side, and about one square mile in Delaware. It protects ducks and muskrats. The Delaware area is used for the spoilbanks from river dredging operations of the Corps of Army Engineers. The refuge is administered by the manager of Bombay Hook Refuge.

New Mexico

Bitter Lake, established in 1937, is thirty-eight square miles on the Pecos River near Roswell. It protects ducks, snowy plovers, scaled quail and nutrias. The latter is a large rat-like rodent native to South America. It has been introduced here. One of the two largest wintering flocks of the little brown crane is on this refuge. A resident manager is in charge, and the address is Roswell.

Bosque del Apache, established in 1939, is eighty-eight square miles in area on the Rio Grande south of San Antonio. It protects waterfowl, including the rare New Mexico or mottled duck, Gambel's and scaled quail, mourning doves, beavers, and muskrats. A resident manager is in charge, and his address is San Antonio.

San Andres, established in 1941, is eighty-nine square miles in area, north of Las Cruces. A mountainous desert refuge, it protects bighorns, mule deer, white-winged doves, and Mearns's, Gambel's and scaled quail. The refuge is administered jointly by the U. S. Forest Service and the Bureau of Land Management. Most of it is closed except to Atomic Energy Commission personnel. The address of the manager is Las Cruces.

New York

Elizabeth Morton, established in 1954, is an area of 187 acres on the narrow, sandy peninsula of Jessup Neck on eastern Long Island, eight miles north of Southampton. Waterfowl, shorebirds and waders are present, as well as deer, gray squirrels, cottontails, opossums, raccoons, foxes and weasels. The manager's address is Box 771, Southampton, Long Island.

Montezuma, established in 1938, is ten square miles in area at the north end of Cayuga Lake near Seneca Falls. It protects ducks, herons, egrets and muskrats. The resident manager's address is Seneca Falls. Montezuma is the only refuge on the long flight lanes between the Canadian breeding grounds around Hudson Bay and our Atlantic coast refuges. In spite of its strategic position and importance to waterfowl, the New York Department of Public Works demanded and was given permission, in 1951, by the U. S. Department of the Interior, to run an east-west throughway—a super highway—across the refuge, cutting the area in two. At the time this invasion was threatening, a number of local and national nature protection organizations did all in their power to have the highway routed around the marsh area (on solid ground), but to no avail. The value of this little refuge to wildlife has been seriously reduced.

Oak Orchard, established in 1958, is seven square miles of swamp and marsh in western New York, midway between Rochester and Buffalo. It is a key area on the Atlantic flyway. The manager's address is Basom.

North Carolina

Mackay Island, established in 1960, contains more than seven square miles in Currituck County, North Carolina, and Princess Anne County, Virginia. This area attracts and holds a wintering population of snow geese and other waterfowl. It is administered from Back Bay Refuge.

Pea Island, established in 1938, is nine square miles in area on the coastal barrier island south of Oregon Inlet and north of Cape Hatteras. It protects greater snow and Canada geese, Atlantic brant, shorebirds, gulls, terns, otters and diamond-backed terrapins. A hard surface road makes the refuge available to birdwatchers. The manager's office is in Manteo.

North Dakota

Arrowwood, established in 1935, is twenty-five square miles, and is located north of Jamestown. It protects prairie chickens, sharp-tailed grouse and waterfowl, including whistling swans. The resident manager's address is Kensal.

Long Lake, established in 1932, is thirty-five square miles in area, south of Driscoll. Development of this refuge eliminated one of the worst botulism death traps in North Dakota. It protects waterfowl, Franklin's gulls, sharp-tailed grouse and shorebirds. A resident manager is in charge, and the address is Moffit.

Lostwood, established in 1935, is forty-one square miles in area, located north of Stanley. It is one of the best pot hole waterfowl nesting areas remaining. It protects ducks, sharp-tailed grouse, sandhill cranes, shorebirds and muskrats. The address is Route 1, Lostwood.

Snake Creek, established for waterfowl in 1956, is twenty-one square miles in area and is superimposed on a Corps of Army Engineers flood control project. It adjoins a state wildlife management area of about nineteen square miles. The refuge is two miles north of Coleharbor, and forty miles south of Minot. The manager's address is Coleharbor.

Sullys Hill National Game Preserve, established in 1914, is two and a half square miles in area adjacent to Devils Lake, southwest of the town of Devils Lake. Popular as a recreational area, it is one of the Service's four fenced refuges. It protects bison, elk and deer. A resident manager is in charge, and his address is Fort Totten.

In addition to the four North Dakota refuges given above, and the three on the Souris watershed described or mentioned in the preceding chapter, there are nearly seventy other national wildlife refuges in North Dakota, established generally on lands for which easements have been granted the government to manage them for wildlife. Most of them are small. Their principal purpose is to protect waterfowl breeding habitat, for this is the southern extremity of the vast northern breeding area of ducks, which extends far into Canada.

The following areas were not included in the original edition of this book. At the time, they contained some easement land. Since then, acquisition has proceeded and these are now considered full-fledged refuges:

	Date	*Acres*	
Kellys Slough	3-19-16	1,620	
Lake Ilo	6-12-39	4,038	
Lake Zahl	6-12-39	1,286	
McLean	6-12-39	760	
Slade	10-10-44	3,000	Manager — Dawson
Stump Lake	3-9-05	27	
Tewaukon	6-26-45	6,293	Manager — Cayuga
White Lake	2-3-41	1,040	

Ohio

Ottawa was established in 1961. An anticipated acquisition of about 4,915 acres lies along the southwestern shore of Lake Erie, in northern Ohio. The refuge is fifteen miles east of Toledo.

West Sister Island, established in 1938, is eighty-two acres in area, and is at the west end of Lake Erie, about twenty miles east of Toledo. It protects great blue and black-crowned night herons.

Oklahoma

Salt Plains, established in 1930, is forty-nine square miles on the Great Salt Plains Reservoir east of Cherokee. Over a thousand acres of grain crops are grown here for waterfowl. Besides waterfowl, there are Mississippi kites, white pelicans, quail, mourning doves, herons and thousands of Frankin's gulls. The resident manager's address is Jet.

Tishomingo, established in 1946, is twenty-seven square miles on the north arm of Lake Texoma, a Corps of Army Engineers flood control project. It protects waterfowl. A resident manager is in charge, and the address is Tishomingo.

Washita, established in 1961, in Custer County, contains thirteen square miles. This is a reservoir constructed by the Bureau of Reclamation in western Oklahoma. The refuge is attractive to migrant waterfowl.

Oregon

Cape Meares, established in 1938, is 139 acres in area on the Pacific coast at the town of Wheeler. It protects shorebirds, band-tailed pigeons and blacktail deer.

Cold Springs, established in 1909, is five square miles near the Columbia River east of Umatilla, on a Bureau of Reclamation project. It protects waterfowl and shorebirds.

Klamath Forest, about eight miles east of Crater Lake National Park, was established in 1958. It comprises twenty-six square miles, and was acquired from tribal Indian lands as a nesting and migration area for waterfowl. It is administered by the manager of Tule Lake National Wildlife Refuge.

McKay Creek, established in 1927, is three square miles in area south of Pendleton. It protects waterfowl and sandhill cranes.

Oregon Islands, established in 1935, covers an aggregate of twenty-one acres off the coast at Gold Beach. The refuge protects cormorants, gulls, murres and puffins.

Three Arch Rocks, established in 1907, is seventeen acres in area, off the coast near Wheeler. This is one of the early colonial nesting bird rock refuges established to protect cormorants, gulls, murres, puffins and sea lions.

Pennsylvania

Erie, established in 1959, contains more than four square miles in northwestern Pennsylvania, thirty-five miles south of Lake Erie. It is used by ducks and geese migrating between Hudson Bay and the Atlantic Coast. The manager's address is Guys Mills.

South Carolina

Carolina Sandhills, established in 1939, is seventy square miles in area southwest of Cheraw. It protects turkeys, quail, mourning doves, beavers, bobcats and gray foxes. The last two are controlled if they become too numerous. A resident manager is in charge, and the address is McBee.

Santee, established in 1941, is 155 square miles in area, and is south of Summerton. It includes two reservoirs of the South Carolina Public Service Authority. It protects waterfowl, mourning doves, herons, otters and raccoons. The manager's address is Summerton.

South Dakota

Bear Butte, established in 1948, is more than a half square mile in area a few miles north of Sturgis. It protects waterfowl.

Belle Fourche, established in 1909, is twenty-one square miles on Belle Fourche Reservoir, a Bureau of Reclamation project northeast of the town of the same name. It protects waterfowl, shorebirds, gulls and herons.

Lacreek, established in 1935, is sixteen square miles in area, and is north of Merriman, Nebraska. It protects waterfowl, sandhill cranes, sharp-tailed grouse, shorebirds and muskrats. The refuge manager's address is Martin.

Lake Andes, established in 1936, is smaller than a square mile, and is east of the town of Lake Andes, where the manager resides. Huge concentrations of mallards winter here except during severe weather.

Sand Lake, established in 1935, is thirty-three square miles in area, and extends for fifteen miles along the James River from Hecla nearly to Columbia. It protects muskrats, cormorants, white pelicans, Franklin's gulls, and blue and snow geese. The resident manager's address is Columbia.

Waubay, established in 1935, is seven square miles, and is located east of Waubay Lake, northeast of Webster. Seventeen species of ducks nest here, and there are Franklin's gulls, shorebirds, muskrats and deer. The address of the manager is Waubay.

Tennessee

Lake Isom, established in 1938, is three square miles in area, and is south of Tiptonville. It protects ducks, mourning doves and herons. The manager's address is Samburg.

Tennessee, established in 1945, is seventy-nine square miles, and is on the Tennessee

River south of Mobley. While primary use of this area is regulated by the Tennessee Valley Authority, tremendous numbers of waterfowl use the refuge. It serves also for recreation. Address of the refuge manager is Paris.

Texas

Buffalo Lakes, established in 1958, contains twelve square miles in the northern panhandle of Texas. This reservoir and former land-utilization area was transferred from the Forest Service. Winter concentrations reach a million ducks, principally mallards and pintails. An extensive recreational program was developed before its transfer. Address of the resident manager, Box 37, Umbarger.

Hagerman, established in 1946, is eighteen square miles on Lake Texoma, a Corps of Army Engineers flood control project, northwest of Sherman. It protects waterfowl. A resident manager is in charge, and the address is Route 3, Box 123, Sherman.

Muleshoe, established in 1935, is nine square miles, and is southeast of Clovis, New Mexico. It protects waterfowl, a huge wintering flock of sandhill cranes, scaled quail, mourning doves and shorebirds. A resident manager is in charge, and the address is Muleshoe.

Utah

Fish Springs, established in 1959, contains twenty-eight square miles near the western edge of the state. The area provides a resting, feeding, and breeding area for large numbers of ducks and geese. Some public domain is included. Address of the resident manager is Dugway.

Locomotive Springs, established in 1931, is one and a half square miles, and is northwest of Great Salt Lake, close to the Utah-Idaho state line. It protects waterfowl.

Ouray, established in 1960, will eventually contain over twenty square miles. The area is on the Green River in Uintah County, twenty-five miles south of Vernal. Periodic overflows of the oxbow lakes provide excellent habitat for nesting of the Great Basin Canada goose. Address of the manager is Vernal.

Vermont

Missisquoi, established in 1948, is five square miles in area on Lake Champlain at Saint Albans. It protects waterfowl and woodcock. The manager's address is Swanton.

Virginia

Back Bay, established in 1938, is seven square miles on the coast south of Virginia Beach. It includes a bay area and islands and part of the barrier beach. It provides winter protection for waterfowl, including whistling swans and greater snow geese. The manager's address is Route 1, Princess Anne.

Presquile, established in 1952, is a man-made island of two square miles in area, situated in the James River near Hopewell. It is important to migrating waterfowl and to a large summer population of song and insectivorous birds, including a colony of bank swallows. The manager's address is Box 658, Hopewell.

Washington

Columbia, established in 1944, is more than forty-three square miles in area south of Vantage. It protects waterfowl. The address of the resident manager is Othello.

Copalis, established in 1907, is a five-acre nesting rock on the coast south of Queets. It protects cormorants, petrels, murres, auklets, guillemots and puffins.

Dungeness, established in 1915, is 556 acres in area, superimposed on a Coast Guard project, and is on the north coast of the Olympic Peninsula east of Port Angeles. It provides a feeding area for shorebirds, black brant and other waterfowl.

Flattery Rocks, established in 1907, is 125 acres in area, situated on the Pacific Ocean side of Cape Flattery. It is used by a nesting colony of auklets, petrels, guillemots and puffins.

Jones Island, established in 1937, is 179 acres in area in the Strait of Georgia southwest of Bellingham. It protects white-winged scoters, band-tailed pigeons and guillemots.

Little Pend Oreille, established in 1939, is sixty-five square miles in area south of Medicine Falls. Acquired by the Resettlement Administration, it serves as a demonstration timber and wildlife area. It protects Franklin's, blue and ruffed grouse, deer and black bears. The manager's address is Route 1, Colville.

Matia Island, established in 1937, is 145 acres in area north of Jones Island in the Strait of Georgia. It protects cormorants, guillemots, harlequin ducks and band-tailed pigeons.

McNary, established in 1955, is about four square miles in area, and is located in the Columbia River Valley, twenty miles upstream from McNary Dam on part of the McNary Lock and Dam project. It protects Canada geese, occasional snow geese, whistling swans and white pelicans, as well as many kinds of ducks, marsh, shore and upland birds, hawks, owls, eagles, muskrats, mink, badgers, rabbits, coyotes and deer. The manager's address is Box 19, Burbank.

Quillayute Needles, established in 1907, is 117 acres on the coast north of Queets. It contains a nesting colony of petrels, cormorants, auklets and puffins.

San Juan, established in 1960, contains fifty-two acres of rocky islands off the coast of Washington in the strait of Juan de Fuca. These islands provide a natural haven for oyster-catchers, gulls, cormorants, puffins, guillemots, band-tailed pigeons, and other migratory birds.

Smith Island, established in 1914, is sixty-five acres in the Strait of Georgia south of Jones Island. It protects waterfowl, shearwaters and gulls.

Turnbull, established in 1937, is twenty-five square miles, and is southwest of Spokane. It protects ducks, shorebirds, ruffed grouse and valley quail. A resident manager is in charge, and the address is Cheney.

Willapa, established in 1937, is twelve square miles on the coast west of Raymond. It protects muskrats, raccoons, blacktail deer, black bears, shorebirds, blue grouse and waterfowl, including black brant. The manager's address is Ilwaco.

Wisconsin

Gravel Island, established in 1913, is twenty-seven acres in area in Lake Michigan off Green Bay Peninsula. It protects great blue herons, herring gulls and Caspian terns.

Green Bay, established in 1912, is two acres on an island in Lake Michigan north of Gravel Island off Green Bay Peninsula. It protects herring gulls and Caspian terns.

Horicon, established in 1941, contains thirty-two square miles, about fifty miles northeast of Madison. Following delayed development of the area, waterfowl use has been astounding. In addition, there are thousands of muskrats and many mink and raccoons. Shortly after acquisition and development, the boundary line of this refuge, as on many others, was purchased or leased by private hunting interests. During the fall of 1953, a marginal area just inside the boundary was opened by the Fish and Wildlife Service for public shooting. This action was severely criticized and opposed by a number of organizations. Address of the refuge manager is Mayville.

Necedah, established in 1939, is sixty-one square miles near the Wisconsin River north of New Lisbon. It protects waterfowl, ruffed and sharp-tailed grouse, prairie chickens, beavers, deer, muskrats, mink and raccoons. The manager's address is Necedah.

Trempealeau, established in 1936, is one square mile on the Mississippi River at Fountain City. It protects ducks, mourning doves and American egrets. It is administered jointly with the Upper Mississippi River Wild Life and Fish Refuge.

Wyoming

Bamforth, established in 1932, is two square miles in area north of Laramie. It protects waterfowl, shorebirds and pronghorns.

Hutton Lake, established in 1932, is three square miles in area south of Laramie. It protects waterfowl, shorebirds and pronghorns. The address of the manager, who also administers Bamforth and Pathfinder, is Box 293, Laramie.

Pathfinder, established in 1909, is seventy-two square miles on the Pathfinder Reservoir, a Bureau of Reclamation project southwest of Casper. It protects shorebirds, waterfowl and pronghorns.

For Further Reading

AMERICAN BISON, by Martin S. Garretson. *New York Zoological Society*, New York, 1938.
ANIMAL WORLD OF ALBERT SCHWEITZER, THE. *Beacon Press*, Boston, 1950.
ARCTIC WILD, by Lois Crisler. *Harper and Brothers*, New York, 1958.
ARIZONA AND ITS BIRD LIFE, by Herbert Brandt. *The Bird Research Foundation*, Cleveland, 1951.
ARMADILLO: ITS RELATION TO AGRICULTURE AND GAME, THE, by E. R. Kalmbach. *Game, Fish and Oyster Commission*, Austin, Texas, 1943.
AUDUBON BIRD GUIDE, by Richard H. Pough. *Doubleday*, New York, 1953.
AUDUBON WATER BIRD GUIDE, by Richard H. Pough. *Doubleday*, New York, 1951.
BIRDS AND MAMMALS OF THE SIERRA NEVADA, by Lowell Sumner and Joseph S. Dixon. *University of California Press*, Berkeley, 1953.
BIRDS OF ARCTIC ALASKA. *Colorado Museum of Natural History*, Denver, 1948.
BIRDS OF LAYSAN AND THE LEEWARD ISLANDS, HAWAIIAN GROUP, by Walter K. Fisher. *Government Printing Office*, 1903.
BIRDS OF MASSACHUSETTS AND OTHER NEW ENGLAND STATES, three volumes, by Edward Howe Forbush. *Commonwealth of Massachusetts*, Boston, 1925-1929.
BIRDS OF NEWFOUNDLAND, by Harold S. Peters and Thomas D. Burleigh. *Department of Natural Resources*, St. John's, Newfoundland, 1951.
BIRDS OF THE PACIFIC STATES, by Ralph Hoffman. *Houghton Mifflin*, Boston, 1927.
BIRDS OF WASHINGTON STATE, by John W. Aldrich and others. *University of Washington Press*, Seattle, 1953.
BIRDS OVER AMERICA, by Roger Tory Peterson, *Dodd, Mead*, New York, 1948.
BUFFALO HUNTERS, THE, by Mari Sandoz. *Hastings House*, New York, 1954.
CANADIAN SPRING, by Florence Page Jaques. *Harpers*, New York, 1947.
CANVASBACK ON A PRAIRIE MARSH, THE, by M. Albert Hochbaum. *American Wildlife Institute*, Washington, D. C., 1944.
CONDOR, THE CALIFORNIA, by Carl B. Koford. *National Audubon Society*, New York, 1953.
COYOTE, THE CLEVER, by Stanley P. Young and Hartley H. T. Jackson. *Wildlife Management Institute*, Washington, D. C., 1951.
COYOTE, THE VOICE OF THE, by J. Frank Dobie. *Little, Brown*, Boston, 1949.
CROSSBILLS OF COLORADO, THE RED, by Alfred M. Bailey, Robert J. Niedrach and A. Lang Baily. Museum Pictorial No. 9, *Denver Museum of Natural History*, Denver, 1953.
DESERT, THE, by John C. VanDyke. *Scribners*, New York, 1908.
DRIFTWOOD VALLEY, by Theodora C. Stanwell-Fletcher. *Little, Brown*, Boston, 1946.
DUCKS, GEESE AND SWANS OF NORTH AMERICA, THE, by F. H. Kortright. *American Wildlife Institute*, Washington, D. C., 1942.
ELK OF NORTH AMERICA, THE, by Olaus J. Murie. *Wildlife Management Institute*, Washington, D. C., 1951.
ERNEST THOMPSON SETON'S AMERICA, edited by Farida A. Wiley. *The Devin-Adair Co.*, New York, 1954.
EXPEDITION OF LEWIS AND CLARK, THE, two volumes. *A. C. McClurg*, Chicago, 1905.
EXPLORING OUR NATIONAL PARKS AND MONUMENTS, by Devereux Butcher. *Houghton Mifflin*, Boston, 1954.
EXPLORING THE NATIONAL PARKS OF CANADA, by Devereux Butcher. *National Parks Association*, Washington, D. C., 1951.
EXTINCT AND VANISHING MAMMALS OF THE WESTERN HEMISPHERE, by Glover M. Allen. Special Publication No. 11, *American Committee for International Wildlife Protection*, 1942.
FADING TRAILS, THE STORY OF OUR ENDANGERED WILDLIFE, edited by Charles N. Elliott. *Macmillan*, New York, 1942.
FAUNA SERIES. National Park Service, *Government Printing Office.*
No. 1. PRELIMINARY SURVEY OF FAUNAL RELATIONS IN NATIONAL PARKS, by George M. Wright, Joseph S. Dixon and Ben H. Thompson, 1932.
No. 2. WILDLIFE MANAGEMENT IN THE NATIONAL PARKS, by George M. Wright and Ben H. Thompson, 1943.
No. 3. BIRDS AND MAMMALS OF MOUNT MCKINLEY NATIONAL PARK, by Joseph S. Dixon, 1938.
No. 4. ECOLOGY OF THE COYOTE IN THE YELLOWSTONE, by Adolph Murie, 1940.
No. 5. THE WOLVES OF MOUNT MCKINLEY, by Adolph Murie, 1944.
FIELD GUIDE TO ANIMAL TRACKS, by Olaus J. Murie, *Houghton Mifflin*, Boston, 1954.
FIELD GUIDE TO THE BIRDS, by Roger Tory Peterson. *Houghton Mifflin*, Boston, 1948.
FIELD GUIDE TO THE MAMMALS, by W. H. Burt and R. P. Grossenheider. *Houghton Mifflin*, Boston, 1952.

FIELD GUIDE TO WESTERN BIRDS, by Roger Tory Peterson. *Houghton Mifflin*, Boston, 1941.
FLORIDA BIRD LIFE, by Alexander Sprunt, Jr. *Coward-McCann*, New York, 1954.
FOREST LIFE SERIES, by Sam Campbell. *Bobbs-Merrill*, New York.
A TIPPY CANOE AND CANADA TOO, 1946.
EENY, MEENY, MINEY, MO—AND STILL-MO, 1945.
HOW'S INKY?, 1943.
MOOSE COUNTRY, 1950.
ON WINGS OF CHEER, 1948.
TOO MUCH SALT AND PEPPER, 1944.
FUR-BEARING MAMMALS OF CALIFORNIA, by Joseph Grinnell, Joseph S. Dixon and Jean Linsdale, two volumes. *University of California Press*, Berkeley, 1937.
GUIDE TO BIRD FINDING EAST OF THE MISSISSIPPI, by Olin S. Pettingill, Jr. *Oxford University Press*, New York, 1951.
GUIDE TO BIRD FINDING WEST OF THE MISSISSIPPI, by Olin S. Pettingill, Jr. *Oxford University Press*, New York, 1953.
GUIDE TO THE MAMMALS OF COLORADO, by Hugo G. Rodeck. *University of Colorado Museum*, Boulder, 1952.
HAWKS ALOFT, THE STORY OF HAWK MOUNTAIN, by Maurice Broun. *Dodd, Mead*, New York, 1949.
HOW TO KNOW THE AMERICAN MAMMALS, by Ivan T. Sanderson. *Little, Brown*, Boston, 1951.
HUNTING WILD LIFE WITH CAMERA AND FLASHLIGHT, two volumes, by George Shiras, 3rd, *National Geographic Society*, Washington, D. C., 1935.
ICEBOUND SUMMER, by Sally Carrighar. *Alfred A. Knopf*, New York, 1953.
INTERNATIONAL PROTECTION OF WILDLIFE, AN EXAMINATION OF TREATIES AND OTHER AGREEMENTS FOR THE PRESERVATION OF BIRDS AND MAMMALS, by S. S. Hayden. *Columbia University Press*, New York, 1942.
IVORY-BILLED WOODPECKER, THE, by James T. Tanner. *National Audubon Society*, New York, 1942.
JOHN BURROUGHS' AMERICA, edited by Farida A. Wiley. *The Devin-Adair Co.*, New York, 1952.
LET THEM LIVE, by Dorothy P. Lathrop. *Macmillan*, 1951.
LIFE HISTORIES OF NORTH AMERICAN BIRDS, by Arthur Cleveland Bent. Bulletin 130, *U. S. National Museum*, Washington, D. C., 1925.
LIVES OF GAME ANIMALS, eight volumes, by Ernest Thompson Seton. *Charles T. Branford Co.*, Boston, 1953.
MAMMAL GUIDE, THE, by Ralph S. Palmer. *Doubleday*, New York, 1954.
MAMMALS OF EASTERN UNITED STATES, by W. J. Hamilton, Jr. *Comstock Publishing Co.*, Ithaca, 1943.
MAMMALS OF NORTH AMERICA, by Victor H. Cahalane. *Macmillan*, New York, 1947.
MEETING THE MAMMALS, by Victor H. Cahalane. *Macmillan*, New York, 1943.
NATURALIST IN ALASKA, by Adolph Murie. *Devin-Adair*, New York, 1961.
NATURE'S MESSAGES, by Sam Campbell. *Rand McNally*, Chicago, 1952.
NORTH AMERICAN FAUNA. Fish and Wildlife Service. *Government Printing Office.*
No. 54. ALASKA-YUKON CARIBOU, by Olaus J. Murie, 1935.
No. 57. ATTWATER'S PRAIRIE CHICKEN, by Valgene W. Lehmann, 1941.
No. 58. HABITS, FOOD, AND ECONOMIC STATUS OF THE BAND-TAILED PIGEON, by Johnson A. Neff, 1947.
No. 60. RACCOONS OF NORTH AND MIDDLE AMERICA, by Edward A. Goldman, 1950.
NORTH AMERICAN MOOSE, by Randolph L. Peterson. *University of Toronto Press*, Toronto, 1955.
NORTH AMERICAN WATERFOWL, by Albert M. Day. *Stackpole and Heck*, Harrisburg, 1949.
NORTH WITH THE SPRING, by Edwin Way Teale. *Dodd, Mead*, New York, 1951.
ONE DAY AT TETON MARSH, by Sally Carrighar. *Alfred A. Knopf*, New York, 1947.
ONE DAY ON BEETLE ROCK, by Sally Carrighar. *Alfred A. Knopf*, New York, 1944.
OTTER'S STORY, AN, by Emil E. Liers. *The Viking Press*, New York, 1953.
OUR ANIMAL NEIGHBORS, by Alan Devoe. *McGraw-Hill*, New York, 1953.
OUR VANISHING WILDLIFE, by William T. Hornaday. *New York Zoological Society*, New York, 1913.
OUR WILDLIFE LEGACY, by Durward L. Allen. *Funk and Wagnalls*, New York, 1954.
PASSENGER PIGEON, THE, by A. W. Schorger. *University of Wisconsin Press*, Madison, 1955.
PASSENGER PIGEON, THE, by W. B. Mershon. *The Outing Publishing Co.*, New York, 1907.
PELICAN, HISTORY AND PRESENT STATUS OF THE BREEDING COLONIES OF THE WHITE, by Ben H. Thompson. U. S. Department of the Interior, *Government Printing Office*, 1932.
PRACTICE OF WILDLIFE CONSERVATION, by Leonard W. Wing. *John Wiley and Sons*, New York, 1951.
PRONGHORN ANTELOPE AND ITS MANAGEMENT, THE, by Arthur S. Einarsen. *Wildlife Management Institute*, Washington, D. C., 1948.
PUMA, MYSTERIOUS AMERICAN CAT, THE, by Stanley P. Young and Edward A. Goldman. *American Wildlife Institute*, Washington, D. C., 1946.

SHARP-TAILS INTO THE SHADOW?, by Frederick and Frances Hamerstrom and Oswald E. Mattson. Wisconsin Wildlife No. 1, *Wisconsin Conservation Department*, Madison, 1952.
SIERRA OUTPOST, by Lila Lofberg and David Malcolmson. *Duell, Sloan and Pearce*, New York, 1941.
SPOONBILL, THE ROSEATE, by Robert Porter Allen. *National Audubon Society*, New York, 1943.
THIRTY YEARS WAR FOR WILDLIFE, by William T. Hornaday. *Scribners*, New York, 1931.
THIS FASCINATING ANIMAL WORLD, by Alan Devoe. *McGraw-Hill*, New York, 1951.
THOSE OF THE FOREST, by Wallace Byron Grange. *The Flambeau Publishing Co.*, Babcock, Wisconsin, 1953.
TUNDRA WORLD, THE, by Theodora C. Stanwell-Fletcher. *Little, Brown*, Boston, 1952.
UPPER MISSISSIPPI, A WILDERNESS SAGA, by Walter Havighurst. *Farrar and Rinehart*, New York, 1937.
WHALES AND MEN, OF, by R. B. Robertson. *Alfred A. Knopf*, New York, 1954.
WHOOPING CRANE, THE, by Robert Porter Allen. *National Audubon Society*, New York, 1952.
WILD ANIMALS OF THE ROCKIES, by William M. Rush. *Harpers*, New York, 1942.
WILDLIFE CONSERVATION, by Ira N. Gabrielson. *Macmillan*, New York, 1941.
WILD LIFE ON THE ROCKIES, by Enos A. Mills. *Houghton Mifflin*, Boston, 1909.
WILDLIFE REFUGES, by Ira N. Gabrielson. *Macmillan*, New York, 1943.
WILDWOOD WISDOM, by Ellsworth Jaeger. *Macmillan*, New York, 1945.
WINGS AT MY WINDOW, by Ada Clapham Govan. *Macmillan*, New York, 1939.
WOLF IN NORTH AMERICAN HISTORY, THE, by Stanley P. Young. *The Caxton Printers*, Caldwell, Idaho, 1946.
YEARLING, THE, by Marjorie Kinnan Rawlings. *Scribners*, New York, 1938.

Periodicals

ATLANTIC NATURALIST. Published five times yearly by the Audubon Naturalist Society of the Central Atlantic States, Inc., 1621 Wisconsin Ave., N. W., Washington 7, D. C.
AUDUBON MAGAZINE. Published bimonthly by the National Audubon Society, 1130 Fifth Avenue, New York 28, N. Y.
DEFENDERS OF WILDLIFE BULLETIN, 809 Dupont Circle Building, Washington 6, D. C.
NATIONAL PARKS MAGAZINE. Published monthly by the National Parks Association, 1300 New Hampshire Ave., N. W., Washington 6, D. C.
SIERRA CLUB BULLETIN. Published monthly, except July and August, by the Sierra Club, 1050 Mills Tower, San Francisco 4, California.
THE LIVING WILDERNESS. Published quarterly by The Wilderness Society, 2144 P Street, N. W., Washington 7, D. C.

INDEX

Page numbers in bold-faced type refer to illustrations.